What readers are saying about *FXRuby*

Learning a GUI framework should be easy, but it's usually hard. Reading this book, I realized by contrast that the reason it's usually hard is that it's no fun. Lyle's results-oriented approach to teaching makes learning FXRuby fun, and therefore easy. This book is a motivating, well-written tutorial about *getting things done* in one of Ruby's most established widget toolkits from its most authoritative sour

► **Chad Fowler**
CTO, InfoEther
Founding Co-director, Ruby Central

FXRuby is a rich, mature GUI toolkit that Lyle has maintained and documented very well for years. With the addition of this excellent book, this toolkit becomes only that much more usable.

► **Hal Fulton**
Author, *The Ruby Way*

I was paid to develop a GUI app using Ruby back in 2003, and I quickly settled on FOX/FXRuby as the right toolkit because of the exceptional quality of the bindings and the high level of support Lyle provided. My only regret? That I didn't have this book! With it open on your desk and the online references loaded in your browser, nothing should be stopping you from building an amazing desktop application using Ruby.

► **Nathaniel Talbott**
Founder and Developer, Terralien, Inc.

Lyle's deep knowledge of FXRuby ensures that this engaging book will prepare you to make cross-platform GUIs in very little time at all.

► **Austin Ziegler**
Software Designer and Developer

FXRuby: Create Lean and Mean GUIs with Ruby is a well-written text straight from the horse's mouth: a book about FXRuby from the author of FXRuby. You can't get better than that, unless, of course, the library wrote the book itself.

► **Jeremy McAnally**
Developer/technical writer, ENTP

This book is an excellent introduction to FXRuby programming. Lyle does a good job of getting you started with the basics and moving on to more advanced topics at just the right pace.

► **Daniel Berger**
Software Engineer, Qwest, Inc.

FXRuby

Create Lean and Mean GUIs with Ruby

FXRuby

Create Lean and Mean GUIs with Ruby

Lyle Johnson

The Pragmatic Bookshelf
Raleigh, North Carolina   Dallas, Texas

Our Pragmatic courses, workshops, and other products can help you and your team create better software and have more fun. For more information, as well as the latest Pragmatic titles, please visit us at

http://www.pragprog.com

Printed in the United States of America.

ISBN-10: 1-934356-07-7

ISBN-13: 978-1-934356-07-4

Printed on acid-free paper with 50% recycled, 15% post-consumer content.

First printing, March 2008

Version: 2008-3-14

Contents

Foreword

The FOX Toolkit is a library for designing user interfaces and has been under development for more than ten years. FOX got its start as my hobby project, called Free Objects for X (FOX), because my initial target environment was the X Window system.

One of the early FOX adopters was CFD Research Corporation, where Lyle and I worked. The user interface developers at the company were pleasantly surprised with the concise coding needed to lay out their interfaces, having been used to Motif, where placing a single button would often require a dozen lines of code. The same task would often require only a single line of code in FOX. Bolstered by this success, the FOX library rapidly went through a number of changes; the library got ported to Microsoft Windows, and support for 3D programming was added. All the key ingredients were in place to transfer the company's GUI applications to the FOX platform.

FOX has now reached a point where developers can write code and be reasonably confident that it will compile and run on numerous platforms, from PCs running Windows to "big-box" Unix machines from Sun and IBM. FOX continues to grow. In the past few years, the focus has been on internationalization and localization, as well as multiprocessing support.

The FOX Toolkit is written in C++, and until other language bindings became available, you had to program in C++ to use FOX. Now, with the creation of the FXRuby library, the capabilities of the FOX Toolkit have become available in the Ruby programming language.

In this book, you'll learn how to build FOX-based graphical user interfaces within Ruby. In Part I, you'll write your first small FXRuby application, starting with detailed instructions on how to get FXRuby extensions installed in your Ruby programming environment. You'll work through several iterations toward a functional application that illustrates many critical features of FXRuby programs.

In Part II, the book goes into more detail on event-driven programming and how to connect the user interface to useful executable Ruby code. Moving on to the available controls and widgets, you'll learn how to use layout managers to place your user interface elements (this is a particularly useful chapter, because automatic layout is a foreign concept even to many seasoned Windows programmers).

After you've read this book, you'll be able to design great user interfaces for your Ruby programs!

Jeroen van der Zijp (Principal FOX Toolkit Developer)
January 2008

Acknowledgments

I've been wanting to write a book about FXRuby development for a long time. When I decided I was finally ready to do that, I knew I wanted to work with the Pragmatic Programmers to make it happen. Many thanks to Dave and Andy for giving me this opportunity.

Obviously, FXRuby would not exist were it not for the FOX Toolkit. I'd like to thank my friend and former co-worker Jeroen van der Zijp for letting me play a small part in FOX's development over the years and for all that I've learned from him in the process.

This book could easily have run off the rails if it weren't for the hard work and dedication of my editor, Susannah Davidson Pfalzer. Susannah, thanks so much for your attention to detail and your expert guidance as we worked through all of those revisions. The result is so much better than it would have been without your help.

One of the realities of working on a book like this for months at a time is that you get way too close to the text to be objective about it, and you become unable to spot its flaws. For that reason, I owe many thanks to the book's reviewers: Dan Berger, Joey Gibson, Chris Hulan, Sander Jansen, Chris Johnson, Joel VanderWerf, and Austin Ziegler. Their comments and suggestions were invaluable. Thanks are likewise due to the numerous beta book readers who took the time to point out problems with the early releases of the book.

Finally, thanks to my wife, Denise, for her support and encouragement and for putting up with a frequently distracted husband over the past nine months. We are *so* going to the beach now that this is done.

Lyle Johnson
January 30, 2008
`lyle@lylejohnson.name`

Chapter 1

Introduction

FXRuby is a library for developing powerful and sophisticated cross-platform graphical user interfaces (GUIs) for your Ruby applications. It's based on the FOX Toolkit, a popular open source C++ library developed by Jeroen van der Zijp. What that means for you as an application developer is that you're able to write code in the Ruby programming language that you already know and love, while at the same time taking advantage of the performance and functionality of a fully featured, highly optimized C++ toolkit.

Although FOX doesn't have the same level of name recognition as some other GUI toolkits, it has been available since 1997 and is still under continuous development. FXRuby has been under development since late 2000, and the first public release was in January 2001. I've been the lead developer during that entire time, with a number of community volunteers contributing patches along the way. It's a tricky proposition to guess the size of the user community for an open source project, but according to the RubyForge statistics there have been close to 45,000 downloads of FXRuby since the project was moved there (and almost 18,000 before that, when it was hosted at SourceForge). Questions posted to the FXRuby users mailing list are often answered by myself, Jeroen van der Zijp (the developer of FOX), or one of the other longtime members of the FXRuby community.

1.1 What's in This Book?

The purpose of this book is to give you a head start on developing GUI applications with Ruby and FXRuby through a combination of tutorial exercises and focused technical information.

This isn't a comprehensive book on FXRuby programming, and it's not a reference manual.[1] A nearly complete reference manual is available, and it's included with the standard FXRuby distribution. What this book *will* do is get you over the initial conceptual hurdles and equip you with the practical information that you need to build your own applications.

1.2 Who Is This Book For?

This book is for software developers who want to learn how to develop GUI applications using the Ruby programming language. If you're new to Ruby programming in general, you should understand that while we'll highlight certain Ruby programming techniques along the way, this book isn't intended to teach you how to program in Ruby. You don't need to be a Ruby guru, but it is important that you're comfortable with programming in Ruby, and object-oriented programming concepts in general, before diving in.

Having said that, it's not necessary for you to have any prior experience with GUI programming to read this book. As new topics are introduced, we'll take the time to explain how they fit into the bigger picture and how they might relate to things you've encountered in other contexts. If you *do* have some previous experience with GUI application development, you'll be able to use this book to quickly identify similarities and differences between this and other GUI toolkits that you've used in the past. Regardless of your experience level, this book will provide a means for you to get over the initial "hump" and learn the fundamentals that you need to understand so that you can move on to developing powerful user interfaces for your applications.

1.3 How to Read This Book

The first part of this book starts with installation instructions and then moves on to an extended example, in which we incrementally build up a full-fledged FXRuby application. This is the place to start if you're looking to get a feel for FXRuby programming. In fact, most folks seem to enjoy building the application along with the book.

---

1. Let's face it, you don't have time to read a book that long, what with all of those books about Rails that you haven't gotten around to reading yet.

If you don't want to do all of that typing, you can cheat and download the source code (a compressed tar archive or a zip file).[2]

In the second part of the book, we'll revisit some of the topics that we covered while developing the example application, and we'll go into more detail about why things work the way they do. We'll also cover some additional topics that wouldn't have fit neatly into the example application but that are still important for you to be familiar with.

Along the way, you'll see various conventions we've adopted.

Live Code

Most of the code snippets we show come from full-length, running examples that you can download. To help you find your way, if a code listing can be found in the download, there'll be a bar above the snippet (just like the one here):

hello.rb

```
require 'fox16'

app = Fox::FXApp.new
main = Fox::FXMainWindow.new(app, "Hello, World!",
  :width => 200, :height => 100)
app.create
main.show(Fox::PLACEMENT_SCREEN)
app.run
```

This contains the path to the code within the download. If you are reading the PDF version of this book and your PDF viewer supports hyperlinks, you can click the bar, and the code should appear in a browser window. Some browsers (such as Safari) will mistakenly try to interpret some of the templates as HTML. If this happens, view the source of the page to see the real source code.

1.4 Where to Get Help

The best places to get help on FXRuby (other than this book, of course) are the mailing lists and the various sources of online documentation.

Mailing Lists

Two different mailing lists are dedicated to FXRuby. The announcements list is a very low-traffic list that's primarily used to notify users

2. http://www.pragprog.com/titles/fxruby has the links for the downloads.

of new releases of FXRuby, while the users list is a higher-traffic list where general discussion of FXRuby programming issues takes place. You can find instructions on how to subscribe to these lists, as well as the mailing list archives, at the RubyForge project page for FXRuby.[3]

In addition to the FXRuby lists, you may find it valuable to subscribe to the regular FOX users mailing list. Many of the issues you'll encounter when developing FXRuby applications are the same as those faced by developers working with the FOX library for C++ GUI applications. For instructions on how to subscribe to the FOX users mailing list and for archives of that list, see the SourceForge project page for FOX.[4]

Online Documentation

Despite rumors to the contrary, there is actually a good deal of online documentation for both FOX and FXRuby, if you know where to look for it.

FOX Documentation Page

The Documentation page at the FOX website has a number of articles with in-depth information on topics such as layout managers, icons and images, fonts, and drag and drop.[5] These articles tend to have more hard-core technical details and are of course aimed at users of the C++ library, so they aren't necessarily appropriate for beginning users of FXRuby. Once you've finished this book, however, you may want to turn to these articles to obtain a deeper understanding of some of the mechanics of FOX programming.

FOX Community Wiki

The FOX Community[6] is a wiki written by and for FOX developers. It features an extended FAQ list, and it's a great source of tutorials and other kinds of documentation. A lot of the sample code is geared toward C++ developers who use FOX in their applications, but most of the information there is also relevant to FXRuby application development.

---

3. http://rubyforge.org/mail/?group_id=300
4. http://sourceforge.net/mail/?group_id=3372
5. http://www.fox-toolkit.org/doc.html
6. http://www.fox-toolkit.net/

FXRuby User's Guide

The *FXRuby User's Guide*[7] is really a hodgepodge of information about FXRuby, but it does provide fairly comprehensive information on how to install FXRuby. It also provides tutorials on working with the clipboard and how to integrate drag and drop into your FXRuby applications.

API Documentation

As you (probably) knew before you bought this book, it's not a reference manual. The API documentation for FXRuby is fairly comprehensive and freely available, so there's no point in trying to duplicate that material here. To view the latest and most accurate API documentation, point your web browser to the copy hosted at the FXRuby website.[8] If you installed FXRuby via RubyGems, you should have a local copy of the documentation as well. To view the HTML documentation that RDoc generated when you installed the gem, first start the gem server:

```
$ gem_server
[2007-05-09 17:18:04] INFO  WEBrick 1.3.1
[2007-05-09 17:18:04] INFO  ruby 1.8.6 (2007-03-13) [i686-darwin8.8.1]
[2007-05-09 17:18:04] INFO  WEBrick::HTTPServer#start: pid=427 port=8808
```

Now, point your web browser to http://localhost:8808/. Scroll through the listing of installed gems until you find the entry for FXRuby, and then click the [rdoc] link to view the documentation.

Another nifty trick you can use to look up information about an FXRuby class or one of its methods is to ask the ri command-line tool:

```
$ ri Fox::FXCheckButton#checked?
----------------------------------- Fox::FXCheckButton#checked?
     checked?()
------------------------------------------------------------------
     Return +true+ if this check button is in the checked state.
```

The ri command is awfully convenient and is of course usable for any Ruby libraries that you've installed, including the core and standard library classes and methods. If you installed FXRuby using RubyGems, it should have automatically generated and installed the ri documentation for FXRuby at that time. If you installed FXRuby directly from the source tarball, or via some other means, you may need to generate and install the ri documentation yourself before you can successfully use the ri command to look up the FXRuby documentation.

---

7. http://www.fxruby.org/doc/book.html
8. http://www.fxruby.org/doc/api/

Regardless, if for some reason `ri` isn't properly installed on your system, do yourself a favor and get it working!

1.5 A Word About Versions

The discussion and examples in this book are based on FXRuby 1.6, the current release at the time this book was written.

Generally speaking, it's in your best interest to use the latest available versions of FOX and FXRuby, because those versions will have the latest bug fixes and enhancements. Note, however, that the major version number for a given FXRuby release indicates the major version number of the FOX release that it's compatible with; for example, FXRuby 1.6 is intended for use with FOX 1.6. This is important because the latest release of FOX is often tagged as an unstable or "development" release, and those versions *aren't* guaranteed to work with the latest release of FXRuby.

Now that we've got that squared away, let's get started!

Part I

Building an FXRuby Application

Chapter 2

Getting Started with FXRuby

This chapter is your jump start to FXRuby application development. We'll spend a few pages looking at FXRuby and how it works with FOX before moving on to instructions for installing FXRuby on several of the most popular operating systems. We'll wrap up the chapter by building a simple "Hello, World!" application so you can learn how FXRuby applications are typically structured and verify that the software is properly installed.

FXRuby is packaged as an extension module for Ruby. That means that it's a C++ library that the Ruby interpreter loads at runtime, introducing a bunch of new Ruby classes and constants in the process. Figure 2.1, on the following page, illustrates the relationship between your application code (written in Ruby), the FXRuby extension, the FOX library, and the operating system. From the application developer's perspective, FXRuby looks like any other "pure Ruby" library that you might use; the difference is that this library's source code isn't actually written in Ruby.[1] FXRuby exposes all the functionality of the FOX library, but it's more than just a simple "wrapper" around the API. FXRuby takes advantage of Ruby language features and uses them to provide an even higher-level interface to FOX. For example, it's somewhat tedious to write all the C++ code required to map user interface events to executable code in traditional FOX applications. In FXRuby, you're able to connect a Ruby block directly to a widget with just a few lines of code.

1. Actually, a good bit of FXRuby is written in Ruby, but that doesn't change how you use it.

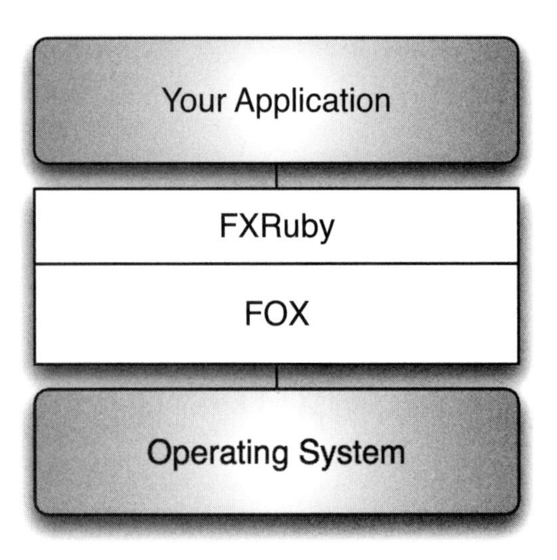

Figure 2.1: RELATIONSHIP BETWEEN THE OPERATING SYSTEM, FOX, FXRUBY, AND YOUR RUBY APPLICATION

When I first started working on FXRuby, there weren't a lot of options in terms of cross-platform GUI development for Ruby, other than the built-in support for Tk. Today, the situation is quite different. If you're looking for a cross-platform GUI, there are mature and well-supported Ruby bindings for GTK+ and Qt, and bindings for other popular GUIs such as wxWidgets and FLTK are under development. Given such a wide selection, it's pretty common for someone to post a question to the Ruby-Talk mailing list asking which GUI is The Best One™.

Just like the questions of which is the best editor, operating system, or programming language, the question of which GUI is the "best" depends on what you're looking for. Instead of trying to talk you out of any particular choice, I encourage you to at least experiment with all the options that you think might be appropriate for your needs. You'll want to keep in mind a few major points as you try to decide, however.

For starters, there are a lot of things that you can *do* with FOX and FXRuby. If you want to put together a simple GUI front-end for a command-line tool, FXRuby certainly fits the bill. Since FOX provides support for all the standard kinds of user interface elements like labels, buttons, and text fields, it's also a great choice for developing straightforward forms-based GUIs. It's FOX's advanced functionality that really sets it apart from some of its competitors, however. FOX's extensive support for the display and manipulation of image data makes it ideal for developing visually rich user interfaces, and thanks to its sophisticated support for OpenGL, FOX has also become a popular choice for applications that require 3-D visualization functionality.

Another characteristic that's important to consider is whether a GUI uses lightweight or heavyweight widgets, as well as which of those you prefer. FOX uses *lightweight* (or non-native) widgets. What this means is that a FOX-based application relies on only the very basic capabilities of the platform that it's running on to create the user interface, instead of providing wrapper classes and methods around existing widgets. This approach has several advantages:

Some people use the terms "native" and "non-native" widgets to describe this difference, but they're talking about the same basic issue.

- Since FOX defines the behavior of the widgets that it creates, rather than relying on the native widgets' behaviors, that behavior is consistent across platforms.
- Since FOX draws it own widgets, your application will look the same regardless of which platform it's running on.[2]
- Since FOX was designed from the start to be highly object-oriented and extensible, you have a lot more flexibility in terms of subclassing existing FOX widgets to create your own application-specific widgets. A good deal of this flexibility is lost when you're using a GUI library that is a wrapper around some other legacy toolkit.
- Since FOX reduces the number of layers of code that you must go through, FOX-based applications tend to be more performant and responsive.

Last, but not least, is the question of how a particular GUI library is licensed. For example, some GUI libraries require you to purchase a commercial development license if you want to use them to develop proprietary (closed-source) applications. FOX and FXRuby are both licensed under the relatively permissive Lesser GNU Public License (LGPL),[3] which permits the use of those libraries in both free and proprietary (commercial) software applications.

Now, let's get started by installing FXRuby and then using it to develop a simple "Hello, World!" program.

2. Some people consider this a *disadvantage* of using lightweight widgets.
3. http://www.gnu.org/licenses/lgpl.html

2.1 Installing FXRuby

Installing FXRuby is a bit more challenging than installing other Ruby libraries, because it's written in C++ and must therefore be compiled into a shared library that the Ruby interpreter can load at runtime. It's further complicated by the fact that there are several dependencies to account for, including the FOX library on which FXRuby is based, as well as the third-party libraries that provide support for various image file formats.

The good news is that if you're installing FXRuby on Windows or Mac OS X, the installation is pretty painless. If you're installing FXRuby on Linux, you'll have a little more work to do, but the steps are pretty easy to follow, and you can count on support from the FOX and FXRuby community for any installation problems that may arise.

The following sections provide some basic instructions on how to get FXRuby installed on the most common operating systems. For some of the more exceptional situations, we'll defer to the online documentation for FOX and FXRuby, which has the most complete and up-to-date information on installation issues:

- For comprehensive instructions on installing the FOX library, see the installation instructions at the FOX website.[4]
- For comprehensive instructions on installing FXRuby, see the instructions in the *FXRuby User's Guide*.[5]

Installing on Windows

If you used the One-Click Installer for Ruby on Windows,[6] you should already have a version of FXRuby installed. However, since the version of FXRuby that's included with the one-click installer sometimes lags behind the latest released version, you should attempt an update using the gemupdate command:

```
C:\> gem update fxruby
```

If you've installed Ruby by some other means, you're going to need to compile both FOX and FXRuby by hand. If you're using a Unix-like environment for Windows, such as Cygwin or MinGW, you should be able to follow the instructions in Section 2.1, *Installing on Linux*, on the

4. http://www.fox-toolkit.org/install.html
5. http://www.fxruby.org/doc/build.html
6. http://rubyinstaller.rubyforge.org/wiki/wiki.pl

next page, to complete this task. If you're using Microsoft's (or some other vendor's) development tools, your best bet is to refer to the online documentation mentioned at the beginning of this chapter.

Installing on Mac OS X

The easiest way to install FOX and FXRuby on Mac OS X is to use MacPorts:[7]

```
$ sudo port install rb-fxruby
```

If you'd prefer to install FXRuby via some other means, such as the source gem, you should at least consider using MacPorts to install its dependencies (such as FOX and the libraries for manipulating JPEG, PNG, and TIFF images).

If you're unable to install the software via MacPorts, you can always just build it using the installation process described in Section 2.1, *Installing on Linux*.

Installing on Linux

Getting FOX and FXRuby working on Linux can be a time-consuming process. You may get lucky: some of the more recent Linux distributions include packages for FOX and/or FXRuby. When that's the case, I strongly recommend you use those packages to avoid some of the inevitable headaches associated with tracking down dependencies and building those by hand. For example, if you're running Ubuntu Linux[8] and have enabled the "universe" component of the Ubuntu software repository, you should be able to install FOX directly from the libfox-1.6-dev package:

```
$ sudo apt-get install libfox-1.6-dev
```

Since Ubuntu Linux doesn't provide a package for FXRuby, you'll need to install it from the gem, as described later in this section.

If you're using a Linux distribution that doesn't yet include FOX or FXRuby as a standard installation package, you'll need to look for third-party packages or (worst case) build them from the source code. In that case, first download the distribution for the latest release in the FOX 1.6 series from the FOX downloads site.[9]

---

7. http://www.macports.org/
8. http://www.ubuntu.com/
9. http://www.fox-toolkit.org/download.html

The distribution will have a filename like fox-1.6.29.tar.gz. Use the tar command to unpack the distribution:

```
$ tar xzf fox-1.6.29.tar.gz
```

This action will create a directory named fox-1.6.29. Change to that directory and then use the standard configure, make, make install sequence to build and install FOX:

```
$ cd fox-1.6.29
$ ./configure
«output of "configure" command»
$ make
«output of "make" command»
$ sudo make install
«output of "make install" command»
```

Now that you've built and installed FOX, you're ready to install FXRuby. The most straightforward method is to use the gem install command to fetch the gem from the remote gem repository hosted at RubyForge:

```
$ sudo gem install fxruby --remote
Bulk updating Gem source index for: http://gems.rubyforge.org
Building native extensions.  This could take a while...
```

As the message indicates, this process can take some time to complete.

2.2 Instant Gratification

Now that you have FXRuby installed and working on your development system, we'll move on to the fun part. We'll start with a simple FXRuby application in this section to get your feet wet, and then we'll move on to a more complicated example in the following chapters that will teach you a lot about how to structure real-world FXRuby applications.

"Hello, World!"

In the time-honored tradition of programming books throughout history, we'll start out with the FXRuby version of "Hello, World!" Let's begin with the absolute bare minimum and make sure that it works.

Create a new file in your editor of choice, and write the first line of your very first FXRuby program:

hello.rb

```
require 'fox16'
```

Setting Up the RubyGems Environment

If you've installed FXRuby using RubyGems, the example programs in this book may not work properly unless you've told Ruby to automatically load the RubyGems runtime and use the libraries stored in the RubyGems repository. There's a discussion of the various options in the RubyGems Users Guide at http://rubygems.org/read/chapter/3; I personally prefer to set the RUBYOPT environment variable as described in that discussion.

Note that if you're running Ruby 1.9.0 or later, the RubyGems runtime is fully integrated with the Ruby interpreter, so these sorts of precautions aren't necessary.

Feels good already, doesn't it? This imports the Fox module and all of its contents into the Ruby interpreter. The feature name (the string you pass to require()) is "fox16" because we want to use FXRuby version 1.6, and not one of the earlier versions.

Now, it's only a one-line program so far, but humor me: save this file as hello.rb, and go ahead and try to run it now:

```
$ ruby hello.rb
```

If Ruby churns for a few seconds and then quietly returns to the command prompt, you're good to go. That's all that the program *should* do if FXRuby is installed correctly. If, on the other hand, you see one or more error messages, stop right there and figure out what's wrong, because nothing past this point matters if you don't have a working installation.[10] One common problem that crops up at runtime has to do with the setup of the RubyGems environment; see the sidebar on the current page for more information on that issue.

10. As mentioned in the previous chapter, there are some useful hints in the *FXRuby User's Guide* about things that sometimes go wrong when you install FXRuby, especially when you're building it from the source code. See http://www.fxruby.org/doc/build.html for more details.

Next, construct an instance of the FXApp class, which is defined in the Fox module:

hello.rb

```
app = Fox::FXApp.new
```

FXApp is short for "application." The application object is responsible for the event loop, as well as a lot of work behind the scenes in an FXRuby program. It's the glue that holds everything together. For now, though, it's enough to know that every FXRuby program that you write will need to construct an FXApp object.

The example application needs a main window, so let's add one of those next:

hello.rb

```
main = Fox::FXMainWindow.new(app, "Hello, World!",
  :width => 200, :height => 100)
```

Now you see one of the many uses for the FXApp object. By passing it in as the first argument to FXMainWindow.new(), you're saying that your application (and not some other application) is responsible for the main window. The second argument is the main window's title and will be displayed in the window's title bar. You also specify the initial width and height of the main window, in pixels. There's more that you could specify about the main window, but for now this will do.

Next, add a call to the create() method. This ensures that all the server-side resources for your application get created. We'll discuss this in more detail later. For now, just know that this is another one of those things that you'll need to do in any FXRuby application:

hello.rb

```
app.create
```

Next, call show() on the main window with PLACEMENT_SCREEN to ensure that it's visible when the program starts running:

hello.rb

```
main.show(Fox::PLACEMENT_SCREEN)
```

The PLACEMENT_SCREEN placement hint is just a request that the window be centered on the screen when it's first shown.[11]

11. The API documentation for the FXTopWindow class (the base class for FXMainWindow) lists some of the other placement hints that you can pass in to the show() method.

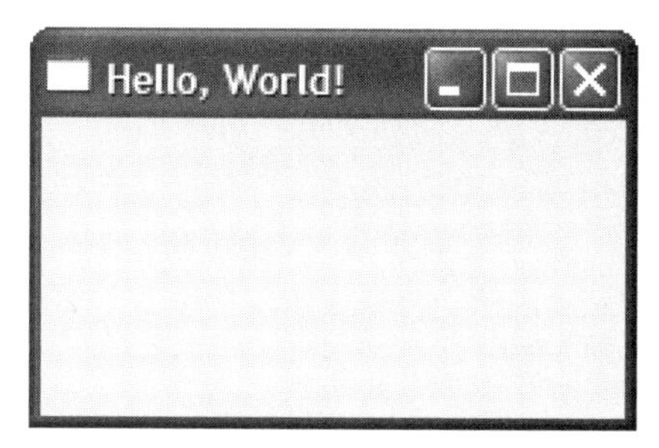

Figure 2.2: "HELLO, WORLD!" ON WINDOWS

Finally, call run() on the FXApp object to kick off the main application loop. Your complete program should look like this:

hello.rb

```
require 'fox16'

app = Fox::FXApp.new
main = Fox::FXMainWindow.new(app, "Hello, World!",
  :width => 200, :height => 100)
app.create
main.show(Fox::PLACEMENT_SCREEN)
app.run
```

Now you can run the program as you would any typical Ruby program:

```
$ ruby hello.rb
```

Your result should look something like the window shown in Figure 2.2, which is a screenshot of the program running in Windows.

Idiomatic FXRuby Programs

If I were going to write a new FXRuby program from scratch, that's not quite how I'd set it up. There are a few idioms that are fairly common in FXRuby programs, and all the rest of the examples that you'll see in this book follow those. The first is that it's common to include the Fox module in Ruby's global namespace so that you don't have to use the fully qualified names for FXRuby classes and constants throughout your program.

With this change, hello.rb becomes a bit easier to read:

hello2.rb

```
require 'fox16'

include Fox

app = FXApp.new
main = FXMainWindow.new(app, "Hello, World!",
  :width => 200, :height => 100)
app.create
main.show(PLACEMENT_SCREEN)
app.run
```

Generally speaking, this practice could lead to clashes between names defined in the Fox module and names defined in other modules, but in practice I've never seen this cause problems.

Another change you can make is to rethink the application's main window as a subclass of FXMainWindow:

hello3.rb

```
require 'fox16'

include Fox

class HelloWindow < FXMainWindow
  def initialize(app)
    super(app, "Hello, World!", :width => 200, :height => 100)
  end

  def create
    super
    show(PLACEMENT_SCREEN)
  end
end

app = FXApp.new
HelloWindow.new(app)
app.create
app.run
```

Take a minute or two to compare this iteration to the previous one, and make sure you understand the changes. Note that everything that has to do with our customization of the main window has been moved into the HelloWindow subclass, including the fact that it calls show() on itself after it has been created.

This introductory program is so trivial that it's overkill to take this step, but as we'll see in subsequent example programs, it becomes convenient to focus the application control inside a custom main window class like this.

As a final modification, move the FXApp and HelloWindow construction into a start-up block:

hello4.rb

```
require 'fox16'

include Fox

class HelloWindow < FXMainWindow
  def initialize(app)
    super(app, "Hello, World!", :width => 200, :height => 100)
  end

  def create
    super
    show(PLACEMENT_SCREEN)
  end
end

if __FILE__ == $0
  FXApp.new do |app|
    HelloWindow.new(app)
    app.create
    app.run
  end
end
```

I also took advantage of this step to show how the block form of the FXApp constructor works. This is something you can do with any FXRuby class, when you want to do some additional initialization. None of these refactorings has changed the basic operation of the program, but they serve to demonstrate a typical structure for FXRuby programs.

It may not feel like it, but we've covered a lot of ground in this chapter. We installed FXRuby and ensured that it's working properly. We also developed a simple but functional program to become familiar with the basic pattern that every FXRuby application will follow. In the process of a few refactorings, we saw that the classes that FXRuby provides can be subclassed and customized just like any other Ruby class. Now that we've gotten our feet wet, we're ready to take on the development of a much more complicated project that we'll be building over the next few chapters.

Chapter 3

The Picture Book Application

Now that you've installed FXRuby and gotten an initial test program working, it's time to move on to something more challenging. For the next few chapters, we're going to be developing a photo library manager application, Picture Book, using FXRuby.

One of the more difficult tasks in writing this book was deciding on a sample application that I could use to demonstrate FXRuby development. I am not a big fan of reinventing the wheel, and needless to say, there are plenty of fine photo album applications available already. The purpose of this exercise is not so much to achieve world domination by building the best-ever photos application but instead to learn how to use the tools that FXRuby provides to build a more complex GUI application.[1]

3.1 What Picture Book Does

As noted in the introduction to this chapter, we're aiming for an application that will touch on a lot of the kinds of features that you'd want to incorporate into your own applications, while keeping the overall scope of the application in check. One of the most important things you'll learn as we work through this exercise is how to combine FOX's powerful layout managers, such as FXMatrix, FXSplitter, and FXSwitcher, to create complex layouts. You'll also get comfortable with subclassing built-in widgets, such as FXList and FXImageFrame, to create customized, application-specific views. Along the way, you'll pick up tricks for using

1. We'll get back to the whole world domination thing later if there's time.

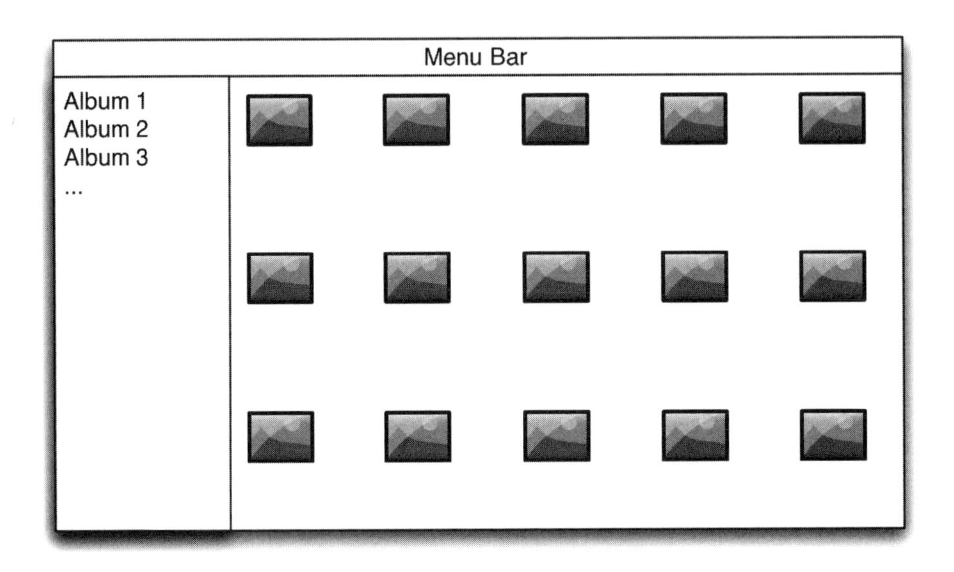

Figure 3.1: USER INTERFACE CONCEPT FOR PICTURE BOOK APPLICATION

FOX's image manipulation and display capabilities. By the time you've completed the application, you'll have a lot better sense of the kinds of details and decisions that go into FXRuby application development.

But first things first. Let's make some decisions about the basic functionality of the Picture Book application. We're looking for a program that will let us organize a bunch of existing digital photos stored on disk into one or more named albums. I'm imagining a user interface like the mocked-up version that appears in Figure 3.1. When the program starts up, you should see a list of the existing albums along the left side of the main window, and if you select one of those albums, the pane on the right side should display all the photos in that album.

Let's stipulate that the user should be able to create new albums and add photos to those albums. We'll pass on some more advanced features such as photo editing and sharing, although my hope is that by the time you've finished reading this book, you'll have some ideas about how to implement those kinds of features as well.

One decision that we'll need to make has to do with how the photos are stored. One option is to leave the imported photos where they are and just keep references to their locations on disk. An advantage of this approach is that you can store your photo albums on devices that may not always be present, such as external hard drives or DVDs. A different option is to actually make copies of the imported photos and stash those copies away in a location known only by the application.

The latter option (making copies of the imported photos) introduces some complexity that, regardless of whether it is a better or worse choice, doesn't really tell us much about FXRuby application development. So, we'll go with the simpler choice and just keep up with the paths to existing photo files on disk.

3.2 Application Data

Now that we've sketched out some of the preliminary requirements for the application, we need to consider what kinds of data structures we're talking about. We're going to (loosely) adopt a Model-View-Controller[2] (MVC) style of architecture for the Picture Book application, which simply means the domain-specific data (namely, photos, albums, and album lists) are represented by one set of classes while the user interface elements (the photo, album, and album list views) are represented by a different set of classes. This approach solves a number of problems that software developers run into when the application data and user interface are too tightly coupled. We'll be using a slightly modified version of the traditional MVC pattern, in that the user interface components will handle both the view and controller aspects of the architecture.

We'll introduce the model classes (the *M* in MVC) here, since they're fairly straightforward and they won't change much during the development of the application. We'll talk more about the view classes starting in the next chapter; they are more complicated, and as you will see, they will change a good bit as we develop successive iterations of the application.

Let's start by looking at a single photo. We know that it will need to hold a reference to a file on disk, so we should store the path to that file. There may be more that we want to say about a photo later, but let's just go with that for now.

---

2. See http://en.wikipedia.org/wiki/Model-view-controller for more information on the MVC architectural pattern.

picturebook_a/photo.rb

```
class Photo

  attr_reader :path

  def initialize(path)
    @path  = path
  end
end
```

What do we want to say about an album? It should have a title, such as "Beach Vacation 2007," and should hold a collection of photos. It's a safe bet that we'll need methods to add a photo to an album and iterate over the photos in an album. We may need to say more about it later, but here's a first cut at the Album class:

picturebook_b/album.rb

```
class Album

  attr_reader :title

  def initialize(title)
    @title = title
    @photos = []
  end

  def add_photo(photo)
    @photos << photo
  end

  def each_photo
    @photos.each { |photo| yield photo }
  end
end
```

Finally, we need a class for managing the list of albums. Following our pattern for the Photo and Album classes, we're going to start out with a really basic AlbumList class and then add to it as needed. Our initial implementation has methods for adding and removing albums, as well as iterating over the albums in the list:

picturebook_e/album_list.rb

```
class AlbumList

  def initialize
    @albums = []
  end
```

```
  def add_album(album)
    @albums << album
  end

  def remove_album(album)
    @albums.delete(album)
  end

  def each_album
    @albums.each { |album| yield album }
  end
end
```

Now that we've developed preliminary implementations of the three model classes, we can move on to building the user interface itself. Note that it's not necessary to fully specify the model's classes before you begin developing the user interface, especially if you're adopting an iterative approach as we are for this application.

3.3 Let's Code

Now that we have a basic idea of what we want the program to do and what kinds of data we're going to use as a model, you're probably itching to get to work on the first iteration of the user interface. We now face the question of how to get started. What comes next?

There is no one right answer to this question. Over time, as you become more and more familiar with FXRuby application development, you'll gain the confidence and skill you need to be able to dive into a new application from scratch and quickly build up its functionality, if that's how you prefer to work. Personally, however, I like to start with the simplest possible solution and then build on that toward the final goal. For that reason, we'll start by building a version of Picture Book that does just one thing: display a single photo.

Chapter 4

Take 1: Display a Single Photo

We're going to start developing the Picture Book application as simply as possible so that we can quickly get something working and see some results. The first task, then, is to display a single photo. To do that, we're going to create our first view class, PhotoView, as a subclass of an existing FXRuby widget. We'll learn what sorts of issues are involved in making sure that view classes are properly initialized and located in the correct spot in the main window. We'll also get an introduction to FOX's image display capabilities by way of the FXJPGImage class.

4.1 Get Something Running

By the end of the "Hello, World!" exercise in Chapter 1, we had established what a basic FXRuby application looks like, so let's create a similar structure for the Picture Book application. Fire up your editor, and define a PictureBook class as a subclass of FXMainWindow. Your code should resemble the following:

picturebook_a1/picturebook.rb

```
require 'fox16'

include Fox

class PictureBook < FXMainWindow
  def initialize(app)
    super(app, "Picture Book", :width => 600, :height => 400)
  end

  def create
    super
    show(PLACEMENT_SCREEN)
  end
end
```

```
if __FILE__ == $0
  FXApp.new do |app|
    PictureBook.new(app)
    app.create
    app.run
  end
end
```

Save this file as picturebook.rb, and then run it to make sure that everything is working so far:

```
$ ruby picturebook.rb
```

You should see an empty main window, with the application name, Picture Book, in the title bar. Even though we don't expect the program to do much of interest at this point, it provides us with some confidence that our working environment is set up properly. Now let's move on to something a little more interesting.

4.2 Create the View

Now that the main window is in place, the next order of business is to build the view for a single photo. We're going to learn how to create a custom view class as a subclass of one of FXRuby's built-in widgets and see how to place that widget inside the main window.

There are a number of different widgets in the FXRuby library that are capable of displaying images, but for this exercise we'll use FXImageFrame. The FXImageFrame widget is a simple widget whose sole purpose is to display an FXImage object. It doesn't really have any behavior other than that. Your initial instinct might be to use an image frame directly as the view, but as we'll see shortly, subclassing FXImageFrame provides us with a bit more flexibility in terms of providing application-specific functionality.

Create a new document in your editor, and set up the definition for the PhotoView class:

picturebook_a2/photo_view.rb

```
class PhotoView < FXImageFrame
  def initialize(p, photo)
    # We'll add code here soon...
  end
end
```

Take a look at the initialize() method for PhotoView. Since PhotoView is a subclass of FXImageFrame, the very first thing we need to do inside PhotoView's initialize() method is call the base class initialize() method.

Our initialize() method for the PhotoView class will use super() to invoke the FXImageFrame implementation of initialize(). This is an important step to remember whenever you subclass an FXRuby class to customize it: be sure to invoke the base class initialize() method from your overridden version. Some programming languages, like C++ and Java, will automatically invoke a default base class constructor for you; Ruby is not one of those languages!

Now, if you inspect the API documentation for the FXImageFrame class,[1] you'll see that the first two arguments for its initialize() method are required arguments—there are no default values for them. The first argument is the parent (container) widget for the image frame, and the second is a reference to the image that it displays. For now, don't worry about all the other arguments that we could pass to initialize(); we'll just accept their default values.

By convention, the first argument to a widget's initialize() method is the parent widget, so let's make the first argument to our initialize() for PhotoView its parent. That way, we can just pass that first argument through to super() as is. And since the purpose of PhotoView is to display a photo, we'd really like to pass in a Photo instance as the second argument for initialize(). We can't pass this along as the second argument to super(), though, because the FXImageFrame class doesn't know anything about our Photo class. In fact, according to the API documentation, the FXImageFrame.new() method is expecting an FXImage object instead. So, how do we get our hands on one of those FXImage objects?

Slow it down, there, sister. As it turns out, we can just pass in nil for the image frame's image. The only consequence of this decision is that the image frame won't have anything to display. We will correct that problem in the next iteration. For now, modify the initialize() method for PhotoView so that it looks like this:

picturebook_a2/photo_view.rb

```
class PhotoView < FXImageFrame
  def initialize(p, photo)
    super(p, nil)
  end
end
```

Now we need to tie this back in to our main window. Return to picturebook.rb, modify the initialize() method for PictureBook to create a Photo object corresponding to some photo that you have lying around, and

1. http://www.fxruby.org/doc/api/classes/Fox/FXImageFrame.html

then add a PhotoView for that photo. I'm using shoe.jpg, which is a picture of the shoe that my niece left behind the last time she visited us, but any JPEG that you have handy should work. Your initialize() method for PictureBook should look something like this:

picturebook_a2/picturebook.rb

```
def initialize(app)
  super(app, "Picture Book", :width => 600, :height => 400)
  photo = Photo.new("shoe.jpg")
  photo_view = PhotoView.new(self, photo)
end
```

By passing in **self** as the first argument in the call to PhotoView.new, we're saying that the PictureBook object (our application's main window) is the parent for the PhotoView.

Don't forget to add the necessary require() statements at the top of the program so that Ruby can see the definitions of the Photo and PhotoView classes. The entire listing should look like this:

picturebook_a2/picturebook.rb

```
require 'fox16'

include Fox

require 'photo'
require 'photo_view'

class PictureBook < FXMainWindow
  def initialize(app)
    super(app, "Picture Book", :width => 600, :height => 400)
    photo = Photo.new("shoe.jpg")
    photo_view = PhotoView.new(self, photo)
  end

  def create
    super
    show(PLACEMENT_SCREEN)
  end
end

if __FILE__ == $0
  FXApp.new do |app|
    PictureBook.new(app)
    app.create
    app.run
  end
end
```

Run the program and see how things look so far:

```
$ ruby picturebook.rb
```

You will still see what appears to be an empty main window; that's because the image frame doesn't yet have an FXImage to display. It's time to correct that problem.

4.3 Construct an Image from a File

FXRuby provides support for displaying many different kinds of image data, including all the major formats, such as BMP, GIF, JPEG, PNG, and TIFF. We'll discuss this functionality in more detail in Chapter 11, *Creating Visually Rich User Interfaces*, on page 139. For now, we're going to learn how to use FXRuby's built-in FXJPGImage class to construct an onscreen image directly from a JPEG file on disk and then assign that image to an instance of our PhotoView class.

An image is represented by an instance of the FXImage class or, more commonly, one of its subclasses, such as FXJPGImage. Let's write some code to load the image data from a file on disk and then build an FXJPGImage object from it. Return in your editor to the PhotoView class, and add the following method:

picturebook_a/photo_view.rb

```
def load_image(path)
  File.open(path, "rb") do |io|
    self.image = FXJPGImage.new(app, io.read)
  end
end
```

The first line of load_image() uses the "transaction" form of open() to ensure that the file is closed properly when we're done with it. We pass in path as the first argument to open(); this is just a string containing the path to a file on disk, something like shoe.jpg. The second argument to open() tells it that we're opening the file for read and that the file contains binary data. On some operating systems, you can safely leave out the b specifier and the file will load properly, but on other operating systems (namely, Windows) I've run into problems when I omitted it. To be safe, always use both r and b when you're dealing with image files.

Inside the block, we read the contents of the file and construct an FXJPGImage instance from them. FXJPGImage is a subclass of FXImage that knows how to display a JPEG image.

So, our load_image() method opens a named JPEG file, reads its contents, and constructs an FXJPGImage object corresponding to the photo. Obviously, if path refers to a GIF or some other kind of image file, this is going to fail. To keep things simple, our program is going to restrict itself to displaying JPEG images only, but for some ideas on how to expand this and support other image types, see Chapter 11, *Creating Visually Rich User Interfaces*, on page 139.

Careful reader that you are, you may be wondering about that app parameter that we are passing in as the first argument to FXJPGImage.() new(). Elsewhere in our program we're constructing an FXApp object and passing that into the PictureBook.new() method when we construct the main window, but how does this instance method way down in the PhotoView class know about all of that?

It turns out that every class representing an FXRuby widget inherits an instance method named app() that returns a reference to the application object. For historical reasons, it's still necessary to pass a reference to the application object into some methods (such as FXJPGImage.new()), even though in practice you can construct only one FXApp instance per FXRuby application.

Now take a closer look at the middle part of load_image(), where we actually construct the FXJPGImage object. We're assigning the newly created object to self.image. What does **self** mean in this context, assuming that load_image() is an instance method for the PhotoView class? That's right, **self** is just a reference to the PhotoView object. Now, our PhotoView class doesn't define an attribute named image, but its base class does. So, *this* is how we tell the photo view which image it should display.

Before we forget, let's add a call to load_image() from the photo view's initialize() method. Your PhotoView class should now look like this:

picturebook_a/photo_view.rb

```
class PhotoView < FXImageFrame
  def initialize(p, photo)
    super(p, nil)
    load_image(photo.path)
  end

  def load_image(path)
    File.open(path, "rb") do |io|
      self.image = FXJPGImage.new(app, io.read)
    end
  end
end
```

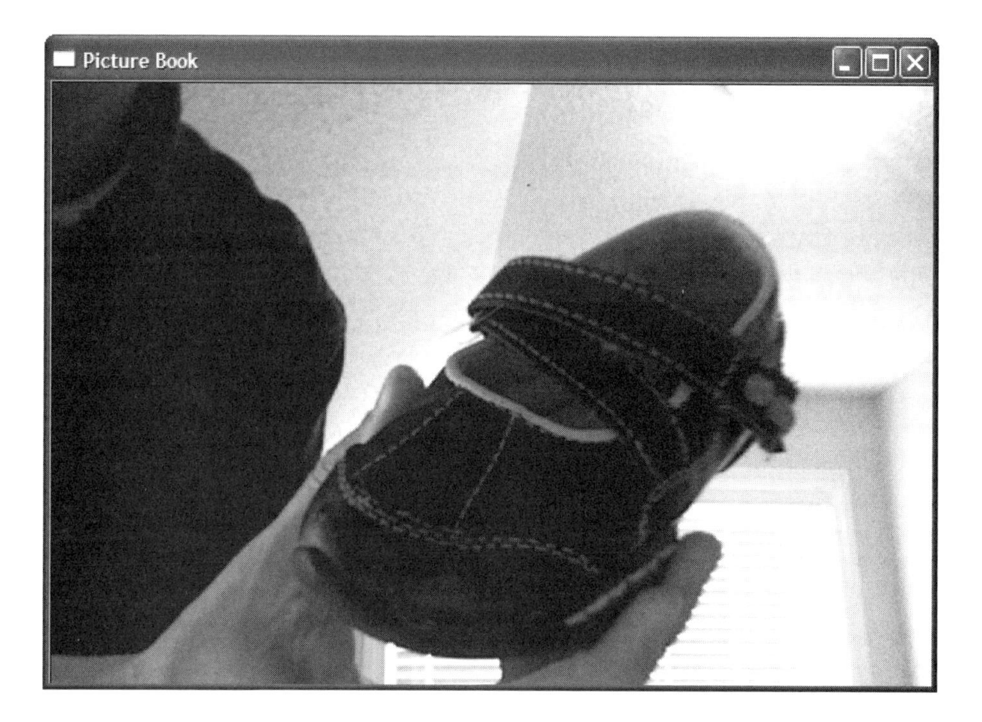

Figure 4.1: PICTURE BOOK, DISPLAYING A SINGLE IMAGE

Finally, we should be able to see something really interesting. Run the program and see what happens:

```
$ ruby picturebook.rb
```

Figure 4.1 shows what it looks like running under Windows. Note that if your photo of choice is too large to fit inside the window, you're going to see only the upper-left portion of it. Don't worry, we're going to fix that soon!

We've made some good progress in this chapter. Picture Book is all about displaying photos, and so with just a little bit of code, we already have the core functionality of the application in place. We've seen that built-in widgets like FXImageFrame can be subclassed like any other Ruby class to provide custom behavior. We've also learned how to use the FXJPGImage class to construct an in-memory representation of a JPEG photo on disk, in one line of code. There's still plenty of work to do, of course, because we're able to display only one photo, and we've hard-coded the path to that photo. In the next chapter, we'll take some steps to improve on that situation.

Chapter 5

Take 2: Display an Entire Album

Maybe you don't get out much, and you really just have that one special photo you're interested in seeing. If so, congratulations! You're finished and can move on to developing some other FXRuby application. If you're not quite that discriminating, however, you probably have a much larger library of photos to deal with. The next order of business, then, is to upgrade Picture Book so that we can display an entire album full of photos.

We eased our way into FXRuby development in the previous chapter, but now it's time to pick up the pace. We're going to cover a lot of ground in this chapter and learn a great deal about some key FXRuby concepts. For example, an understanding of how layout managers work together in constructing the user interface is critical if you want to develop anything other than trivial user interfaces with FXRuby. We'll get an introduction to layout managers when we learn how to use the FXMatrix and FXScrollWindow layout managers to tackle some layout challenges in Picture Book. In the previous chapter, we saw how easily we could construct an image object from a file and then display it onscreen. In this chapter, we're learn a little bit more about FOX's image manipulation capabilities when we create thumbnails of the album's photos. We're also going to learn how to add to our application a menu bar with pull-down menus and how to implement the actions associated with those menu commands. By the time you've completed this upgrade to Picture Book, you'll have a much better feel for how serious FXRuby applications are built.

5.1 Add Album View

FOX provides a number of special-purpose widgets known as *layout managers*. The purpose of a layout manager is to automatically arrange the sizes and placement of its child windows, according to some layout policy that is unique to that layout manager. We'll discuss several of these layout managers in more detail in Chapter 12, *Managing Layouts*, on page 157. In this section, we'll get an introduction to the FXMatrix layout manager.

To display all the photos in an album, we need some kind of view class that's capable of managing a number of PhotoView instances. There are a lot of ways we could do this. For this example we'll use the FXMatrix layout manager, which lays out its child windows in rows and columns.[1] So, our AlbumView class is derived from FXMatrix:

picturebook_b/album_view.rb

```
class AlbumView < FXMatrix

  attr_reader :album

  def initialize(p, album)
    super(p, :opts => LAYOUT_FILL)
    @album = album
  end
end
```

The first argument to initialize() is the parent widget for the album view, and the second argument is a reference to an Album object. As we learned in the previous chapter, we need to be sure to call the base class initialize() method whenever we subclass a widget from FXRuby. Taking a look at the documentation for the FXMatrix class,[2] the only required argument for the base class initialize() method is the parent widget, so at the least we need to be sure to pass that argument into the call to super(). We'll also pass in the LAYOUT_FILL layout hint, which tells the matrix to be greedy and stretch to take up as much room as it can. Otherwise, it will just take up as much room as it needs.

Next, we want to iterate over all the photos in the album and add them to the view. Add the following line of code to the end of the initialize() method for the AlbumView class:

---

1. We discuss the FXMatrix layout manager in detail in Section 12.2, *Arranging Widgets in Rows and Columns with a Matrix Layout*, on page 170.
2. http://www.fxruby.org/doc/api/classes/Fox/FXMatrix.html

picturebook_b/album_view.rb

```
@album.each_photo { |photo| add_photo(photo) }
```

The add_photo() method for the AlbumView class looks like this:

picturebook_b/album_view.rb

```
def add_photo(photo)
  PhotoView.new(self, photo)
end
```

Note that when we construct a PhotoView object, we're again passing in **self** as the first argument to PhotoView.new. This time, though, **self** doesn't refer to the main window, does it? No, now we're creating these photo views as children of the AlbumView window.

Speaking of that, we need to modify the initialize() method for PictureBook so that it creates an Album and an AlbumView, instead of a PhotoView:

picturebook_b/picturebook.rb

```
def initialize(app)
  super(app, "Picture Book", :width => 600, :height => 400)
  @album = Album.new("My Photos")
  @album.add_photo(Photo.new("shoe.jpg"))
  @album.add_photo(Photo.new("oscar.jpg"))
  @album_view = AlbumView.new(self, @album)
end
```

Don't forget to add the necessary **require** statements to album_view.rb and picturebook.rb so that the definitions of the Album, AlbumView, Photo, and PhotoView classes are visible. Here's what your copy of album_view.rb should look like now:

picturebook_b/album_view.rb

```
require 'photo_view'

class AlbumView < FXMatrix

  attr_reader :album

  def initialize(p, album)
    super(p, :opts => LAYOUT_FILL)
    @album = album
    @album.each_photo { |photo| add_photo(photo) }
  end

  def add_photo(photo)
    PhotoView.new(self, photo)
  end
end
```

And here's the updated version of picturebook.rb:

picturebook_b/picturebook.rb

```
require 'fox16'

include Fox

require 'album'
require 'album_view'
require 'photo'

class PictureBook < FXMainWindow
  def initialize(app)
    super(app, "Picture Book", :width => 600, :height => 400)
    @album = Album.new("My Photos")
    @album.add_photo(Photo.new("shoe.jpg"))
    @album.add_photo(Photo.new("oscar.jpg"))
    @album_view = AlbumView.new(self, @album)
  end

  def create
    super
    show(PLACEMENT_SCREEN)
  end
end

if __FILE__ == $0
  FXApp.new do |app|
    PictureBook.new(app)
    app.create
    app.run
  end
end
```

Run the program and see how things look so far:

```
$ ruby picturebook.rb
```

Figure 5.1, on the next page, shows what it looks like running on my machine, but it looks like there's a problem. Depending on the sizes of the photos you're trying to display, you may see it too. As the total size of the album increases, we're running out of space to display the photos, and some of them are being partially (or completely) clipped. Manually resizing the window may allow you to see a little more than you can by default, but that's obviously not going to work in general. We're going to make a couple of changes to address this problem, and the first is to scale down the sizes of the images a bit.

Figure 5.1: PICTURE BOOK, DISPLAYING AN ALBUM

5.2 Display Images as Thumbnails

In addition to simply displaying images, FOX provides support for a number of different image manipulation effects. In this section, we'll learn how to use the scale() method from the FXImage API to scale down the size of our imported photos.

The FXJPGImage class that we're using to represent JPEG images is a subclass of FXImage, and FXImage provides a number of really useful APIs for manipulating images. To tackle the problem at hand, we'll use the image's scale() method to shrink the image from its natural size so that it fits more comfortably in the album view. Since the PhotoView class is responsible for displaying the photo, all of the changes for this iteration will be isolated to that class.

We want the resulting image to fit inside a given bounding box, while maintaining its original aspect ratio. For the time being, let's assume that the dimensions of the bounding box are fixed and are defined by the class constants MAX_WIDTH and MAX_HEIGHT:

picturebook_b/photo_view.rb

```
MAX_WIDTH  = 200
MAX_HEIGHT = 200
```

The scaled-down width of the image thumbnail will be the lesser of its original width or MAX_WIDTH. Similarly, the scaled-down height of the thumbnail will be the lesser of its original height or MAX_HEIGHT. Let's add some helper methods to compute the scaled width and height of the thumbnail:

picturebook_b/photo_view.rb

```
def scaled_width(width)
  [width, MAX_WIDTH].min
end

def scaled_height(height)
  [height, MAX_HEIGHT].min
end
```

Now we can write the code that actually performs the scaling. Let's call it scale_to_thumbnail():

picturebook_b/photo_view.rb

```
def scale_to_thumbnail
  aspect_ratio = image.width.to_f/image.height
  if image.width > image.height
    image.scale(
      scaled_width(image.width),
      scaled_width(image.width)/aspect_ratio,
      1
    )
  else
    image.scale(
      aspect_ratio*scaled_height(image.height),
      scaled_height(image.height),
      1
    )
  end
end
```

The aspect ratio is simply the ratio of the image's width to its height, but we need to consider two cases. If the image is wider than it is tall, then we want to scale down the image's width so that it fits inside the bounding box and then adjust the height accordingly. On the other hand, if the image is taller than it is wide, it's the image height that is the important dimension.

Finally, we can add a call to our new scale_to_thumbnail() method at the end of load_image(). So that you can see all these changes in context, here's the complete listing for our new-and-improved version of PhotoView:

picturebook_b/photo_view.rb

```
class PhotoView < FXImageFrame

  MAX_WIDTH  = 200
  MAX_HEIGHT = 200

  def initialize(p, photo)
    super(p, nil)
    load_image(photo.path)
  end

  def load_image(path)
    File.open(path, "rb") do |io|
      self.image = FXJPGImage.new(app, io.read)
      scale_to_thumbnail
    end
  end

  def scaled_width(width)
    [width, MAX_WIDTH].min
  end

  def scaled_height(height)
    [height, MAX_HEIGHT].min
  end

  def scale_to_thumbnail
    aspect_ratio = image.width.to_f/image.height
    if image.width > image.height
      image.scale(
        scaled_width(image.width),
        scaled_width(image.width)/aspect_ratio,
        1
      )
    else
      image.scale(
        aspect_ratio*scaled_height(image.height),
        scaled_height(image.height),
        1
      )
    end
  end
end
```

Figure 5.2: DISPLAYING IMAGES AS THUMBNAILS

If you run the program now, you should be able to see both photos, at approximately the same size. Figure 5.2 shows what the top part of the main window looks like when the program is running under Windows. This looks so much better that it's a shame we have only two photos to show off. We know, of course, that we could programmatically add even more photos by constructing additional Photo objects and adding them to the album, but that's not really an ideal solution. What we need to do is give the user some means of selecting JPEG files from disk and building up the album interactively. Let's add that functionality next.

5.3 Import Photos from Files

So far, we've been manually constructing an Album and adding Photo objects to it. This obviously isn't going to work moving forward; we need to be able to display a file selection dialog box, pick one or more photo files, and create an album from that list. In this iteration, we'll learn about how the FXMenuBar, FXMenuPane, FXMenuTitle, and FXMenuCommand classes can work together to outfit an application with a menu bar with pull-down menus. We'll see how to use the connect() method to connect widgets such as FXMenuCommand buttons to blocks of Ruby code. Finally, to provide the user with a means to select the files that she wants to import into the album, we'll display an FXFileDialog dialog box and then retrieve the names of the selected files from it.

When Picture Book's users start looking for a command to import photos, the first place they'll want to look will be the File menu. We don't have one of those yet, so let's add one now. To keep the initialize()

method for the PictureBook class as clean as possible, let's put all the code related to constructing the menu bar in a new instance method named add_menu_bar(). The first thing that this method needs to do is construct an FXMenuBar instance, as a child of the main window:

picturebook_c/picturebook.rb

```
def add_menu_bar
  menu_bar = FXMenuBar.new(self, LAYOUT_SIDE_TOP|LAYOUT_FILL_X)
end
```

Since you're an old pro at this point, you've already taken a look at the API documentation for the FXMenuBar class by this point and seen that there are actually two overloads for the initialize() method.[3] We'll use the version that constructs a "nonfloatable" menu bar, and it has two required arguments: the parent window (no surprise there) and an options value. As an old pro, you also already know that the **self** that we're passing in as the menu bar's parent refers to the PictureBook window, since this is an instance method for the PictureBook class. The LAYOUT_SIDE_TOP and LAYOUT_FILL_X layout hints tell FXRuby to place the menu bar at the top of the main window's content area and to stretch it as wide as possible.

Next, we construct an FXMenuPane window, as a child of the FXMenuBar:

picturebook_c/picturebook.rb

```
file_menu = FXMenuPane.new(self)
```

The menu pane will hold all the commands for the File menu. A menu pane is a kind of pop-up window, which means that it makes only brief appearances in public. When it's summoned, it "pops up." You interact with it by choosing a menu command, and then it "pops down" again. You summon a menu pane by clicking the FXMenuTitle widget associated with that menu pane.

picturebook_c/picturebook.rb

```
FXMenuTitle.new(menu_bar, "File", :popupMenu => file_menu)
```

This one is a little tricky. The FXMenuTitle is a child of the FXMenuBar, but it also needs to know which menu pane it should display when it is activated, so we pass that in as the :popupMenu argument. Now we have a menu bar, as well as a File menu, so it's time to add our first command:

---

3. Ruby doesn't actually support overloaded methods per se, at least not in the same sense that some other programming languages implement overloaded methods. Ruby does allow methods to inspect the types of incoming arguments, however, and this is how FXRuby mimics the overloaded methods found in the standard FOX API.

picturebook_c/picturebook.rb

```
import_cmd = FXMenuCommand.new(file_menu, "Import...")
import_cmd.connect(SEL_COMMAND) do
  # ...
end
```

We create the FXMenuCommand object as a child of the menu pane. By calling connect() on import_cmd, we're associating a block of Ruby code with that command. When the user selects the Import... command from the File menu, we want to display a file selection dialog box. To make that happen, here's what should go inside the connect() block:

picturebook_c/picturebook.rb

```
dialog = FXFileDialog.new(self, "Import Photos")
dialog.selectMode = SELECTFILE_MULTIPLE
dialog.patternList = ["JPEG Images (*.jpg, *.jpeg)"]
if dialog.execute != 0
  import_photos(dialog.filenames)
end
```

We start by constructing an FXFileDialog as a child of the main window, with the helpful title Import Photos. Next, we set the file selection mode for this dialog box to SELECTFILE_MULTIPLE, which means the user is allowed to pick any number of existing files for import. We also set the pattern list for the dialog box so that it will display only those filenames that end with the .jpg or .jpeg extension, since these are the only files we're interested in seeing anyway. Finally, we call execute() to display the dialog box and wait for the user to select some files.

The execute() method for a dialog box returns a completion code of either 0 or 1, depending on whether the user clicked Cancel to dismiss the dialog box or OK to accept the selected files. If the user clicked Cancel, we don't really need to do anything else for this command. Otherwise, we want to call the as-yet nonexistent import_photos() method to import the selected photos into our album. Let's add that method to the PictureBook class now:

picturebook_c/picturebook.rb

```
def import_photos(filenames)
  filenames.each do |filename|
    photo = Photo.new(filename)
    @album.add_photo(photo)
    @album_view.add_photo(photo)
  end
  @album_view.create
end
```

The import_photos() method iterates over the filenames collected from the FXFileDialog and adds a new photo to the AlbumView for each of them. Note that since importing photos is now the preferred way to get new ones into the album, you can remove those hard-coded calls to add_photo() that we had in the initialize() method.

If you're paying close attention, you may have noticed that call to the album view's create() method at the tail end of import_photos(). I *hope* you noticed it, because as you'll discover if you leave it out, you won't be able to see any of the newly imported photos unless it's there.

We've run into the create() method before, back in the first chapter when we were building our "Hello, World!" application. At that time, we noted that calling create() ensures that all the server-side resources for the application get created, and for now we'll leave it at that and kick that can a little farther down the street. We're going to talk about this topic in great detail later, in Section 7.7, *Client-Side vs. Server-Side Objects*, on page 89.

But back to the task at hand. As long as we're here, why don't we add an Exit command to the File menu? Add these lines to the add_menu_bar() method, right after the code that sets up the Import... command:

picturebook_c/picturebook.rb

```
exit_cmd = FXMenuCommand.new(file_menu, "Exit")
exit_cmd.connect(SEL_COMMAND) do
  exit
end
```

To complete this iteration, all we need to add is a call to add_menu_bar() from the initialize() method. Your PictureBook class should look like this:

picturebook_c/picturebook.rb

```
require 'fox16'

include Fox

require 'album'
require 'album_view'
require 'photo'

class PictureBook < FXMainWindow
  def initialize(app)
    super(app, "Picture Book", :width => 600, :height => 400)
    add_menu_bar
    @album = Album.new("My Photos")
    @album_view = AlbumView.new(self, @album)
  end
```

```
  def add_menu_bar
    menu_bar = FXMenuBar.new(self, LAYOUT_SIDE_TOP|LAYOUT_FILL_X)
    file_menu = FXMenuPane.new(self)
    FXMenuTitle.new(menu_bar, "File", :popupMenu => file_menu)
    import_cmd = FXMenuCommand.new(file_menu, "Import...")
    import_cmd.connect(SEL_COMMAND) do
      dialog = FXFileDialog.new(self, "Import Photos")
      dialog.selectMode = SELECTFILE_MULTIPLE
      dialog.patternList = ["JPEG Images (*.jpg, *.jpeg)"]
      if dialog.execute != 0
        import_photos(dialog.filenames)
      end
    end
    exit_cmd = FXMenuCommand.new(file_menu, "Exit")
    exit_cmd.connect(SEL_COMMAND) do
      exit
    end
  end

  def import_photos(filenames)
    filenames.each do |filename|
      photo = Photo.new(filename)
      @album.add_photo(photo)
      @album_view.add_photo(photo)
    end
    @album_view.create
  end

  def create
    super
    show(PLACEMENT_SCREEN)
  end
end

if __FILE__ == $0
  FXApp.new do |app|
    PictureBook.new(app)
    app.create
    app.run
  end
end
```

Run the program at this point to see whether things are looking correct so far. The album view should be empty when the program starts, but you should be able to use the Import... command from the File menu to choose some photos and add them to the album. Figure 5.3, on the facing page, shows what the program looks like running on Windows, after I imported a few photos into my album.

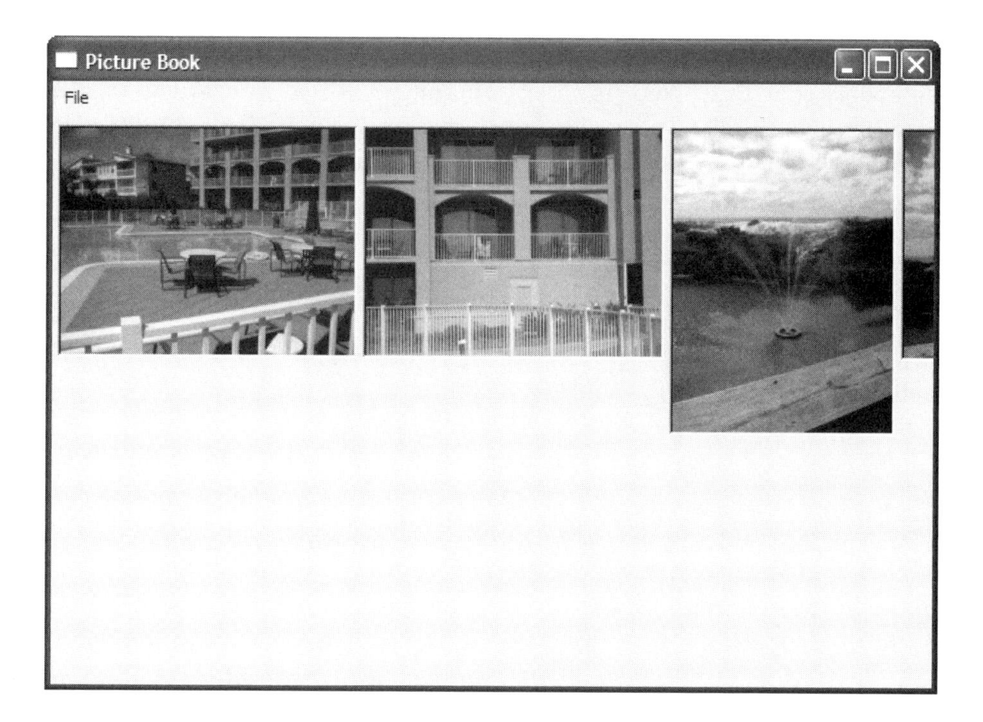

Figure 5.3: NOW WITH MENUS

If you take a close look at the rightmost edge of the window, you'll see that the last photo is clipped. It's not really even the last photo that I imported; it's just that the others are completely offscreen! It looks like our newfound freedom to add as many photos as we want has caused us to once again run out of room. We need to make a little change to the AlbumView class to work around this problem.

5.4 Dynamically Reconfigure the Album View

The default configuration for the FXMatrix layout manager that we're using as the basis for our AlbumView class isn't quite working for us: it's simply placing all the photos on a single row, one right after the other. We'd prefer that it place as many photos as will comfortably fit on a row and then use additional rows as needed to display the remaining photos. To do that, we need to make a couple of changes.

The first change we need to make has to do with the overall layout algorithm used by the FXMatrix layout manager. A matrix can be configured to lay out its children either with a fixed number of rows (the default behavior) or with a fixed number of columns. Since we want to fix the number of columns and let the number of rows vary, we need to pass in the MATRIX_BY_COLUMNS option to the list of construction options for the album view. Our modified version of initialize() for the AlbumView class looks like this:

picturebook_d/album_view.rb

```
def initialize(p, album)
  super(p, :opts => LAYOUT_FILL|MATRIX_BY_COLUMNS)
  @album = album
  @album.each_photo { |photo| add_photo(photo) }
end
```

Next, we need to determine how many columns the matrix should display. The problem is that the number depends on how much space we have to work with and how many columns' worth of photos we can make fit. For example, if the album view window were 800 pixels wide and the photos were each 200 pixels wide, we could fit about four photos on each row. However, if the window were resized so it became narrower or wider, we'd need to reconsider.

To account for the fact that our desired number of columns depends on the current width of the album view, we'll override the album view's layout() method. Whenever the amount of screen "real estate" allocated to a particular window changes, FOX ensures that that window's layout() method is called so that it can update the positions and sizes of its child windows.[4] We're going to take advantage of this to recalculate the number of columns for the matrix before it performs the layout. Add the following method to the AlbumView class:

picturebook_d/album_view.rb

```
def layout
  self.numColumns = [width/PhotoView::MAX_WIDTH, 1].max
  super
end
```

The second line of our overridden version of layout() uses **super** to invoke the base class version of layout(). As usual, that's a step we don't want to overlook. But let's focus on the first line, which is where we actually assign the number of columns.

4. We'll talk more about how layout managers work in Chapter 12, *Managing Layouts*, on page 157.

Starting with the expression on the right side of the assignment, width refers to the width of the album view window in pixels. It may look like we're referring to a variable, but we're actually calling a method on the FXMatrix class that returns the window's width. If you look for the width() method in the API documentation, you'll find that it's actually defined way up in the FXWindow class, from which FXMatrix and many other FXRuby classes are derived.

The PhotoView::MAX_WIDTH reference lets us know the maximum possible width of a photo. Remember, the child windows for the album view are just PhotoView instances. We divide the total width by the maximum possible width of a photo and assign the result to the matrix's numColumns attribute.[5]

Finally, on the off chance that the user shrinks the album view window so that it's actually narrower than PhotoView::MAX_WIDTH, we need to protect ourselves from setting the number of columns to zero. If we build a two-element array containing the number 1 and our calculation for numColumns, we can then call the array's max() method as shown here to return the larger of the two values. This will ensure that we end up with at least one column.

Let's see whether our work has paid off. If you run the application and import a bunch of photos, you should now see that when a row in the album view gets too "full," a new row is added. Figure 5.4, on the following page, shows what the program looks like running on my machine, with several photos in place. You should also be able to resize the main window, to make it narrower or wider, and see that the number of columns in the album view changes dynamically depending on how much space is available.

Unfortunately, this change solves only part of our problem. Before we made this change, the photos that didn't fit inside the album view were spilling off the right edge of the window. Now, if you import too many photos, you'll see that the ones that don't fit start spilling off the *bottom* edge of the window. To address this problem, we need to enlist the help of yet another layout manager.

---

5. Again, although I refer to numColumns as an attribute, we're really just calling an FXMatrix instance method named numColumns=().

Figure 5.4: MAKING THE ALBUM RESIZABLE

5.5 Make the Album View Scrollable

We got an introduction to FOX's layout managers when we decided to use the FXMatrix layout manager as the basis for our AlbumView class. In this section, we'll take a look at another layout manager, the FXScrollWindow, and see how to use it to solve our latest layout dilemma.

Sometimes, the content that you want to display inside a window is simply too large to fit inside the viewable area for that window. For example, many digital cameras are now capable of taking photographs of such high resolution that they can't be displayed in their true dimensions on a typical computer monitor. When that's the case, you have at least a couple of options. One option is to somehow scale down the dimensions of the content so that it fits inside the window. If the content doesn't really lend itself to scaling, however, or if you're afraid that scaling down will cause you to lose some of the finer details of the content, another option is to place the content inside a scrolling window.

FOX provides for this latter option by way of the FXScrollArea and FXScrollWindow classes. FXScrollWindow is a subclass of FXScrollArea, and in most cases it's the class that you'll want to use when you need to provide scrollable content windows in your applications. To apply this technique to the Picture Book application, we're going to begin by modifying our AlbumView class to make it a subclass of FXScrollWindow:

picturebook_e/album_view.rb

```
class AlbumView < FXScrollWindow
  # ...
end
```

The next set of changes that we need to make involves the initialize() method for AlbumView. A quick check of the API documentation for FXScrollWindow[6] reveals that its initialize() method has only one required argument, and as was the case for the initialize() method for FXMatrix, that argument is the parent window. We're going to make one little change to how we invoke the base class initialize() method, however. In addition to the parent window, we're going to pass in the LAYOUT_FILL layout hint as one of our construction options:

picturebook_e/album_view.rb

```
def initialize(p, album)
  super(p, :opts => LAYOUT_FILL)
  # ...
end
```

You'll learn all about layout managers and layout hints in Chapter 12, *Managing Layouts*, on page 157. For now, it's enough to know that this layout hint tells FXRuby that we'd like the album view to stretch in the horizontal and vertical directions in order to take up as much room as possible.

Now that we've initialized the base class part of the album view, we need to say what it is that we will be scrolling. An FXScrollWindow has a single child window that is designated as its *content window*. For our application, the FXMatrix instance is that content that we want to make scrollable. So, the album view is now an FXScrollWindow, which contains an FXMatrix, which in turn contains a bunch of PhotoView instances:

picturebook_e/album_view.rb

```
def initialize(p, album)
  super(p, :opts => LAYOUT_FILL)
  @album = album
  FXMatrix.new(self, :opts => LAYOUT_FILL|MATRIX_BY_COLUMNS)
  @album.each_photo { |photo| add_photo(photo) }
end
```

6. http://www.fxruby.org/doc/api/classes/Fox/FXScrollWindow.html

Figure 5.5: MAKING THE ALBUM SCROLLABLE

Take a good look at this, and make sure you understand what's going on before you read ahead. What does it mean, for example, on the third line when we pass in **self** as the argument to FXMatrix.new? What does **self** refer to in this context? Are you beginning to understand what it means for one window, like an FXMatrix window, to be a child window of another window, like an FXScrollWindow?

The final changes to the AlbumView class for this iteration take place in the add_photo() and layout() methods. First, here's what the new and improved version of add_photo() looks like:

picturebook_e/album_view.rb

```
def add_photo(photo)
  PhotoView.new(contentWindow, photo)
end
```

The difference between this version of add_photo() and the previous version is subtle. Instead of passing in **self** to PhotoView.new, we're passing in the result of the scroll window's contentWindow() method. As I mentioned earlier, the content window for an FXScrollWindow is just the first (and only) child window that you add to it—in this case, the FXMatrix widget. So, we're still constructing our PhotoView objects as children of the FXMatrix object, even though it's not as obvious as it was before.

We need to make a similar change to the layout() method, since **self** no longer refers to the matrix widget but rather the scroll window. Here's what the new version of layout() looks like:

picturebook_e/album_view.rb

```
def layout
  contentWindow.numColumns = [width/PhotoView::MAX_WIDTH, 1].max
  super
end
```

After you've made all of the modifications to the AlbumView class, it should look something like this:

picturebook_e/album_view.rb

```
require 'photo_view'

class AlbumView < FXScrollWindow

  attr_reader :album

  def initialize(p, album)
    super(p, :opts => LAYOUT_FILL)
    @album = album
    FXMatrix.new(self, :opts => LAYOUT_FILL|MATRIX_BY_COLUMNS)
    @album.each_photo { |photo| add_photo(photo) }
  end

  def layout
    contentWindow.numColumns = [width/PhotoView::MAX_WIDTH, 1].max
    super
  end

  def add_photo(photo)
    PhotoView.new(contentWindow, photo)
  end
end
```

Now when you rerun the application, you should see a vertical scroll bar appear on the right side of the window whenever the album contains more photos than can be displayed onscreen. It should look something like Figure 5.5, on the facing page. Here, I've scrolled the album down a bit so that I can see some of the additional photos in my album.

We've made a lot of progress in this chapter. We've taken our program from a pretty rudimentary single-image viewer to an application that's able to load any number of photos from disk and display them as thumbnails in a scrollable window. We're still restricted to dumping all our photos into the same album, however, and there are a number of other issues that we need to address, so let's press on.

Chapter 6

Take 3: Manage Multiple Albums

We've made some really good progress over the past few chapters in building up the foundation for the Picture Book application. By the time you finish this chapter, you may feel like we've torn up all of our previous work and started over from scratch. That won't quite be the case, but we will need to make some serious structural changes to the application in order to keep track of multiple photo albums.

We'll begin by creating a view that will allow us to display a listing of the names of the albums in the album list and that will allow the user to switch back and forth between albums to view the photos they contain. Along the way, we'll make a number of other changes as we continue to push toward providing useful functionality.

As in the previous chapters, we're going to continue to build on our knowledge of FXRuby development as we extend the application. We'll begin by getting an introduction to the FXList widget when we use it as the basis of our AlbumListView class. When we encounter some new layout challenges, we're going to turn to the FXSplitter and FXSwitcher layout managers for help. We'll use an FXInputDialog as a dead simple way to collect information from the user. Perhaps most important, we'll get an introduction to FOX's powerful GUI update mechanism when we use it to automatically update the album view's contents whenever the user selects a new album from the list. So, let's get back to work.

6.1 Create the Album List View

The first order of business is to think about the view for the album list and how we might implement that. In this section, we'll learn how to use the FXList widget to display lists of items from which the user can select.

If you'll let your mind wander back to the notional user interface that's pictured in Figure 3.1, on page 22, you'll recall that we're looking for a simple listing of the album names to appear on the left side of the window. As you'll read later, in Chapter 9, *Sorting Data with List and Table Widgets*, on page 111, FXRuby provides a number of kinds of widgets for dealing with listlike data, so we have plenty of options to choose from. Let's go with the most obvious choice, which is the basic FXList widget.

Create a new AlbumListView class as a subclass of FXList, and give it an initialize() method that accepts arguments for the parent window, some construction options, and an AlbumList instance:

picturebook_f/album_list_view.rb

```
class AlbumListView < FXList

  attr_reader :album_list

  def initialize(p, opts, album_list)
    super(p, :opts => opts)
    @album_list = album_list
  end
end
```

Now we want to hop over to the PictureBook class, which implements the main window, and add some code to its initialize() method to construct an AlbumListView as a child of the main window. Note that since the main window already has a couple of child windows—the album view and the menu bar—this list view will be a “sibling” to those windows. Here's what the modified version of initialize() should look like:

picturebook_f/picturebook.rb

```
def initialize(app)
  super(app, "Picture Book", :width => 600, :height => 400)
  add_menu_bar
  @album = Album.new("My Photos")
  @album_list = AlbumList.new
  @album_list.add_album(@album)
  @album_list_view = AlbumListView.new(self,
    LAYOUT_FILL_Y|LAYOUT_SIDE_LEFT, @album_list)
  @album_view = AlbumView.new(self, @album)
end
```

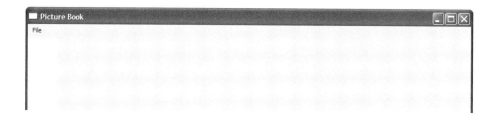

Figure 6.1: AFTER ADDING LIST VIEW

Don't forget to add the necessary **require** statements to import the definitions for the AlbumList and AlbumListView classes:

picturebook_f/picturebook.rb

```
require 'album'
require 'album_list'
require 'album_list_view'
require 'album_view'
require 'photo'
```

Now let's run the program and see how it looks. Figure 6.1 shows what the top part of the main window looks like when the program is running under Windows. Clearly, something has changed, but is that white strip along the left side of the window supposed to be a list?

Part of the problem is that our list doesn't actually have anything in it yet. First, we'll add a helper method for AlbumListView that appends a new list item for a given album:

picturebook_f/album_list_view.rb

```
def add_album(album)
  appendItem(album.title)
end
```

Now, let's add some code to the initialize() method for AlbumListView so that it iterates over all the albums in the album list and adds each of them:

picturebook_f/album_list_view.rb

```
@album_list.each_album do |album|
  add_album(album)
end
```

Figure 6.2: BARELY WIDE ENOUGH

Now run the program again. This time, the name of our single album (creatively named "My Photos") should appear in the list. The problem now (as shown in Figure 6.2) is that the list is just barely wide enough to display the entire album name. In fact, depending on the size of the default font that FOX selects on your computer, the list may be too narrow to display the album's name, or it may be disproportionately wide. The point is that you can't really make any assumptions about the default width of an empty list.

FOX does provide options for setting a fixed widget width, so we could just pick some arbitrary width for the album list, and that would take care of the problem—for now. Looking ahead, though, we might add some albums with even longer names, which would then require us to change the fixed width value for the list again. We could perhaps make it so that the list dynamically resizes itself, becoming just wide enough to hold the widest list item's text, but that seems likely to become a visual distraction. What we need is a layout that will allow the user to dynamically resize the width of the list according to her own preferences. To do that, we're going to use a splitter.

6.2 Use a Split View

FXSplitter is a layout manager that you can use to display user-resizable windows. The FXSplitter is a special kind of layout manager that manages two child windows. When it's configured as a horizontal splitter, the two child windows are side by side; when it's a vertical splitter, one child window is on top, and the other is on the bottom. We're going to use the horizontal flavor of FXSplitter.

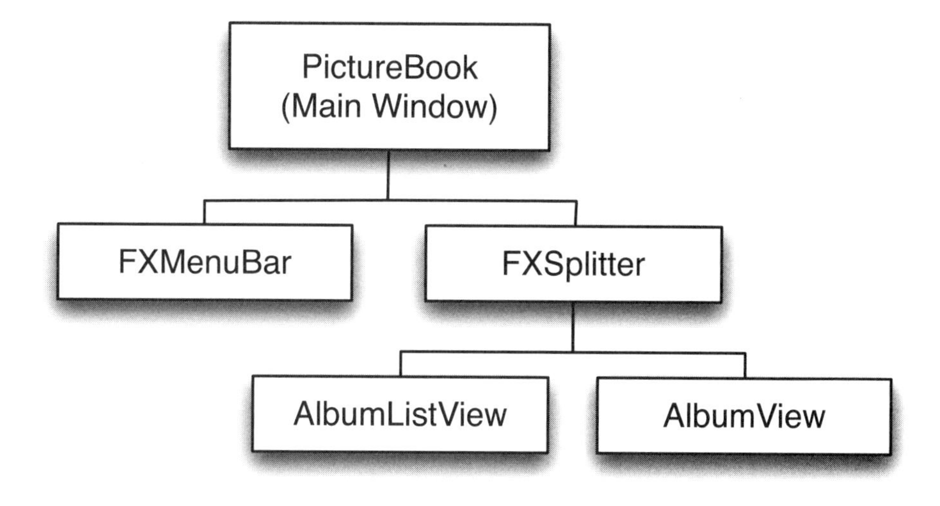

Figure 6.3: LAYOUT HIERARCHY

Here's the plan: we're going to create a splitter window as a child of the main window and then make the album list view and the album view children of the splitter. Since the nesting of these windows is starting to get deep, take a look at Figure 6.3 to see what's taking place.

First, create the splitter as a child of the main window:

picturebook_g/picturebook.rb

```
splitter = FXSplitter.new(self,
  :opts => SPLITTER_HORIZONTAL|LAYOUT_FILL)
```

Next, make the album list view and album view windows children of the splitter:

picturebook_g/picturebook.rb

```
@album_list_view = AlbumListView.new(splitter,
  LAYOUT_FILL, @album_list)
@album_view = AlbumView.new(splitter, @album)
```

Note that it's no longer necessary to specify the LAYOUT_SIDE_LEFT hint on the album list view. Since we're adding the album list view first, it's automatically assigned to the left side of the split, and the album view is assigned to the right side.

Here's what the initialize() method for the PictureBook class looks like after this set of changes:

picturebook_g/picturebook.rb

```
def initialize(app)
  super(app, "Picture Book", :width => 600, :height => 400)
  add_menu_bar
  @album = Album.new("My Photos")
  @album_list = AlbumList.new
  @album_list.add_album(@album)
  splitter = FXSplitter.new(self,
    :opts => SPLITTER_HORIZONTAL|LAYOUT_FILL)
  @album_list_view = AlbumListView.new(splitter,
    LAYOUT_FILL, @album_list)
  @album_view = AlbumView.new(splitter, @album)
end
```

Now when you run the program, if the mouse is on the edge between the list and the album view, the mouse cursor should change its shape to a set of vertical lines with arrows pointing outward. When the mouse cursor is this shape, you can press the left mouse button to "grab" the splitter, drag it left and right to resize the split, and then release the mouse button.

6.3 Switch Between Albums

By now you should be getting pretty comfortable with the notion of layout managers and how to use them to solve different kinds of layout problems. We learned about the FXMatrix layout manager when we created the album view, and in the previous section we learned how to use an FXSplitter to manage windows that may need to be resized by the user. In this section, we're going to learn about yet another layout manager, FXSwitcher.

When the user selects a new album from the album list, we want the album view to update itself so that it shows the photos from the newly selected album. One way to do this would be to first remove all the PhotoView instances associated with the previously selected album and then repopulate the AlbumView using the photos from the newly selected album. This could certainly work; FOX is very efficient in terms of creating and destroying windows, and it's likely that the user wouldn't notice much of a delay for switching back and forth between albums that contained a relatively small number of photos. It's not a very resource-friendly solution, however, and for larger albums the time required to reload all the image files and then create FXJPGImage objects for them would be too great.

A better solution is to construct one AlbumView instance for every album in the library and then use FOX's FXSwitcher layout manager to quickly switch back and forth between those album views. A switcher can contain any number of child windows, but it displays only one of them at a time. One way to think of it is as a deck of cards, where only the topmost card is visible.[1]

We're going to change our layout once again so that the right pane of the FXSplitter contains an FXSwitcher. Then we'll make the AlbumView window a child of FXSwitcher. Figure 6.4, on the following page, shows the revised parent-child hierarchy. The first step is to create the switcher as a child of the splitter, where it will take over the spot previously held by the album view:

picturebook_h/picturebook.rb

```
@switcher = FXSwitcher.new(splitter, :opts => LAYOUT_FILL)
```

Now modify the first argument in the call to AlbumView.new to make the switcher the new parent of the album view:

picturebook_h/picturebook.rb

```
AlbumView.new(@switcher, @album)
```

Note that we no longer need to keep a reference to the single AlbumView instance in @album_view. If we are going to be dealing with multiple albums, we really need to start thinking in terms of operations on the *current* album's view. In fact, let's code up a little convenience function that asks the album list for the index of the currently selected album and then returns the switcher child with the same index:

picturebook_h/picturebook.rb

```
def current_album_view
  @switcher.childAtIndex(@switcher.current)
end
```

We can then piggyback off this to provide a current_album() method:

picturebook_h/picturebook.rb

```
def current_album
  current_album_view.album
end
```

---

1. If you've ever used Java's Swing toolkit, you'll recognize this as FOX's equivalent of the CardLayout layout manager.

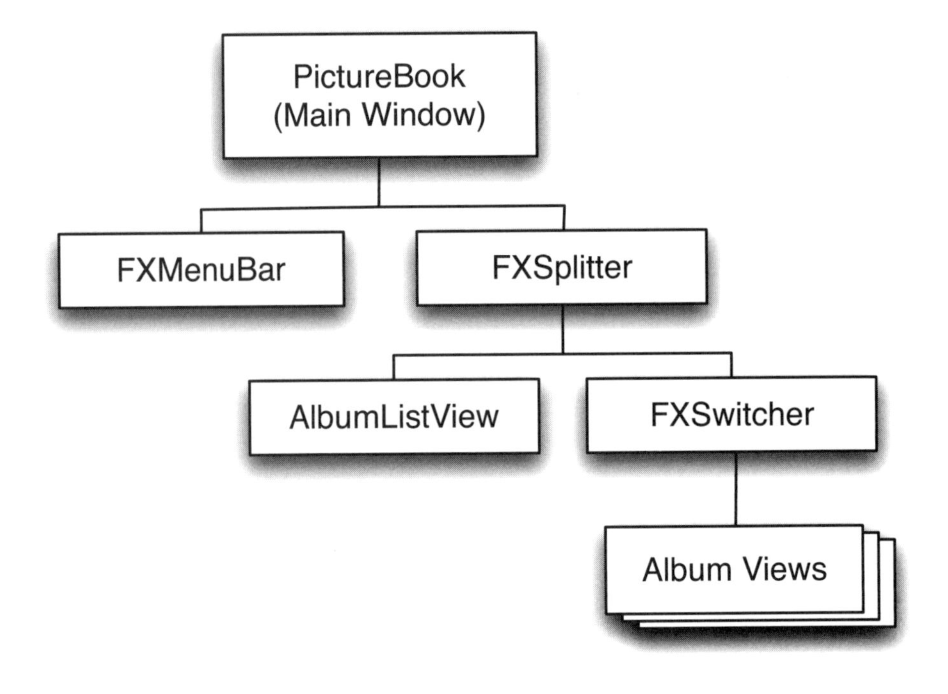

Figure 6.4: USING A SWITCHER

While we're at it, modify the import_photos() method to ensure that it always imports photos into the currently selected album:

picturebook_h/picturebook.rb

```
def import_photos(filenames)
  filenames.each do |filename|
    photo = Photo.new(filename)
    current_album.add_photo(photo)
    current_album_view.add_photo(photo)
  end
  current_album_view.create
end
```

We sure have been going to a lot of effort to make it possible to view multiple photo albums. What do you say we finally get around to actually adding another album or two to the collection?

6.4 Add New Albums

In the previous chapter, you learned how to use one kind of dialog box, the FXFileDialog, to provide the user with an interface to the file system for selecting files. In this section, we'll learn how to use the FXInputDialog to collect a different sort of input from the user. We'll also get an introduction to FOX's GUI update mechanism, a powerful and useful way to keep the user interface in sync with the overall application state.

Until this point, we've been dealing with only a single album, even though we've been making a lot of changes to the code to accommodate multiple albums. Let's head into the home stretch by adding a new command to the File menu. Find your way to the add_menu_bar() method, and set up the scaffolding for the New Album... command. You know how:

picturebook_h/picturebook.rb

```
new_album_command = FXMenuCommand.new(file_menu, "New Album...")
new_album_command.connect(SEL_COMMAND) do
  # ...
end
```

All we need to do is prompt the user for the name of the new album, create a new album by that name, and add it to the album list and the album list view. To get the name, we're going to use the FXInputDialog class:

picturebook_h/picturebook.rb

```
album_title =
  FXInputDialog.getString("My Album", self, "New Album", "Name:")
```

If the user clicks the Cancel button, the getString() method will return nil. Otherwise, getString() will return the new album's title, and we can use that to carry out the rest of the command:

picturebook_h/picturebook.rb

```
if album_title
  album = Album.new(album_title)
  @album_list.add_album(album)
  @album_list_view.add_album(album)
  AlbumView.new(@switcher, album)
end
```

The final product should look like this:

picturebook_h/picturebook.rb

```
new_album_command = FXMenuCommand.new(file_menu, "New Album...")
new_album_command.connect(SEL_COMMAND) do
  album_title =
    FXInputDialog.getString("My Album", self, "New Album", "Name:")
  if album_title
    album = Album.new(album_title)
    @album_list.add_album(album)
    @album_list_view.add_album(album)
    AlbumView.new(@switcher, album)
  end
end
```

If you run the program at this point and try adding an album, you should see the new album's name show up in the album list. If you then click that item in the list, you might expect to see a fresh, empty album show up in the album view. If that's what you do and that's what you're expecting, well, you're going to be disappointed. That's because we haven't told the switcher that you've selected a new item from the album list—so far, there's no connection there.

In many GUI toolkits, the way you'd address this problem is to go back to the album list widget and write some code that reacts to the new list selection by updating the switcher. You could do it that way in FXRuby, too, but I'm going to show you a slightly different approach. We will instead use FOX's GUI update mechanism to let the switcher update itself based on the list selection.

Jump back up to the initialize() method for PictureBook, and add this block after the switcher creation:

picturebook_h/picturebook.rb

```
@switcher.connect(SEL_UPDATE) do
  @switcher.current = @album_list_view.currentItem
end
```

By defining a SEL_UPDATE handler for the switcher, we're telling FOX how to update the state of the switcher whenever the state of the application changes. The currently shown switcher item should reflect the currently selected list item. This update handler is called for us automatically. We'll talk about the GUI update mechanism in more detail in Section 7.4, *Syncing the User Interface with the Application Data*, on page 85.

Now we should have everything wired up properly. Let's do a little experiment. Start the program, and import a set of photos into the initial album. Now, add a new album to the list, and select that album. The switcher should properly update itself and show you the new (and empty) album. Import some photos into this album, and then confirm that you can switch back and forth between the two. If you really feel like going crazy, add another album or two. Maybe invite the neighbors over to watch.

6.5 Serialize the Album List with YAML

In this final step, we'll learn how to use Ruby's YAML Ain't Markup Language (YAML) library to save the application data to a file and then read that data back in when the program starts. Although this doesn't directly have much to do with FXRuby development, we'll see that we do need to make some changes to the application code to ensure that the user interface is updated properly after new album data is loaded.

If you've been running the application along the way, you've probably picked up on an annoyance. Every time the program starts, you're presented with a blank slate, and you have to re-create the albums and reimport your photos. We clearly need to make some provisions for persisting the album list to disk when the program exits and then reloading those albums when the program starts back up.

We could do this in several ways. If you're coming from a Java programming background, your first instinct may be to devise an XML schema that describes the relationships between the album list, the albums, and the photos contained therein. XML wouldn't be the worst choice you could make, and it is a well understood, human-readable way to store structured data. Ruby's standard library even includes REXML, a great module for reading and writing XML documents. Despite its popularity, however, XML is not always the best solution for every data storage problem.

Another option is to store the information in a relational database. Once again, Ruby provides excellent support for working with databases if that makes sense for your application, but it feels like a pretty heavyweight solution for our current needs. Ruby's standard library provides support for two lightweight serialization schemes, by way of the Marshal and YAML modules.

I'm not a big fan of data that's not human readable, and since Ruby's Marshal module stores its data in a proprietary binary format, we'll use a YAML file as our persistent store for the Picture Book application data.

First, the easy part. Let's write some code to save the contents of the album list to a file. The store_album_list() method creates a file named picturebook.yml and uses the YAML.dump method to write out the album list data:

picturebook_i/picturebook.rb

```
def store_album_list
  File.open("picturebook.yml", "w") do |io|
    io.write(YAML.dump(@album_list))
  end
end
```

We want this to happen when the user selects the Exit command from the File menu, so let us modify the exit handler to add a call to store_() album_list() before the call to exit():

picturebook_i/picturebook.rb

```
exit_cmd.connect(SEL_COMMAND) do
  store_album_list
  exit
end
```

Now, the tricky part. Obviously, the key thing we need to do is try to load the saved album list file, if it exists. If it doesn't exist, we'll fall back on our default behavior to this point and construct a new album list with one album in it:

picturebook_i/picturebook.rb

```
begin
  @album_list = YAML.load_file("picturebook.yml")
rescue
  @album_list = AlbumList.new
  @album_list.add_album(Album.new("My Photos"))
end
```

Don't forget to add a **require** statement at the top of picturebook.rb to import the YAML library:

picturebook_i/picturebook.rb

```
require 'yaml'
```

Let's factor the code related to populating the AlbumListView from the album list's contents out into an accessor method:

picturebook_i/album_list_view.rb

```
def album_list=(albums)
  @album_list = albums
  @album_list.each_album do |album|
    add_album(album)
  end
end
```

Whenever a new AlbumList instance is assigned to the AlbumListView, this code will call add_album() for each album in the list. Now that this accessor method is in place, we don't really need to pass the album list into the list view's initialize() method, so let's remove that parameter from the argument list:

picturebook_i/album_list_view.rb

```
def initialize(p, opts)
  super(p, :opts => opts)
end
```

We also need to modify the line in PictureBook where we actually construct the AlbumListView and ensure that we no longer pass in the album list to AlbumListView.new():

picturebook_i/picturebook.rb

```
@album_list_view = AlbumListView.new(splitter, LAYOUT_FILL)
```

Don't forget to actually assign the album list to the view, though. Otherwise, we'll never actually see the contents of our albums:

picturebook_i/picturebook.rb

```
@album_list_view.album_list = @album_list
```

Now add a line to the add_album() method to create a new AlbumView at the same time we're adding the list item:

picturebook_i/album_list_view.rb

```
def add_album(album)
  appendItem(album.title)
  AlbumView.new(@switcher, album)
end
```

For this to work, we need a way to let the AlbumListView know about the switcher:

picturebook_i/album_list_view.rb

```
def switcher=(sw)
  @switcher = sw
end
```

Here's what the new-and-improved version of AlbumListView looks like:

picturebook_i/album_list_view.rb

```
class AlbumListView < FXList

  attr_accessor :album_list

  def initialize(p, opts)
    super(p, :opts => opts)
  end

  def album_list=(albums)
    @album_list = albums
    @album_list.each_album do |album|
      add_album(album)
    end
  end

  def switcher=(sw)
    @switcher = sw
  end

  def add_album(album)
    appendItem(album.title)
    AlbumView.new(@switcher, album)
  end
end
```

The last little pair of changes takes place in the initialize() method for PictureBook. First, we set the switcher for the album list view:

picturebook_i/picturebook.rb

```
@album_list_view.switcher = @switcher
```

Finally, since assigning the album list to the album list view triggers a call to add_album() for each album in the list and since our updated version of add_album() creates an AlbumView corresponding to the newly added album, we can (and should) remove the line from PictureBook's initialize() method that constructed a default AlbumView object.

Since the ordering of these lines in initialize() is important, here's what the final version of the initialize() method should look like:

picturebook_i/picturebook.rb

```
def initialize(app)
  super(app, "Picture Book", :width => 600, :height => 400)
  add_menu_bar
  begin
    @album_list = YAML.load_file("picturebook.yml")
  rescue
    @album_list = AlbumList.new
    @album_list.add_album(Album.new("My Photos"))
  end
  splitter = FXSplitter.new(self,
    :opts => SPLITTER_HORIZONTAL|LAYOUT_FILL)
  @album_list_view = AlbumListView.new(splitter, LAYOUT_FILL)
  @switcher = FXSwitcher.new(splitter, :opts => LAYOUT_FILL)
  @switcher.connect(SEL_UPDATE) do
    @switcher.current = @album_list_view.currentItem
  end
  @album_list_view.switcher = @switcher
  @album_list_view.album_list = @album_list
end
```

At this point, you should be able to use Picture Book to create albums and add photos to them without fear that all your work will be lost when you exit the program. This is where we're going to draw the line and stop working on Picture Book, but before we move on to other topics, let's take a minute to think about some additional enhancements that you might want to make after you've finished the book.

6.6 So, What Now?

Over the past three chapters, we've managed to substantially extend the functionality of Picture Book with relatively few changes to the code base. As you become more and more comfortable with FXRuby development, you're going to find that it's a really flexible toolkit for building up applications in this fashion.

The purpose of this exercise wasn't so much to build a real-world application as it was to give you a taste of what it's like to develop applications with FXRuby and to introduce you to a lot of the techniques that you will use in your own projects. Having said that, you could make a number of enhancements to Picture Book.

For example, Picture Book currently supports only the import and display of JPEG images. In Chapter 11, *Creating Visually Rich User Interfaces*, on page 139, we'll go into more detail about the various image formats that FOX supports. Armed with that knowledge, you should be able to extend Picture Book so that most any kind of image data could be imported and displayed. You may also get some ideas about other kinds of image manipulations that you'd like for your version of Picture Book to support, such as cropping and rotating images.

Another limitation of Picture Book in its current form is that the size of the image thumbnails is hard-coded to 200 pixels square. In Chapter 8, *Building Simple Widgets*, on page 95, you'll get an introduction to some of the other kinds of widgets that you can build into the user interface to get user input. You may decide that you want to use some of these tools to allow the user to edit the thumbnail sizes, the photo or album names, or some other kinds of application data.

Or consider the album list. Our organizational structure for that list is a little inflexible, in that we can't group together similar albums in folders—it's all one big flat list. In Chapter 9, *Sorting Data with List and Table Widgets*, on page 111, we'll look at (among other things) the FXTreeList widget, which you could use to present a more deeply nested sort of album list.

You're not going to learn about every nook and cranny of FOX and FXRuby from this book, but by the time you finish reading, you'll have a solid enough foundation to go out and investigate some of the even more advanced features that the toolkit has to offer. As you work your way through the rest of the book, and beyond, I hope you'll be inspired to return to Picture Book as a kind of test bed for trying the new things that you learn about GUI development with FXRuby.

Part II

FXRuby Fundamentals

Chapter 7

FXRuby Under the Hood

Now that we've worked our way through the creation of an entire application from start to finish, it's time to dig a bit deeper into how FXRuby actually gets things done. Although you can certainly get by with a superficial understanding of the FXRuby library, taking the time to learn how FXRuby works under the hood can help you write more flexible, maintainable, and efficient applications.

While we were building the Picture Book application, we learned how to use the connect() method to associate a few user actions, such as mouse clicks, with blocks of Ruby code. That functionality is built on top of a powerful event-driven messaging system, and in this chapter we'll learn more about how to take advantage of that system to handle a number of kinds of application events. FOX uses that same event system as the basis of its automatic GUI update mechanism in order to keep your user interface in sync with the application data. We'll take a closer look at how this works with a variety of FXRuby widgets, as well as how to use data targets as a higher-level alternative to dealing directly with the GUI update engine.

FOX's creator takes great pride in FOX being one of the fastest and most resource-friendly GUI toolkits around, and although it's not critical to understand all the optimizations that FOX uses to achieve its performance, we'll explore some of the most significant ones. One way that FOX ensures that your applications remain quick and responsive is by actually delaying the layout calculations and subsequent repainting of the user interface. FOX also makes a much more explicit distinction between the client-side and server-side representations of user interface objects than other GUI toolkits do, so we'll learn how managing those different representations helps you keep your application's resource use at a minimum.

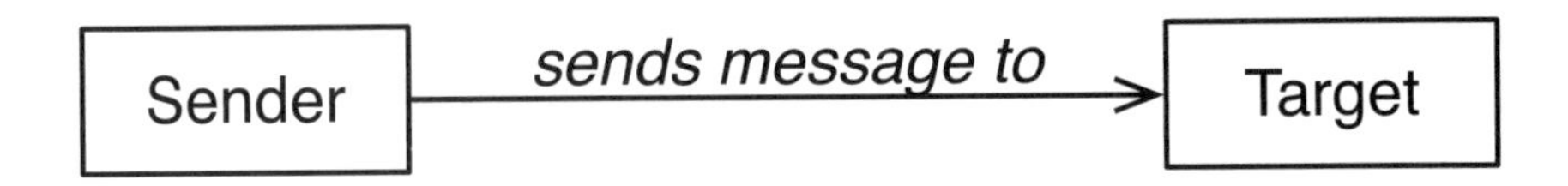

Figure 7.1: OBJECTS SEND MESSAGES TO OTHER OBJECTS

By the end of this chapter, you'll have a much more in-depth understanding of how FXRuby works under the hood, and you'll have the strong foundation that you need to tackle the rest of this book.

7.1 Event-Driven Programming

A lot of the scripts and programs that you write in Ruby follow a fairly predictable path. A typical program might open a file, read in some data, perform computations on that data, and report its results. The program might contain some conditional logic that causes it to branch off and do different things depending on the input data, but you can count on it to do things in an orderly fashion.

FXRuby programs are event-driven and behave somewhat differently. After some initialization, an FXRuby program enters what's known as the *event loop*: the program waits for an event to occur, it responds to that event, and then it resumes waiting for the next event. Most often it's the user who generates an event, whether it's by clicking a mouse button, by typing some text in a text field, or by doing some other action. Other times, it's the operating system or the windowing system that generates an event, such as by raising a signal. Other GUI toolkits implement event-driven programming in a variety of ways, but FXRuby models an event as one object, the *sender*, sending a message to another object, the *target* (see Figure 7.1).

Message Types, Identifiers, and Data

Every message that's sent from one FXRuby object to another consists of a *message type*, a *message identifier*, and some *message data*. The message type is a constant whose name begins with SEL_. You've already seen a number of examples of these, most notably the SEL_COMMAND message type.

The message identifier is also a constant, and it's used by the target (the receiver of the message) to distinguish between different incoming messages of the same type. For example, if the target expects to receive SEL_CHANGED messages from two different senders, it might rely on the senders using two different message identifier values when they send their messages. Along the same lines, if the target wants to implement different behaviors for the same message type, it might require a number of message identifiers. For example, when the FXTextField widget receives a SEL_COMMAND message with an identifier of ID_CURSOR_HOME, it moves the cursor to the beginning of the line, but when it receives a SEL_COMMAND message with an identifier of ID_CURSOR_END, it moves the cursor to the end of the line.

Finally, the message data is just an object that provides some additional context for the message. For example, when an FXText object sends a SEL_INSERTED message to its target, it sends along an FXTextChange object that indicates what text was inserted and where it was inserted.

You can use the API documentation to identify which message types a particular widget sends to its target, as well as the message data for those messages. For example, Figure 7.2, on the following page, shows part of the documentation for the FXTable class.[1] Note that under the "Events" heading, there's a table listing the message types and important information for every message that an FXTable sends to its target. There's similar information in the API documentation for every FXRuby widget.

Messages and Targets

Given that this is how FOX's target-message system works, what do we need to do in our application code so that it actually does something in response to these messages? Suppose that your application incorporates a table widget, and you want to know when the user clicks one of the cells in that table so that you can display some additional details about the data in that cell. You'd start by consulting the API documentation for the FXTable class to see what kinds of messages it sends when the user clicks a table cell. As it turns out, there are a number of candidates (including SEL_COMMAND, SEL_CLICKED, and SEL_SELECTED) that sound like they would fit the bill.

1. You can view this page online at http://www.fxruby.org/doc/api/classes/Fox/FXTable.html.

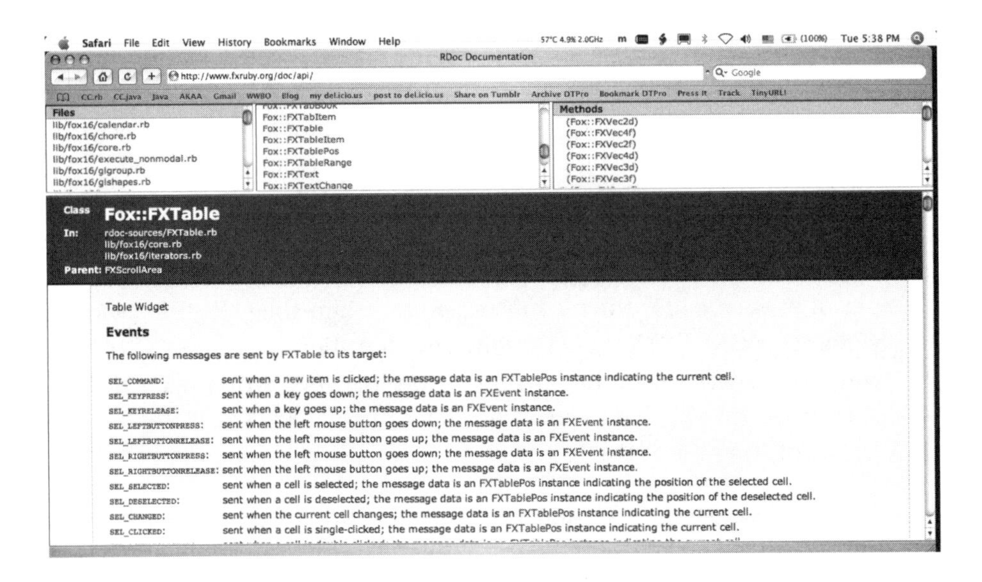

Figure 7.2: API DOCUMENTATION FOR FXTABLE

This isn't an accident. Even though a single action (like clicking a table cell) may lead to many kinds of messages being fired off, different semantics are associated with each message type. For example, a SEL_SELECTED message has to do with a new cell being selected, whether that selection happens interactively as the result of a mouse click or programmatically as a result of a call to the table's selectRange() method. The difference between SEL_CLICKED and SEL_COMMAND is even subtler. The table will send a SEL_CLICKED message if the user clicks anywhere on the table, but it will follow that up with a SEL_COMMAND message only if the click was actually inside a table cell.

For this example, the SEL_COMMAND message is the most suitable candidate. That's also not an accident. In most cases, the most useful message that a widget sends to its target is its SEL_COMMAND message. The specific meaning of SEL_COMMAND is of course different for different kinds of widgets, but you can always think of it as having to do with the primary function of that widget (such as pushing a button or entering text in a text field).

Now that we've settled on SEL_COMMAND as the table message that we'd like to handle, we need to tell the FXTable object which object is its message target and what message identifier it should use when it sends messages to that target. One way to do this is to specify the target and message identifier when you construct the table:

```
table = FXTable.new(p,
  :target => target_object, :selector => message_identifier, ...)
```

You can also assign (or change) the target and message identifier after you construct the table, using the target and selector attributes:

```
table.target = target_object
table.selector = message_identifier
```

Being the clever reader that you are, you've probably picked up on the fact that (for historical reasons) the attribute that you use to read or set the message identifier is named selector. Trust me, it's really just the message identifier.

Now, at this point in the conversation, I could go into a lot of ugly detail about how to set up the message map that tells the target object which of its methods to invoke when it receives a message for a particular message type and identifier. The brave souls who toughed it out during the early years of FXRuby's development had to go through that process, and folks who use the FOX library for their C++ GUI applications *still* have to do so. The good news is that, for the most part, FXRuby users don't have to deal with FOX-style message maps anymore.[2]

Connecting Messages to Code

The connect() method provides a straightforward way to connect messages sent from a widget to a chunk of code that handles them. Under the hood, the connect() method creates an target object and message identifier and then assigns those to the message sender, so we're not fundamentally altering how FOX's event-driven programming model works. But what this means for you as an application programmer is that handling the SEL_COMMAND message from a table takes just a few lines of code:

```
table.connect(SEL_COMMAND) do |sender, selector, data|
  # Handle a click inside a table cell
end
```

In this example, we're just passing a single argument to connect(), and it's the message type that we're interested in handling. There's a variation on this that I'll cover in a moment, but this is the most common form. We "connect" the SEL_COMMAND message from the table to

---

2. For the morbidly curious, this topic is covered in more detail in the *FXRuby User's Guide* at http://www.fxruby.org/doc/events.html.

a Ruby block that expects three arguments. The names that you use for these arguments inside the block are of course up to you, as long as you keep their meanings straight. The first argument, which we've given the name sender, is a reference to the object that sent the message (the table). The second argument, selector, is a value that combines the message type and identifier (more on this in a moment). The third argument, data, is a reference to the message data.

According to the API documentation for the FXTable class, the message data associated with the SEL_COMMAND message is an FXTablePos instance indicating the current cell. From this, we can extract the row and column number of the cell that was clicked:

```
table.connect(SEL_COMMAND) do |sender, selector, data|
  puts "User clicked cell at row: #{data.row}, column: #{data.col}"
end
```

There's a slightly different way to call connect(), and it's useful when you want to use the same handler code for multiple widgets or when you just want to break the handler code out into its own method. This variation involves passing a Method instance (or some other kind of callable object, like a Proc instance) as the second argument to connect():

```
def table_cell_clicked(sender, selector, data)
  puts "User clicked cell at row: #{data.row}, column: #{data.col}"
end

table.connect(SEL_COMMAND, method(:table_cell_clicked))
```

These two forms are functionally equivalent, and the choice between them is mostly a matter of preference. I do recommend that you break the handler code out into a separate method if it is more than a handful of lines long, primarily to keep your code readable.

Finally, I mentioned earlier that the second argument to a handler is a value that combines the message type and identifier. You can extract the message type from this value using the FXSELTYPE() method, and you can extract the identifier using the FXSELID() method:

```
table.connect(SEL_COMMAND) do |sender, selector, data|
  puts "The message type is: #{FXSELTYPE(selector)}"
  puts "and the message identifier is #{FXSELID(selector)}"
end
```

In practice, this information isn't all that useful, because you usually know which message type you're handling. It could be useful, however, if you're using the same method to handle messages from more than one object.

7.2 Mouse and Keyboard Events

Depending on the complexity of the application that you're trying to build, you may not have to deal with low-level mouse and keyboard events directly. For example, you've already seen that FOX will synthesize mouse button clicks into SEL_COMMAND and other types of messages from widgets to their targets. Nevertheless, there are some occasions when you really do need to get at the basic mouse and keyboard event data, and we'll take a look at how to do that in this section.

Handling Mouse Events

Most of the time, FOX sends mouse-related messages to the window that the mouse cursor is pointing at.[3] When the left mouse button goes down, FOX will send a SEL_LEFTBUTTONPRESS message to that window, and when the left mouse button is released, FOX will send it a corresponding SEL_LEFTBUTTONRELEASE message. If you're using a two or three-button mouse, there are corresponding SEL_MIDDLEBUTTONPRESS, SEL_MIDDLEBUTTONRELEASE, SEL_RIGHTBUTTONPRESS, as well as SEL_RIGHTBUTTONRELEASE messages, and if your mouse has a scroll wheel, FOX will send a SEL_MOUSEWHEEL message when the wheel is scrolled up or down.

The message data associated with mouse and keyboard events (and a number of other message types) is an FXEvent object. Usually, the only thing that you want to know about button press and release messages is that they occurred, so the associated message data isn't important. However, for some applications you may also want to know exactly where the mouse cursor was pointing when the mouse button was pressed (or released). In those cases, you can inspect the values of the win_x and win_y attributes of the message data, which will tell you the x and y coordinates in the local coordinate system for the window where the event occurred.

```
my_window.connect(SEL_LEFTBUTTONPRESS) do |sender, sel, event|
  p "Button pressed at coordinates (#{event.win_x}, #{event.win_y})"
end
```

Alternately, you can look at the root_x and root_y attributes to learn the root window coordinates for the event.

3. I say "most of the time" because under some circumstances (such as drag-and-drop operations) some other window can temporarily "grab" the mouse and intercept all the mouse-related messages, regardless of which window the mouse cursor is pointing at.

When the mouse moves, you'll get a SEL_MOTION message. As was the case for the button press and release events, the message data will indicate the current position of the mouse cursor (where the mouse has moved *to*). FOX also keeps track of the previous mouse position, in the last_x and last_y attributes. Note that the last_x and last_y values are in window coordinates, not root coordinates.

Handling Keyboard Events

In the previous section, we talked about how mouse-related messages are sent to the window that the mouse cursor is pointing at. Along the same lines, keyboard-related messages are always sent to the window that currently holds the keyboard *focus*.

When the user presses a key on the keyboard (that is, when the key goes down), FOX will send a SEL_KEYPRESS message to the object that currently has the focus. When they release the key, FOX will send a SEL_KEYRELEASE message. In both cases, the data sent with the message is an FXEvent instance that includes information about which keys were pressed when the message was generated. The FXEvent attributes that you'll be most concerned with are the code and state attributes (and, to a lesser extent, the text attribute).

The event code tells you which key was pressed (or released). Its value will correspond to one of the symbolic constants listed in the API documentation for the Fox module.[4] The names of these constants all begin with the prefix KEY_, and in most cases the key code constant will have a sensible name. For example, when you press the a key, the event code will be equal to KEY_a. For some more obscure cases, you may have to do a little bit of "reverse engineering" to figure out which key code FOX is sending you, such as by printing out its numeric value and then looking up the constant name in the documentation.

The event state tells you which (if any) modifier keys were pressed at the time the event was generated. You can test this by logically ANDing the event state with the modifier flags listed in Figure 7.3, on the next page. For example, the following code sets the value of shift_check.checkState to true if the Shift key was pressed when the event was generated:

keyboard.rb

```
self.connect(SEL_KEYPRESS) do |sender, sel, event|
  shift_check.checkState = (event.state & SHIFTMASK) != 0
end
```

4. Available online at http://www.fxruby.org/doc/api/classes/Fox.html

Modifier Flag	**Meaning**
ALTMASK	Alt key is pressed
CAPSLOCKMASK	Caps Lock key is pressed
CONTROLMASK	Ctrl key is pressed
METAMASK	Meta key is pressed
NUMLOCKMASK	NumLock key is pressed
SCROLLLOCKMASK	ScrollLock key is pressed
SHIFTMASK	Shift key is pressed

Figure 7.3: KEYPRESS MODIFIER FLAGS

We'll revisit the issue of keyboard-related events later, in Section 8.1, *Getting Pushy with Buttons*, on page 99, when we look at how to define accelerators and hotkeys for widgets.

7.3 Timers, Chores, Signals, and Input Events

Mouse and keyboard events are always generated by the user directly interacting with the application. However, a number of other kinds of events can occur in an FXRuby application, and the following sections describe how you can deal with those in your applications.

Scheduling Tasks with Timeout Events

When you register a *timeout event* with the application, you're asking FOX to send a message to your application at some point in the future. For example, suppose you'd like to add a timed backup capability to your application and automatically save the user's work every five minutes:

```
app.addTimeout(5*60*1000) do
  # invoke the "save" operation
end
```

The first argument to addTimeout() is the amount of time, in milliseconds, that FOX should wait before triggering the timeout event. The code shown previously doesn't do quite what we want, though, because a timeout event is a one-shot deal; once it has fired, FOX forgets about the original request.

To get the timeout to occur every five minutes, we need to pass in the :repeat parameter:

```
app.addTimeout(5*60*1000, :repeat => true) do
  # invoke the "save" operation, then re-register the timeout
end
```

Note that when you use an instance method as the timeout handler, the method signature must include the three standard dummy arguments, as shown in this example.

If you'd prefer to move the timeout-handling code out of the block and into a method, you can instead pass in a Method object as the second argument to addTimeout():

```
def save_data(sender, sel, data)
  # ...
end

app.addTimeout(5*60*1000, method(:save_data), :repeat => true)
```

The addTimeout() method returns a value that's useful only if you need to determine whether a timeout event is still pending, find out how much time is left before the timeout occurs, or cancel the timeout event before it has fired:

```
timeout = app.addTimeout(5*60*1000, :repeat => true) do
  # invoke the "save" operation, then re-register the timeout
end

# Elsewhere in the application code
if app.hasTimeout?(timeout) && app.remainingTimeout(timeout) < 30000
  app.removeTimeout(timeout)
end
```

This code says that if the previously registered timeout is still active and there are less than thirty seconds remaining before that timeout fires again, the application should unregister that timeout.

Doing Chores in Idle Time

Another way to ask FOX to call back to your application at some point in the future is to register a *chore*. When you're working with an interactive application like the ones you'll build with FXRuby, the computer tends to have a lot of time to kill while it's waiting for you to make your next move. Instead of letting that time go to waste, you can tell FOX to use that idle time to take care of various application-specific maintenance tasks that aren't really time-sensitive. Unlike timeout events, which are handled at specific times, chores are handled as soon as FOX's event queue becomes empty:

```
app.addChore do
  # take out the trash as soon as we get a chance
end
```

Other than that important difference, chores behave very much like timeout events. A chore is handled only once and then discarded, unless you pass in the :repeat parameter to addChore(). You can use the hasChore?() method to determine whether a chore is still waiting to be handled and use the removeChore() to unregister a previously registered chore before it gets handled. Of course, there is no equivalent for the remainingTimeout() method, because even FOX doesn't know in advance when it will have idle time to handle a chore.

Be careful about using repeating chores. Your application will typically have a lot more idle time than you might expect, and that's a good thing. When your application takes a break, that allows your computer to devote some of its time to other applications that are running alongside your GUI. If you schedule a chore that repeats over and over, however, your application will start to eat up CPU time, and both its performance and the performance of other running applications will suffer as a result.

Handling Operating System Signals

The operating system sends a *signal* to an application when it needs to report some kind of exceptional situation. For example, if you've ever written a C/C++ program that tried to dereference a NULL pointer, you've probably encountered the dreaded "segmentation violation" (SIGSEGV) signal.

You can register a signal handler with your application to intercept these signals and do some processing in response to them. For example, most operating systems respond to Ctrl+C by sending the SIGINT signal to the application. By default, the process that your application is running in will be terminated when it receives this signal. To ensure that your application does any necessary cleanup before it's terminated, you could install a signal handler for that signal:

```
app.addSignal("SIGINT") do
  # save the user's work, then exit the application
end
```

The first argument to addSignal() is a string indicating the name of the signal that you want to catch.[5] The signal names are the standard POSIX signal names and are the same ones supported by Ruby's trap() method.

5. You can also use the actual signal number (an integer), but that's a bad idea since the signal numbers can vary from platform to platform. It's better to just use the name.

Speaking of the trap() method, you might be wondering whether it's appropriate to use addSignal() or trap() when you need to respond to a particular signal being raised. It turns out that you can use either one, and it's really just a matter of preference. Note that if you register more than one signal handler for the same signal, the most recently registered handler is the one that will be used:

```
app.addSignal("SIGINT") do
  # this handler for SIGINT is registered first...
end
Signal.trap("SIGINT") do
  # ... but this one replaces it.
end
```

Reacting to I/O with Input Events

We'll wrap up this section by looking at how your FXRuby application can handle input events. You'd want to use this feature to deal with inputs from places other than the GUI itself, namely, pipes or sockets. If your application needs to react to data being written on a pipe, you could set up a timer or chore to periodically check that pipe for new data, but that's a pretty inefficient way to work. The better approach is to take advantage of operating system mechanisms for responding to those changes, and the addInput() method provides a convenient interface for doing that.

You can add an input handler using the addInput() method:

```
@pipe = IO.popen("tail -f /var/log/system.log")
app.addInput(@pipe, INPUT_WRITE) do
  # respond to new data in the I/O stream
  data = @pipe.read_nonblock(256)
end
```

To respond to more than one kind of event for a given source, pass in some combination of the mode flags INPUT_READ, INPUT_WRITE, and INPUT_EXCEPT as the second argument to addInput(). This complicates the processing a little bit, since you now need to determine which message type was sent (SEL_IO_READ, SEL_IO_WRITE, or SEL_IO_EXCEPT):

```
app.addInput(@pipe, INPUT_WRITE|INPUT_EXCEPT) do |sender, sel, data|
  case FXSELTYPE(sel)
    when SEL_IO_WRITE:
      # something was written to the file
    when SEL_IO_EXCEPT:
      # an exception has occurred
  end
end
```

Until now, we've focused on the messages that FOX sends to your application when something happens. In most cases, that "something" is an action that the user takes, such as moving the mouse cursor or tapping the spacebar. In some special circumstances, it's a higher-level sort of event, such as a timer expiring or some data getting written to a file that you're watching.

In the next few sections, we'll look at a very different and powerful application of this target and message-based system, and that's FOX's automatic GUI updating mechanism.

7.4 Syncing the User Interface with the Application Data

FOX's automatic GUI updating mechanism is one of its most powerful features, but it's also one of the trickier concepts to learn for developers who are new to FOX. Many other GUI toolkits, such as Java's Swing toolkit, apply what's known as the Observer pattern to keep the user interface (aka the view) in sync with the model data.[6] With this approach, a user interface event triggers a message from a widget to the model so that the model can update its value. Likewise, a change to the model data triggers a message back to the observers (views) so that they can be synced to the model.

We've already discussed how you can use the connect() method to handle messages from widgets and thus change the model data:

buttonexample.rb

```
activate_button = FXButton.new(p, "Activate Launch Sequence",
  :opts => BUTTON_NORMAL|LAYOUT_CENTER_X)
activate_button.connect(SEL_COMMAND) do |sender, sel, data|
  @controller.activate_launch_sequence
end
```

FOX takes a different approach, however, when it comes to updating the GUI in response to changes in the model. Instead of the model object sending a message to the view objects, telling them that a change has occurred, the application periodically sends a special message of type SEL_UPDATE to every widget, telling it to update its state. A GUI object can register its interest in receiving update requests from the application by calling its connect() method and passing in the SEL_UPDATE message type.

6. See the description of Observer in *Design Patterns* [GHJV95] for more details.

In the following example, the cancel_button enables or disables itself according to the current model state:

buttonexample.rb

```
cancel_button.connect(SEL_UPDATE) do |sender, sel, data|
  sender.enabled = @controller.launch_sequence_activated?
end
```

Another typical use of GUI update is to show or hide a widget depending on the application state:

```
encrypt_drives_button.connect(SEL_UPDATE) do |sender, sel, data|
  sender.visible = @edition.ultimate?
end
```

If you're interested in a different approach to the task of keeping the user interface and model data in sync, you may want to check out Joel VanderWerf's FoxTails library.[7] With FoxTails, you can identify certain model attributes as "observable" and then directly associate them with widgets. When you interact with the widget, it automatically updates the value of the attribute, and vice versa. This can be an extremely convenient alternative to the process of setting up SEL_COMMAND and SEL_UPDATE handlers for widgets that primary deal with simple data values. But while we're on that subject, let me tell you about data targets.

7.5 Using Data Targets for GUI Update

In the previous section, we learned how to keep the GUI view in sync with the model data by handling the SEL_UPDATE message. A common application of this is to keep the setting for a specific widget, such as a text field, in sync with a specific attribute in the model, such as a username. This certainly isn't difficult to do. We know how to handle the SEL_COMMAND message from an FXTextField to update the model data whenever the user types a new value into the widget:

```
user_name_textfield.connect(SEL_COMMAND) do |sender, sel, data|
  @user_name = sender.text # the FXTextField is the sender
end
```

Likewise, we know how to handle the SEL_UPDATE message to update the widget's setting whenever the model data changes:

```
user_name_textfield.connect(SEL_UPDATE) do |sender, sel, data|
  sender.text = @user_name
end
```

7. http://redshift.sourceforge.net/foxtails/

When we consider this example in isolation, it doesn't seem like such a big deal. But what if the username is displayed in multiple locations on the user interface? To keep things consistent, you'd need to write SEL_UPDATE handlers for every widget whose appearance depends on the value of that piece of model data. Generally speaking, when you're dealing with large amounts of model data that may be used in more than one place in the GUI, maintaining all the source code required to keep the model and view in sync can quickly get out of hand.

The FXDataTarget class provides a straightforward solution to this problem. A data target is a special kind of object that keeps up with some bit of data (like the username) and knows how to do the right thing in response to certain message types such as SEL_COMMAND and SEL_UPDATE:

```
@user_name = FXDataTarget.new("Rollie")
user_name_textfield = FXTextField.new(p, 20,
  :target => @user_name, :selector => FXDataTarget::ID_VALUE, ...)
```

Note that we can associate @user_name with a number of widgets in the user interface, if that makes sense. If you change the setting for the username in one of those widgets, all the other widgets connected to the data target will be updated. Likewise, if you change the value of @user_name.value, all of the widgets' settings will be updated to reflect the new value.

We'll see more concrete examples of how to use FXDataTarget in Chapter 8, *Building Simple Widgets*, on page 95. Before we do that, though, we're going to switch gears a bit and take a closer look at some of the optimizations that FOX uses to make it one of the fastest and most resource-friendly GUI toolkits on the block.

7.6 Responsive Applications with Delayed Layout and Repaint

FOX implements a number of optimizations intended to keep your user interface as responsive as possible. In this section we'll take a closer look at two of those optimizations: delayed layout and delayed repaint.

Delayed Layout

Layout is the process of making sure that all the widgets in your user interface are placed in the proper locations and at the proper sizes.[8] FOX uses a technique called *delayed layout* to efficiently recalculate

8. We'll get into the details of the policies used by different layout managers to accomplish this in Chapter 12, *Managing Layouts*, on page 157.

the layout of the user interface in response to changes. When you call recalc() on a window, that window's layout is marked as "dirty," meaning that it needs to be updated, but nothing is done immediately. Instead, that call to recalc() percolates all the way up the hierarchy to that window's shell window, marking all the intermediate windows along the way as dirty. The shell then registers a layout chore with the application to perform the actual layout later whenever there is idle time.

Most of the operations that you'd reasonably expect to mark the layout as dirty will call recalc() for you. For example, if you set the text for an FXLabel to some new string, the label will call recalc() on itself. If you change the frame style for an FXButton from FRAME_RAISED to FRAME_SUNKEN, the button will call recalc() on itself. One notable exception to this rule has to do with adding new child windows to a parent window. In this situation, the parent window's layout isn't marked as dirty, so it's your job to call recalc() on the parent to ensure that the window layout is properly updated:

dynamic.rb

```
FXLabel.new(contents, "Dynamically Added Field")
FXTextField.new(contents, 20)
contents.create # create server-side resources
contents.recalc # mark parent layout as dirty
```

Since FOX uses a chore to carry out this delayed layout, that means it will happen only after all the other pending events have been dealt with. Usually this isn't a problem, but sometimes you just can't wait that long, and you need to get the layout updated right away. In that situation, you can call layout() to immediately reconcile the layout, but be sure to make the call to the topmost widget in the hierarchy.

Delayed Repaint

A closely related subject to delayed layout is *delayed repaint*. Just as constant recalculation of the user interface layout can become computationally expensive, repeated repainting of small sections of the screen can become very expensive. To perform repainting most efficiently, FOX queues up repaint events until there's idle time in your application. You can call update() on a window to mark it as dirty and in need of a repaint, much as you'd call recalc() on a window whose layout has changed. If you call repaint() on a window, all the pending repaint events for that window are processed immediately. Likewise, if you call repaint() on the application object, all the pending repaints for all windows are processed immediately.

Delayed layout and repainting are especially nice optimizations because for the most part, you don't really have to do much in your applications to take advantage of them. Another important optimization that FOX employs is its explicit distinction between what it calls the client-side and server-side representations of user interface objects. You'll have to do a bit more work in your code to properly use this feature, so we'll discuss that in detail next.

7.7 Client-Side vs. Server-Side Objects

One of the important things to understand about FXRuby is how widgets and other user interface objects are constructed and created. When people in the know talk about client-side objects and server-side resources in FOX and FXRuby, they're referring to the separation between the "client" space—that is, the objects that you instantiate in your programs, which are allocated on the heap—and the "server" space—the resources that are allocated in the X server (or in Windows GDI) corresponding to those objects. The terminology may be a little confusing, since we usually use the terms *client* and *server* to talk about the architecture of network-based applications.

To make this picture even more complicated, the Ruby binding adds another object—a Ruby instance—that is linked to the C++ object. Luckily for you, FXRuby handles this linkage automatically, and for the most part, you don't have to worry about it.

Figure 7.4, on the next page, illustrates the life cycle of the client-side objects and their server-side resources. When you call create() on an object, the server-side resource for that client-side object is created. Calling destroy() on an object destroys its server-side peer but otherwise has no effect on the client-side object. The detach() method is a sort of compromise between these two; it breaks the connection between the client-side object and server-side resource but doesn't actually destroy the latter.

So, how does this two-step construction and creation process affect you as an application programmer? Well, you've already seen some evidence of it in the very first program we wrote:

hello.rb

```
require 'fox16'

app = Fox::FXApp.new
main = Fox::FXMainWindow.new(app, "Hello, World!",
  :width => 200, :height => 100)
app.create
main.show(Fox::PLACEMENT_SCREEN)
app.run
```

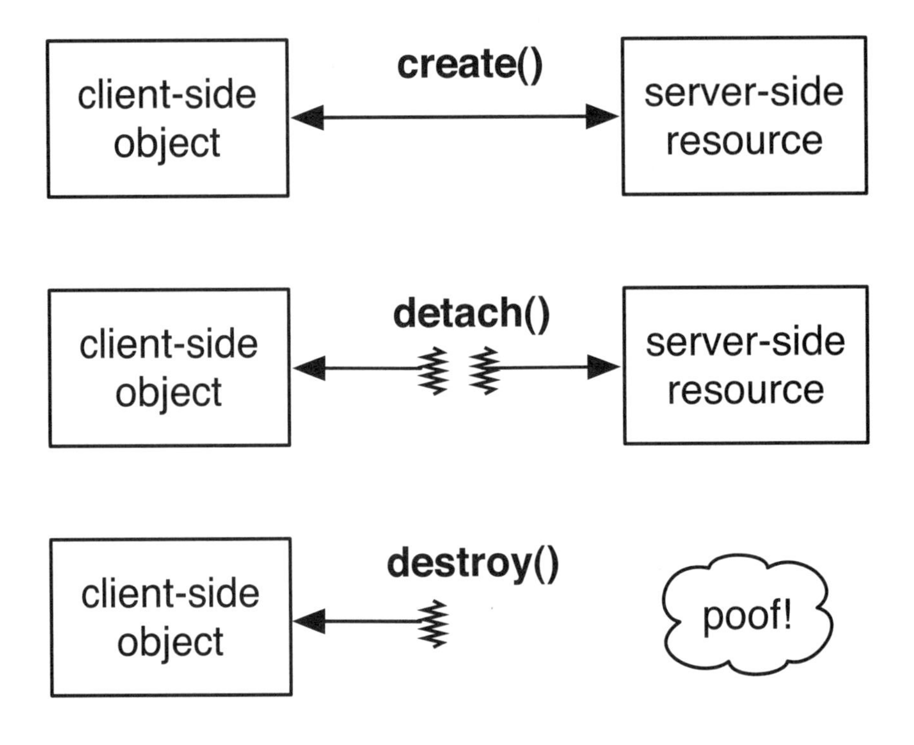

Figure 7.4: THE CREATE, DETACH, AND DESTROY LIFE CYCLE

When we call create() on the FXApp object, the application then walks through the entire collection of widgets, calling create() on each of them and creating server-side windows for them. Up until this point, the FXMainWindow object that you constructed on the previous line didn't have a server-side peer. It's worth noting that this discussion applies not only to windows but to all kinds of user interface objects, including icons, images, and fonts—they all go through this same construction and creation process.

If your program constructed all its user interface objects up front, that initial call to create() would be the only one you'd need. In practice, though, you'll be writing programs that construct new widgets on the fly in response to various events. For example, every time you display a new dialog box in your program, you'll be constructing (and creating) a bunch of new widgets. If you're writing a program that loads and displays image data of any kind, you'll be constructing and creating FXImage objects. FXRuby makes it easy and inexpensive (computationally speaking) to do all of this, so you don't need to worry about preconstructing your entire application. What you *do* need to do, however, is remember to call create() on these objects that you construct dynamically, once the program is up and running.

I can't emphasize that last point enough. The number-one source of errors in FXRuby programs that I've seen (including my own) is failing to call create() on dynamically constructed user interface objects. The best-case scenario is that the user interface won't look like you expected it to look. Consider the following example:

```
# Add a row to the contact information form for providing
# an alternate e-mail address.
add_button.connect(SEL_COMMAND) do
  FXLabel.new(@contact_info, "Alternate e-mail address: ")
  FXTextField.new(@contact_info, 20)
end
```

In this code snippet, we're trying to add a new field to a form when the user clicks add_button. This code will run, but we'll never see that new field on the screen because there's no server-side window for it:

```
# Add a row to the contact information form for providing
# an alternate e-mail address.
add_button.connect(SEL_COMMAND) do
  FXLabel.new(@contact_info, "Alternate e-mail address: ")
  FXTextField.new(@contact_info, 20)
  @contact_info.create # create dynamically constructed widgets
end
```

Adding a call to create() on the parent window solves this problem. The parent will walk through all of its child windows and call create() on them. Note that it doesn't hurt to call create() on an object that's already been created. FXRuby will recognize that the object already has a server-side resource associated with it and will move on to the next object.

The worst-case scenario is that your program crashes because, for example, some bit of code deep in the bowels of the FOX library tried to draw a font that did not have a server-side font resource associated with it:

```
# Change the font for this label
new_font = FXFont.new(app, "helvetica", 14)
label.font = new_font
```

Without a call to create() for new_font, this program will crash spectacularly at some point after you assign the font to the label. I say "some point after" because that point is a little unpredictable—it doesn't become a problem until FXRuby actually needs to redraw that label and access its font. As in the previous example, adding a call to create(), either for the label or for the font itself, will take care of the problem.

Before we wrap up this chapter, there's one more topic to discuss, and that's the basic functionality that all FXRuby widgets (or windows) have in common.

7.8 How Windows Work

Before we begin looking at the specifics of various widgets in the next chapter, we need to talk about something that all FXRuby widgets have in common, namely, that every FXRuby widget class is a descendant of the FXWindow base class. If you check out the API documentation page for the FXWindow class, you'll quickly discover that it's a very complicated class, with a huge number of attributes of methods. I'm obviously not going to try to cover all of them in this section, but we'll hit some of the highlights.

FXRuby makes a distinction between parent windows and child windows. In this case, we're not talking about the class hierarchy, where we might observe that the FXLabel class is the parent of the FXButton class. The relationship that we're describing here has to do with the containment of windows inside other windows: all the child windows for a given parent window will be displayed within the parent's boundaries. You can see this terminology reflected in the names of a number of FXWindow methods and attributes. For example, the parent attribute for a window returns a reference to its parent, while the children() method for a window returns an array of references to its child windows.

FXRuby also makes a distinction between the desktop (or *root*) window, top-level (or *shell*) windows, and other kinds of windows. Shell windows are direct children of the root window, and they're always instances of FXShell or one of its subclasses. So, for example, your application's main window (an instance of FXMainWindow) is a shell window, as are any dialog boxes that your application displays.

Occasionally, you'll have to deal with window coordinate systems. In Section 7.2, *Handling Mouse Events*, on page 79, we talked about how the event data for mouse-related messages includes information about where on the screen the event occurred, in both window-local coordinates and root window coordinates. Unlike the cartesian coordinate systems you learned about in your high-school math classes, these coordinate systems start with (0, 0) in the upper-left corner of the window. The x coordinate increases as you move to the right, and the y coordinate increases as you move downward.

The translateCoordinatesFrom() and translateCoordinatesTo() methods can be used to convert back and forth between differing windows' coordinate systems. Suppose, for example, that you are dealing with a SEL_MOTION event that occurred inside window A, but we'd like to know the mouse cursor's location in terms of window B's coordinate system:

```
window_a.connect(SEL_MOTION) do |sender, selector, event|
  b_x, b_y =
    sender.translateCoordinatesTo(window_b, event.win_x, event.win_y)
end
```

Because the event occurred inside window A, the event.win_x and event.win_y values are in terms of A's coordinate system. The call to translateCoordinatesTo() returns an array containing the coordinates in window B's coordinate system.

We've covered a lot of heavy material in this chapter, and it's material that you'll want to revisit as you begin writing your own applications. Although it's possible to get lucky and hack your way through the development of an FXRuby application, understanding why things work the way that they do has a number of advantages. By understanding how FOX's event-driven programming model is implemented, you can write much more tightly integrated applications that require fewer lines of housekeeping code to tie widgets back to the data they represent. Knowing how the delayed layout and repaint algorithms operate, and recognizing those times when you need to write code to interface with them, will help you avoid some of the pitfalls that less experienced developers run into. Recognizing the distinction between the client-side and server-side representations of FOX objects, and especially understanding when it's necessary to call create() on a newly instantiated object, is a key skill for developing bug-free FXRuby applications.

With this foundation in place, we're ready to move on to learning more about the standard widgets, such as labels, buttons, and text fields, that most every FXRuby application will use.

Chapter 8

Building Simple Widgets

Widgets are the building blocks of GUI applications. They are special-purpose objects that are displayed onscreen and can be manipulated to allow communication between users and software. If you're like most people, a majority of the computer software that you work with on a daily basis incorporates some kind of graphical user interface, so working with widgets is second-nature to you even if you don't consciously think of it in those terms. When you click a drop-down menu in your word processor and choose a command from that menu, you're interacting with the application through widgets. When you grab the scroll bar on the right side of the document pane and drag it up and down to scroll back and forth through the document, you're again using a widget to interact with the software.

In his book *About Face* [Coo95], Alan Cooper talks about the four basic types of widgets, as evaluated in terms of users' goals:

- Imperative widgets, which are used to initiate a function
- Selection widgets, used to select options or data
- Entry widgets, used to enter data
- Display widgets, used to directly manipulate the program visually

Some widgets can of course meet combinations of these goals. Figure 8.1, on the next page is a list of the widgets we'll cover in this chapter, along with advice about when to use them. We don't have enough space in this book to describe all the widgets provided by FXRuby, but if you study some of the most commonly used widgets, you'll pick up on the terminology and naming conventions that are used throughout the library. After you finish reading this chapter and the next few chapters, you will have the skills you need to integrate other more specialized widgets into your application with no problem.

Widget Class	What's It For?
FXLabel	Use a label to display text, with an optional icon, for decorative or informative purposes.
FXButton	Use a button as a "pushable" interface to an imperative command.
FXRadioButton	Use a group of radio buttons when you need the user to select one from many possible options.
FXCheckButton	Use a check button to allow the user to select or deselect an option.
FXTextField	Use a text field to allow the user to edit a single line of text.
FXToolTip	Use a tooltip to display a temporary, informative message about the purpose of some other widget.
FXStatusBar	Use a status bar to display detailed, context-sensitive help about the purpose of some other widget or the state of the application.

Figure 8.1: SIMPLE WIDGETS

8.1 Creating Labels and Buttons

I don't think I've ever developed a GUI application that didn't have at least a few labels and buttons. They're easy to understand and simple to use, so this seems like a good place to start.

Displaying Text with Labels

We can use an FXLabel widget to display a message on a user interface. It can be simple, such as a title string for a feature in the user interface, or more complicated, such as a set of instructions for some task. The label text can consist of one or more lines, separated by newline characters, and the label can optionally display an icon. Technically speaking, the text for a label is optional too, and it's possible to display a "label" widget that has only an icon, but this practice is more common for button widgets (which we'll cover in the next section).

By default, the label text is centered (both horizontally and vertically) inside the label's bounding box. However, the label supports a number of different justification options that we can use to specify how the

Figure 8.2: LABEL DISPLAYING LEFT-JUSTIFIED TEXT

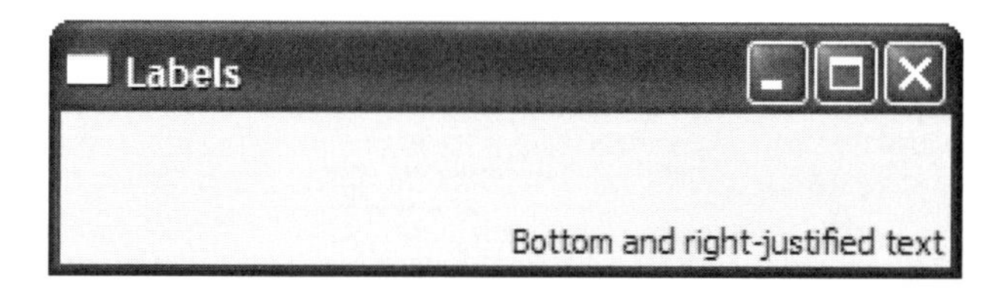

Figure 8.3: LABEL DISPLAYING BOTTOM- AND RIGHT-JUSTIFIED TEXT

label's text is aligned. For example, to left-justify the label text, pass in the JUSTIFY_LEFT option to the FXLabel constructor.

labelexample1.rb

```
label = FXLabel.new(self, "Left-justified text", :opts => JUSTIFY_LEFT)
```

Figure 8.2 shows how this label's text is displayed left-justified. You can also modify the text justification for a label by setting its justify attribute.

labelexample2.rb

```
label.justify = JUSTIFY_RIGHT|JUSTIFY_BOTTOM
```

Figure 8.3 shows the label text, justified against the right and bottom sides of the label's bounding box. For a listing of the text justification options, see the API documentation for the FXLabel class.

By default, a label is drawn without any kind of frame around it. The frame style can be changed by passing in a combination of frame-style flags to the FXLabel constructor. For example, to create a label with a solid line around its border, use the FRAME_LINE frame style.

labelexample3.rb

```
line_frame = FXLabel.new(p, "Line Frame", :opts => FRAME_LINE)
```

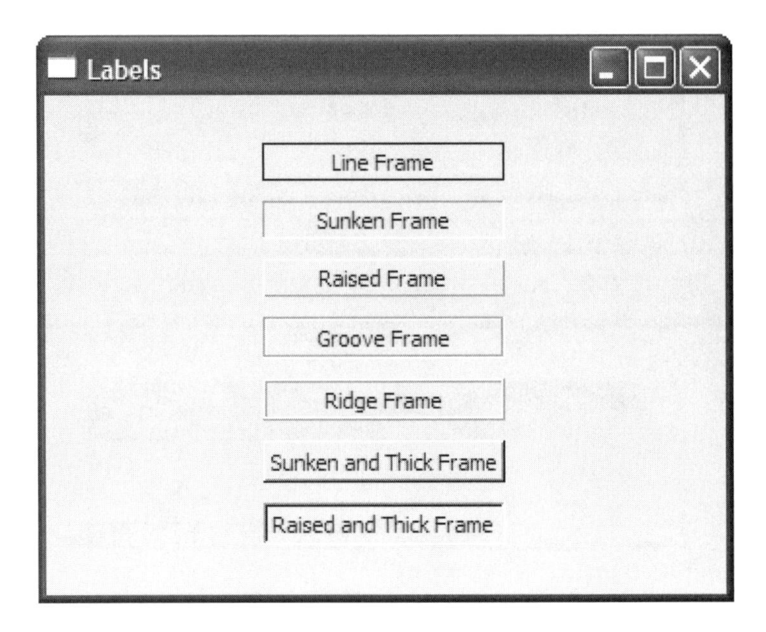

Figure 8.4: LABELS DISPLAYING THE VARIOUS FRAME STYLES

You can also change the frame style by setting the label's frameStyle attribute after it has been created. In this example, we're giving the label a sunken frame.

labelexample3.rb

```
sunken_framed_label = FXLabel.new(p, "Sunken Frame")
sunken_framed_label.frameStyle = FRAME_SUNKEN
```

Figure 8.4 shows examples of labels with all the supported frame styles. For a complete listing of the available frame styles, see the API documentation for the FXWindow class.[1]

As I mentioned earlier, you can also include an icon with a label. For example, you can construct an icon from a GIF format file and then pass it in as an argument to the FXLabel constructor.

labelexample4.rb

```
question_icon =
  FXGIFIcon.new(app, File.open("question.gif", "rb").read)
question_label =
  FXLabel.new(self, "Is it safe?", :icon => question_icon)
```

1. The frame style constants are associated with the FXWindow base class because a lot of different kinds of widgets have associated frame styles, not just labels.

Figure 8.5: A LABEL WITH AN ICON

We'll go into more detail on the topic of how to create icons in Chapter 11, *Creating Visually Rich User Interfaces*, on page 139. For now, it's enough to know that you can construct an icon object from an image file (or some other source) and then use it as decoration for labels, buttons, and several other kinds of widgets.

By default, the icon will appear centered inside the label's bounding box, which could make the label text difficult to read unless the icon is transparent or there's high contrast between the icon's colors and the text color. The label supports a number of options that we can use to specify how the text and icon are positioned with respect to one another. For example, to place the icon before the text (in other words, to its left), use the ICON_BEFORE_TEXT option.

labelexample4.rb

```
question_label.iconPosition = ICON_BEFORE_TEXT
```

Figure 8.5 shows how this example looks running under Windows. Again, refer to the API documentation for the FXLabel class for a complete listing of the available icon position settings.

Getting Pushy with Buttons

An FXButton is a step up from a label in the sense that it can be "pushed" and that, when pushed, it executes some command in your program. Like a label, a button can display a message string and an icon. Unlike a label, a button typically has a 3-D "raised" appearance that makes it stand out. Figure 8.6, on the next page, shows two different buttons, one enabled and one disabled.

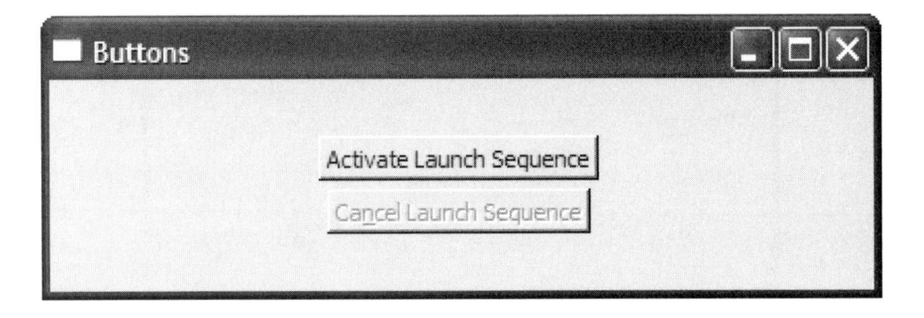

Figure 8.6: UNLIKE LABELS, BUTTONS LOOK "PRESSABLE."

When a button is pressed and released, it sends a SEL_COMMAND message to its target:

buttonexample.rb

```
activate_button = FXButton.new(p, "Activate Launch Sequence",
  :opts => BUTTON_NORMAL|LAYOUT_CENTER_X)
activate_button.connect(SEL_COMMAND) do |sender, sel, data|
  @controller.activate_launch_sequence
end
```

A button will also send a few other messages to its target, but those messages are rarely useful in practice. If you're interested in reading about those, remember that you can always refer to the online API documentation for a class to learn about all the messages it sends to its target.

You can associate accelerators and hotkeys with buttons and other kinds of widgets. An *accelerator* is a combination of keystrokes that invokes an action in your application. For example, pressing Ctrl+C will invoke the Copy action in many applications. A *hotkey* is a special kind of accelerator that is a combination of the Alt key and a letter, such as Alt+F to open the File menu.

Hotkeys are most commonly associated with buttons, or buttonlike widgets, that have an associated text string. You encode the hotkey for the button by doing this:

buttonexample.rb

```
cancel_button = FXButton.new(p, "Ca&ncel Launch Sequence",
  :opts => BUTTON_NORMAL|LAYOUT_CENTER_X)
```

In this example, the ampersand character that precedes the letter *n* in the button's label indicates that the Alt+N keystroke should trigger this button's command, just as if the user had clicked this button with the mouse.

We talked in the previous chapter about how to use the automatic GUI updating feature to update the state of the user interface widgets depending on the application state. There's a fairly common situation in which you might want to use this to change the state of a button, and it's when you want to disable a button because the command associated with that button isn't currently available. For example, we should disable the Cancel Launch Sequence button if the launch sequence hasn't been activated. You can write a SEL_UPDATE handler to account for this:

buttonexample.rb

```
cancel_button.connect(SEL_UPDATE) do |sender, sel, data|
  sender.enabled = @controller.launch_sequence_activated?
end
```

Note that in this block, sender is a reference to the cancel_button widget, since it's the sender of the SEL_UPDATE message.

Making Choices with Radio Buttons

When you need your user to make a selection from a group of mutually exclusive options, you should consider using a group of FXRadioButton widgets. Radio buttons are an appropriate choice when the number of options is fixed and reasonably small. If the number of options is unknown until runtime, you're probably better off using a different user interface object such as a list or combo box that's designed to accommodate an arbitrary number of items. You'll also want to use a list-like widget if you're presenting the user with more than a few choices, because a long column of radio buttons is difficult to deal with visually.

Let's put together a short example program to demonstrate everything you need to know when working with radio buttons. First, although it's not required, it's good practice to use an FXGroupBox widget to visually group radio buttons. You can use either the FRAME_GROOVE or FRAME_RIDGE option with the group box to affect the style of the outline, and you can optionally assign a title to the group box:

radiobuttons1.rb

```
groupbox = FXGroupBox.new(self, "Options",
  :opts => GROUPBOX_NORMAL|FRAME_GROOVE|LAYOUT_FILL_X|LAYOUT_FILL_Y)
```

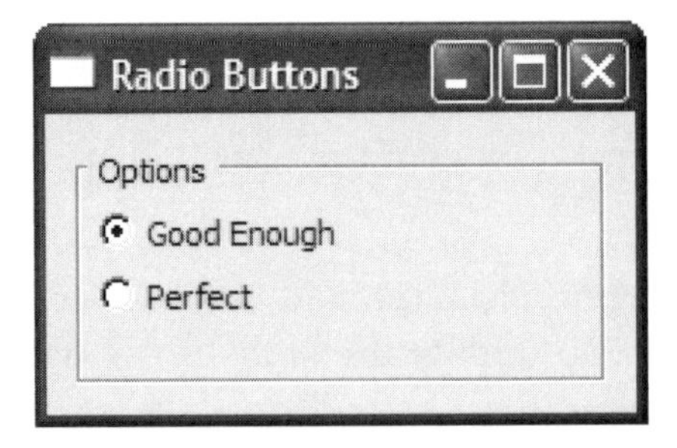

Figure 8.7: USE RADIO BUTTONS FOR MUTUALLY EXCLUSIVE CHOICES.

Now you can add a couple of radio buttons to represent the different options:

radiobuttons1.rb

```
@radio1 = FXRadioButton.new(groupbox, "Good Enough")
@radio2 = FXRadioButton.new(groupbox, "Perfect")
```

While we're at it, let's add an instance variable to hold the index of the currently selected radio button and make sure that the first radio button is checked by default:

radiobuttons1.rb

```
@choice = 0
@radio1.checkState = true
```

Now, since there's still no link between the value of @choice and the radio buttons, let's connect each of the radio buttons to a block that will update @choice whenever one of the radio buttons is selected:

radiobuttons1.rb

```
@radio1.connect(SEL_COMMAND) { @choice = 0 }
@radio2.connect(SEL_COMMAND) { @choice = 1 }
```

Figure 8.7 shows what this example looks like running on Windows. If you run the program at this point and start selecting the two radio buttons, you'll observe a pretty serious problem right off the bat. It turns out that the group box doesn't do anything to enforce the mutual exclusivity of the radio buttons—it's just window dressing. To ensure that only one of the radio buttons in a group is selected at a time, we need to do something in our program to enforce that constraint.

A straightforward way to do this is to just connect each of the radio buttons in the group to a block that updates the state of the radio button based on the value of @choice:

radiobuttons2.rb

```
@radio1.connect(SEL_UPDATE) { @radio1.checkState = (@choice == 0) }
@radio2.connect(SEL_UPDATE) { @radio2.checkState = (@choice == 1) }
```

If you run the program again, you should find that it's behaving much better at this point. When you check the Perfect radio button, the Good Enough radio button is unchecked, and vice versa. Despite this success, we can imagine that this approach won't scale well for a larger number of options. The bookkeeping code required to manage the radio buttons' states would result in a lot of code clutter.

A more elegant way to handle this problem is to create an FXDataTarget instance to hold the selected choice number:

radiobuttons3.rb

```
@choice = FXDataTarget.new(0)
```

Now we can make this data target the target object for each of the radio buttons in the group:

radiobuttons3.rb

```
radio1 = FXRadioButton.new(groupbox, "Good Enough",
  :target => @choice, :selector => FXDataTarget::ID_OPTION)
radio2 = FXRadioButton.new(groupbox, "Perfect",
  :target => @choice, :selector => FXDataTarget::ID_OPTION+1)
```

With this change in place, we can get rid of all those calls to connect() for the radio buttons. Although this is clearly a lot cleaner than our previous attempt, there's a little snag. As things currently stand, we don't have any way of knowing when the value of @choice actually changes. That might be a significant problem if we want to change some other part of the GUI whenever a different choice is selected. Fortunately, an FXDataTarget is like any other FOX object in that we can connect it to a command handler:

radiobuttons3.rb

```
@choice.connect(SEL_COMMAND) do
  puts "The newly selected value is #{@choice.value}"
end
```

With this final change, we get all the benefits of using an FXDataTarget as the gatekeeper for any changes to @choice without losing any visibility we might want when those changes take place. Now we're going to switch gears and take a look at a different technique for offering the user choices, and that's with the FXCheckButton widget.

Check Buttons: Yes? No? Maybe?

When you're dealing with an application setting that can take on one of two possible states, the FXCheckButton widget is probably your best choice to represent that setting.

Well, let me be more specific: it's probably your best choice when those two possible states are *opposites* of each other, like an "on" or "off" setting. Even though our radio button example from the previous section offered the user only two choices, a check button wouldn't have been an appropriate widget since Perfect is not the opposite of Good Enough.[2]

Check buttons can actually be in one of three possible states. In addition to the "checked" and "unchecked" states, a check button can be in an indeterminate, or "maybe," state. I've seen this feature used in different ways. For example, suppose you have a check button that you're using to indicate whether the selected articles in a news feed have been read. If they've all been read, the check button should be in the checked state, and if none of them have been read, the check button should be in the unchecked state. But what if some of the selected articles have been read and others haven't? In this situation, you might want to set the check button state to indeterminate. When a check button is in this state, it will appear to be checked but will also have a dimmed background (see Figure 8.8, on the next page). When the user clicks a check button in the indeterminate state, its state will change to unchecked, and at that point you're back to the basic checked/unchecked toggling. There's no way for the user to "click" a check button back into the indeterminate state.

The FXCheckButton class uses the values true, false, and MAYBE, respectively, to represent the checked, unchecked, and indeterminate states. You can set a check button's state via the checkState attribute and test its state using the checked?(), unchecked?(), and maybe?() queries:

```
checkbutton = FXCheckButton.new(...)
checkbutton.checkState = true
checkbutton.checked?   # returns true
checkbutton.unchecked? # returns false
checkbutton.maybe?     # returns false
```

2. They are merely enemies.

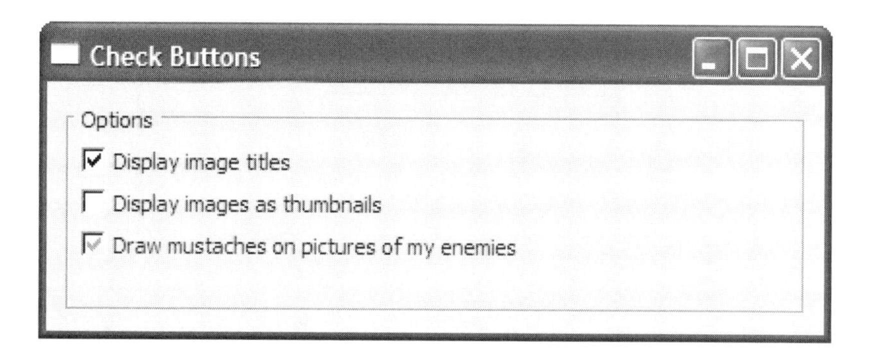

Figure 8.8: CHECK BUTTONS IN THE CHECKED, UNCHECKED, AND MAYBE STATES

As was the case with the FXRadioButton, it's often convenient to connect a check button to a data target:

checkbutton.rb

```
@titles = FXDataTarget.new(true)
@thumbnails = FXDataTarget.new(false)
@mustaches = FXDataTarget.new(MAYBE)
groupbox = FXGroupBox.new(self, "Options",
  :opts => GROUPBOX_NORMAL|FRAME_GROOVE|LAYOUT_FILL)
titles_check = FXCheckButton.new(groupbox,
  "Display image titles",
  :target => @titles, :selector => FXDataTarget::ID_VALUE)
thumbnails_check = FXCheckButton.new(groupbox,
  "Display images as thumbnails",
  :target => @thumbnails, :selector => FXDataTarget::ID_VALUE)
mustaches_check = FXCheckButton.new(groupbox,
  "Draw mustaches on pictures of my enemies",
  :target => @mustaches, :selector => FXDataTarget::ID_VALUE)
@titles.connect(SEL_COMMAND) do
  puts "The new value for 'titles' is #{@titles.value}"
end
```

In this program, we construct a separate FXDataTarget object for each of the settings and then associate those data targets with the corresponding check buttons. Since @mustaches is initialized to the MAYBE value, the third check button (mustaches_check) will start in the indeterminate state. We can also connect each of the data targets to a block of code to be notified when their values change.

Figure 8.9: USE TEXT FIELDS TO EDIT SINGLE LINES OF TEXT.

The FXRadioButton and FXCheckButton widgets are all about letting the user make selections from a fixed set of choices, and they are some of the simplest tools that FXRuby gives you for providing that kind of functionality. Naturally, FXRuby provides other kinds of widgets that don't inherently limit the user's input to a fixed set of choices, and in the next section we'll take a look at one such widget, the FXTextField.

8.2 Editing String Data with Text Fields

The FXTextField widget is appropriate when you need to provide for the input and subsequent editing of single-line text strings. Figure 8.9 shows a couple of text fields from the example program we'll look at in this section. For working with multiline text, you should look at Chapter 10, *Editing Text with the Text Widget*, on page 129.

Most of the time, you're going to want to handle the SEL_COMMAND message from a text field. The FXTextField sends a SEL_COMMAND message to its target when the user presses the Return (or Enter) key after typing some text in a text field. It will also send a SEL_COMMAND message when the text field loses the keyboard focus (because the user clicked somewhere else or pressed the Tab key to shift the focus to some other widget).[3]

If you need a more fine-grained response to changes in the text field's contents, you should instead handle the SEL_CHANGED message. The FXTextField widget will send a SEL_CHANGED message to its target after every keystroke.

3. You can override this behavior by passing in the TEXTFIELD_ENTER_ONLY flag when you construct the FXTextField.

For some applications, you'll want to be able to limit the kinds of text that can be entered into a text field. The FXTextField supports a few different modes out of the box to deal with some of the more common cases. For example, when you're using a text field to accept entry of a password, it's common practice to mask the password text using asterisks. You can do this by passing in the TEXTFIELD_PASSWD flag when you construct the text field. Likewise, you can restrict the input in a text field to integer or floating-point values using the TEXTFIELD_INTEGER and TEXTFIELD_REAL modes.

If your application calls for some more complicated limits on the entered text, you can handle the SEL_VERIFY message that the text field sends to its target. This message is similar to SEL_CHANGED, but with an important difference: the SEL_VERIFY message is sent before the tentative changes are "committed," so to speak. For example, if we wanted to verify that the text begins with a letter and consists of only letters and numbers, we might do something like this:

textfield.rb

```
userid_text.connect(SEL_VERIFY) do |sender, sel, tentative|
  if tentative =~ /^[a-zA-Z][a-zA-Z0-9]*$/
    false
  else
    true
  end
end
```

Note that if the text *doesn't* match the expected pattern, the block returns true. This seems a little counterintuitive, but it's our way of telling FOX that the SEL_VERIFY message has been "handled" and that no further processing should be done. If the text matches and the block returns false, FOX will proceed and update the text field's contents.

Finally, as with the other widgets that we've talked about in this chapter, you can associate a text field with a data target:

textfield.rb

```
@name_target = FXDataTarget.new("Sophia")
name_text = FXTextField.new(p, 25,
  :target => @name_target, :selector => FXDataTarget::ID_VALUE)
@name_target.connect(SEL_COMMAND) do
  puts "The name is #{@name_target.value}"
end
```

If you don't require the SEL_VERIFY handling, this is the most convenient way to work with a text field. As shown, you can also connect the data target to some downstream target object if you want to be notified of changes to the data target's value.

We are going to wrap up this chapter by looking at how you can incorporate help messages via tooltips and the status bar. Although these are both technically just another kind of display widget, not unlike labels, they're unusual in the sense that they always work in conjunction with other widgets to provide a kind of higher-level service for the application.

8.3 Providing Hints with Tooltips and the Status Bar

The tooltip is a special kind of pop-up window that knows to show itself whenever the mouse cursor rests in one particular spot for a few seconds. The tooltip asks the widget that the mouse cursor is pointing at what it's tooltip text is, and the tooltip displays that text. The tooltip will display this text for a short time, and then it will hide again; it will also hide as soon as you move the mouse cursor to a new location.

FXRuby makes it easy to add tooltips to your application. First, you need to create the FXToolTip object:

tooltipexample.rb

```
FXToolTip.new(app)
```

Note that there's only one tooltip object for the entire application, which may seem a little counterintuitive since you'll see the tooltip pop up all over the place!

Next, you need to specify the tooltip text that should be displayed for each widget, since the default tooltip text for a widget is empty.[4] For FXButton widgets and other widgets derived from FXButton, you can embed the tooltip text directly in the button label when you construct the button:

tooltipexample.rb

```
upload_button = FXButton.new(self, "Upload\tUpload Files")
```

Note that the tooltip text is separated from the button's label by a tab character.

4. You aren't required to specify tooltip text for widgets that don't need it. The tooltip is smart enough not to show itself when it has no text to display.

Many other widgets that don't have a label associated with them also allow you to set their tooltip text, using the tipText attribute:

tooltipexample.rb

```
dial = FXDial.new(self, :opts => DIAL_HORIZONTAL)
dial.range = 0..11
dial.tipText = "Volume"
```

Like the tooltip, the FXStatusBar widget is capable of displaying a context-sensitive help message about a widget when the mouse cursor hovers over that widget. Unlike the tooltip, the status bar is a permanent fixture on your application's main window—it doesn't just pop up briefly and then disappear again like a tooltip. Traditionally, the status bar is placed along the bottom edge of the main window and stretched to the full width of the main window, but that's not required if your application has some other layout needs.

For FXButton widgets and other widgets derived from FXButton, you can specify the help message for a widget directly in the button's label:

tooltipexample.rb

```
download_button = FXButton.new(self,
  "Download\tDownload Files\tStart Downloading Files in the Background")
```

Note that the status line help text is separated from the tooltip text by a second tab character. You can use the helpText attribute to specify the status line help text for widgets that don't have a label associated with them.

tooltipexample.rb

```
dial.helpText = "This one goes to eleven"
```

The widgets that we've looked at in this chapter are among the simplest widgets that FXRuby has to offer, and they primarily deal with setting and displaying single values. In the next chapter, we'll kick it up a notch and see what tools FXRuby provides for working with lists of values.

Chapter 9

Sorting Data with List and Table Widgets

The simple widgets we learned about in the previous chapter primarily deal with a single value (if they have any real "value" associated with them at all). FXRuby also provides a number of more complicated widgets for dealing with collections of values. Figure 9.1, on the following page, lists the widgets that we'll be looking at in this chapter, along with brief descriptions of when you'd want to consider using them in your applications. We'll begin by looking at the FXList.

9.1 Displaying Simple Lists with FXList

The FXList widget displays a list of items, where each item has an associated text string and an optional icon. If the list contains more items than it can display, it will grow a vertical scroll bar to allow you to scroll up or down in the list.

By default, an FXList is empty. You can add items to the end of a list using the appendItem() method:

listexample.rb

```
groceries = FXList.new(self,
  :opts => LIST_EXTENDEDSELECT|LAYOUT_FILL)
groceries.appendItem("Milk")
groceries.appendItem("Eggs")
groceries.appendItem("Bacon (Chunky)")
```

Widget Class	What's It For?
FXList	Use FXList to display an always-visible, flat list of items and allow the user to select one or more items from it.
FXListBox	Use FXListBox to display a drop-down, flat list of items and allow the user to select a single item from it.
FXComboBox	Use FXComboBox to display a drop-down, flat list of items and allow the user to select a single item from it. Unlike FXListBox, the FXComboBox is editable.
FXTreeList	Use FXTreeList to display a list of hierarchically structured items and allow the user to select one or more items from it.
FXTable	Use FXTable to display a collection of items in tabular form and allow the user to select one or more items from it.

Figure 9.1: LIST WIDGETS

You can of course also prepend an item to the beginning of the list, insert an item at a specific position in the list, or remove an item from the list (using the prependItem(), insertItem(), or removeItem() method, respectively):

listexample.rb

```
groceries.prependItem("Bread")
groceries.insertItem(2, "Peanut Butter")
groceries.removeItem(3)
```

Making Selections in Lists

FXRuby maintains several attributes having to do with the current selection in a list. The *current item* is simply the last list item that you clicked, and it's the item that currently has the keyboard focus. If there is no current item, the currentItem for a list is -1; otherwise, it's the integer index of the current item. When the current item changes, the FXList sends both a SEL_CHANGED message and a SEL_COMMAND message to the list widget's target:

```
groceries.connect(SEL_COMMAND) do |sender, sel, index|
  puts "The new current item is #{sender.currentItem}"
end
```

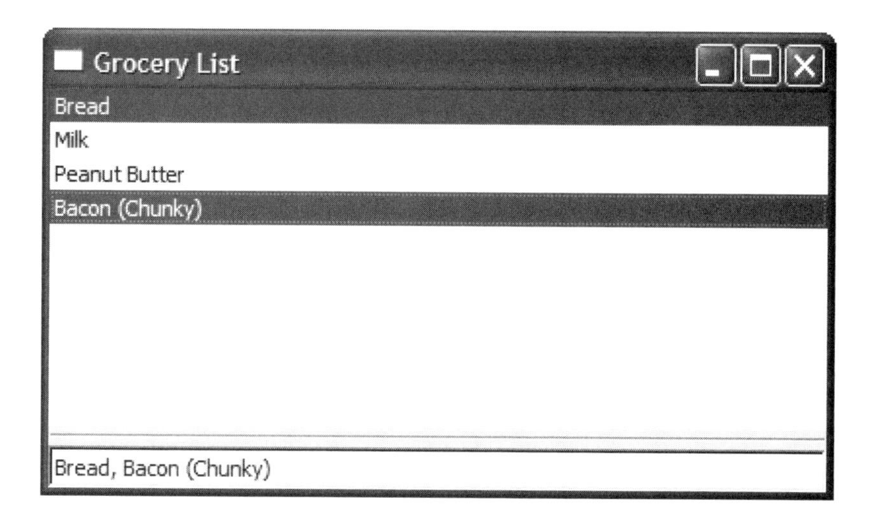

Figure 9.2: FXLIST IN ACTION

The list sends a number of other interesting messages to its target when, for example, the user double-clicks a list item. For a complete listing of all the messages that FXList sends to its target, check the API documentation.

The selection mode for an FXList sets the policy for how many items can be selected at the same time and how you go about changing the selection. One selection mode that you'll use often is the LIST_BROWSESELECT mode. In this mode, there's always exactly one list item selected, and it's the last one you clicked. The other commonly used list selection mode is the LIST_EXTENDEDSELECT mode. In this mode, any number of items can be selected. Ctrl+clicking an item toggles its selected state, and holding down the Shift key while clicking items extends the current selection to include all the intermediate items.

The FXList also provides the less frequently used LIST_SINGLESELECT, LIST_AUTOSELECT, and LIST_MULTIPLESELECT selection modes.

So Which Items Are Selected?

When the list is configured in the LIST_SINGLESELECT, LIST_BROWSESELECT, or LIST_AUTOSELECT mode, you can safely assume that the currentItem is the currently selected item. When the list is configured in either LIST_EXTENDEDSELECT or LIST_MULTIPLESELECT mode, however, you need to check each list item individually to find out whether it's selected.

One way to do this is to iterate over all the item indices:

```
selected_indices = []
0.upto(list.numItems-1) do |index|
  selected_indices << index if list.itemSelected?(index)
end
```

A different approach is to iterate over the FXListItem instances themselves, testing their selected?() states:

listexample.rb

```
selected_items = []
groceries.each { |item| selected_items << item if item.selected? }
```

As you might expect, the FXList and FXListItem classes provide a number of additional methods having to do with the behavior and appearance of a list. For all the gory details, see the API documentation for these classes.

Depending on the number of items in the list and the available "real estate" in your user interface, an FXList might not be the best choice for displaying a collection of data. If you need to display a long list of items but have only a small amount of space to work with, a combo box or list box might work better. We'll take a look at those widgets next.

9.2 Good Things Come in Small Packages: FXComboBox and FXListBox

The FXComboBox and FXListBox widgets are both variations on the FXList widget. Both of these widgets look like a combination of an FXTextField and an FXArrowButton. When you click the arrow button, the text field expands to display the entire list of items. After you select an item from the list, the list "pops" back down to assume its original appearance. Like FXList, they can both be used to display a flat list of items from which the user can select an item. Unlike FXList, they allow you to select only one item at a time from the list.

There are no hard-and-fast rules about when it's preferable to use a regular FXList as opposed to an FXComboBox or FXListBox. Obviously, if you need for the user to be able to pick more than one item, you'd want to go with the FXList. On the other hand, if a single selection is appropriate and if you don't have enough room in the user interface to display a list, a combo box or list box is a nice, compact way to hide the list's contents away when they aren't needed.

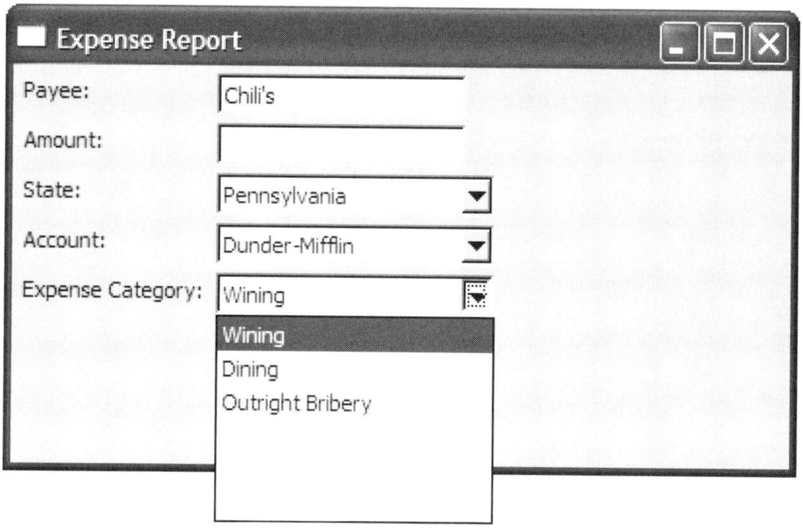

Figure 9.3: SEPARATED AT BIRTH? FXCOMBOBOX AND FXLISTBOX

My personal philosophy is that if a list is going to contain more than a handful of items, I'll use a combo box or list box instead of a plain old list. The differences between combo boxes and list boxes are subtle, however, and depending on how you use them, they're pretty interchangeable. I mean, can *you* tell the difference between the two in Figure 9.3? Neither can I. Basically, if all you need is to be able to select an item from a list, you should use the FXListBox. If you want to be able to type in a text string as an alternative to the existing list items and even see that item added to the list of items, you should use FXComboBox.

Like FXList, both of these widgets provide prependItem(), appendItem(), insertItem(), and removeItem() methods for altering the contents of the list:

comboboxexample.rb

```
states = FXListBox.new(matrix,
  :opts => LISTBOX_NORMAL|FRAME_SUNKEN|FRAME_THICK|LAYOUT_FILL_X)
$state_names.each { |name| states.appendItem(name) }
```

One item can be selected at any time, and the currentItem attribute indicates the index of that item (or -1 if there is no current item).

Since the FXComboBox can be edited, there are a few additional issues we need to address for that widget. One issue has to do with whether text that the user types into the combo box's text field should be added to the list of items.

By default, the combo box uses the COMBOBOX_NO_REPLACE option, which means the list's contents remain the same regardless of what the user types into the text field:

comboboxexample.rb

```
accounts = FXComboBox.new(matrix, 20,
  :opts => COMBOBOX_NO_REPLACE|FRAME_SUNKEN|FRAME_THICK|LAYOUT_FILL_X)
```

When you are using an editable FXComboBox, you can't necessarily depend on the currentItem to lead you to the user's input, since they may have typed some new text into the text field. For that reason, you should instead inspect the value of the combo box's text attribute to determine its current value:

comboboxexample.rb

```
accounts.connect(SEL_COMMAND) do |sender, sel, data|
  assign_expense_account(sender.text)
end
```

Note that the data the combo box sends along with the SEL_COMMAND message is in fact equal to the value of its text attribute, so for this example you could've just passed in data directly to the assign_expense_account() method.

If you'd like for the strings that the user types into the text field to be added to the combo box's list, you have several choices as to where those new items are placed in the list:

- Use the COMBOBOX_INSERT_FIRST option to insert the new item at the beginning of the list.
- Use the COMBOBOX_INSERT_LAST option to insert the new item at the end of the list.
- Use the COMBOBOX_INSERT_BEFORE option to insert the new item before the current item.
- Use the COMBOBOX_INSERT_AFTER option to insert the new item after the current item.

In my experience, the COMBOBOX_INSERT_BEFORE and COMBOBOX_INSERT_AFTER options are a bit confusing, from a user's perspective, and I usually just stick with the COMBOBOX_INSERT_FIRST option. Note that the

FXComboBox doesn't have a built-in option to automatically maintain the sort order of the items, but you can work around this by calling sortItems() on the combo box during the SEL_COMMAND handler:

comboboxexample.rb

```
categories.connect(SEL_COMMAND) do |sender, sel, data|
  assign_expense_category(sender.text)
  sender.sortItems
end
```

The call to sortItems() won't disturb the text entered in the text field, but if you click the arrow button to pop the list pane down, you will see that the newly added item appears at the correct position in the sorted list.

The widgets we've looked at so far in this chapter all deal with flat lists of items. FXRuby also provides support for dealing with hierarchically structured data by way of the FXTreeList widget, and we'll discuss it next.

9.3 Branching Out with Tree Lists

The FXTreeList widget is so named because you can imagine the data that it manages as treelike, starting from a root and reaching out in various directions, with branches leading to other branches. Unlike the FXList, FXComboBox, and FXListBox, which all deal with flat lists of things, the FXTreeList is designed for use with hierarchically structured data.

Although we use the word *tree* to describe this list's data and appearance, you should note that it's not exactly like the classic tree data structure that you may have studied in your computer science classes. One especially confusing point is that the standard documentation for the FXTreeList class uses the term *root item* to refer to any one of the topmost visible items in the tree. From a strict computer-science point of view, the actual root of the tree never appears onscreen, and we can refer to it only indirectly by using the FXTreeList API.

Once you get used to the terminology that FXRuby uses to talk about the FXTreeList class, however, you'll find that it's easy to use in practice. You can modify the content of the tree list using the familiar prependItem(), insertItem(), appendItem(), and removeItem() methods, although the calling conventions are slightly different because of the hierarchical nature of the list. The first argument for the prependItem() and appendItem() methods is a reference to the parent item for the item that you're adding.

If it's a top-level item, pass in nil as the first argument:

treelistexample.rb

```
treelist = FXTreeList.new(treelist_frame,
  :opts => TREELIST_NORMAL|TREELIST_SHOWS_LINES| \
           TREELIST_SHOWS_BOXES|TREELIST_ROOT_BOXES|LAYOUT_FILL)
artist_1    = treelist.appendItem(nil, "Alison Kraus")
album_1_2   = treelist.appendItem(artist_1, "Forget About It")
track_1_2_3 = treelist.appendItem(album_1_2, "Ghost in this House")
track_1_2_2 = treelist.prependItem(album_1_2, "Maybe")
track_1_2_1 = treelist.insertItem(track_1_2_2, album_1_2, "Stay")
album_1_1   =
  treelist.prependItem(artist_1, "Every Time You Say Goodbye")
```

There are three options that you can use to control how the connections between parent and child items in the tree list are displayed. If the TREELIST_SHOWS_LINES option is selected, the tree list will draw a faint dotted line from a parent item to each of its child items. If TREELIST_SHOWS_BOXES is selected, the tree list will display a small box to the left of any tree item that has one or more child items; if that tree item is expanded, the box will contain a dash, and if the tree item is collapsed, it will contain a plus sign. Now, for some reason, the TREELIST_SHOWS_BOXES option applies only to items nested somewhere below the top-level items. If you also want to see the boxes next to top-level items (and remembering that FOX calls these the *root-level* items), you must also pass in the TREELIST_ROOT_BOXES option. Note that the TREELIST_ROOT_BOXES option has no effect unless TREELIST_SHOWS_BOXES is also enabled.

Having said all that, I usually pass in all three options, as shown in the sample code. I've never found a good reason to omit any of them. Figure 9.4, on the facing page, will give you an idea of what the tree list looks like in this case.

Keeping Track of the Selection

FXTreeList supports the same kinds of selection modes that FXList does, and they work in the same ways, so the things you've already learned about them apply here as well. The currentItem attribute still tells you the last item that was clicked, although in this case it's a reference to an FXTreeItem object instead of an integer index.

Determining which items are selected in a tree list can be tricky, however, when the selection mode allows for multiple selected items. The most straightforward way to do this, in my experience, is to track the selected items in an Array (or some other container) and then use the

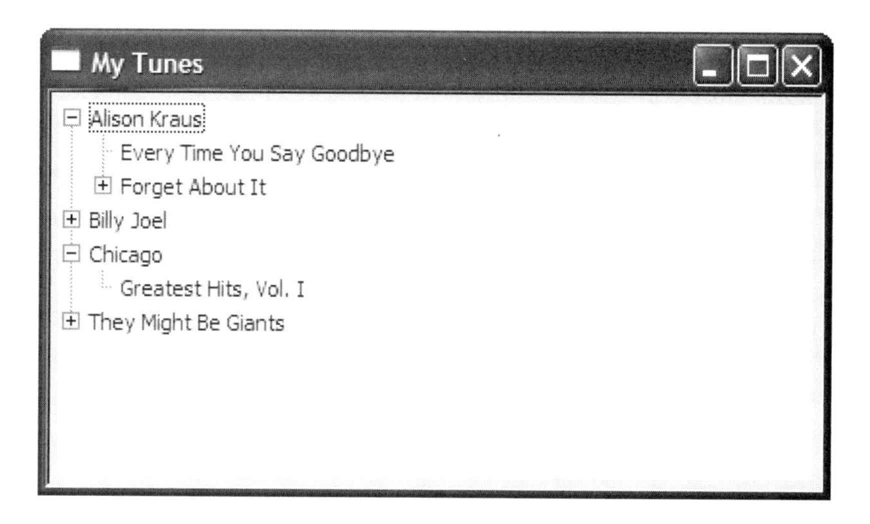

Figure 9.4: A SAMPLE FXTREELIST

SEL_SELECTED and SEL_DESELECTED messages from the FXTreeList to update the array:

treelistexample.rb

```
selected_items = []
treelist.connect(SEL_SELECTED) do |sender, sel, item|
  selected_items << item unless selected_items.include? item
end
treelist.connect(SEL_DESELECTED) do |sender, sel, item|
  selected_items.delete(item)
end
```

This technique works well for any size tree list because it's inexpensive, computationally speaking. If you know that the tree list isn't going to hold all that many items, however, you may find that simply traversing the tree every time the current item changes, and recording which items are selected, is fast enough for your purposes. Just catch the SEL_COMMAND message from the FXTreeList:

treelistexample.rb

```
treelist.connect(SEL_COMMAND) do |sender, sel, current|
  selected_items = []
  treelist.each { |child| add_selected_items(child, selected_items) }
end
```

Here's the add_selected_items(), which traverses the tree in a recursive fashion to see which items are selected:

treelistexample.rb

```
def add_selected_items(item, selected_items)
  selected_items << item if item.selected?
  item.each { |child| add_selected_items(child, selected_items) }
end
```

Now before we end this chapter, we'll see a super-secret bonus trick about associating a right-click pop-up menu with an FXTreeList.

Creating Context Menus for Tree Items

Users have gotten used to the idea of being able to right-click an object in the user interface to display a context-sensitive pop-up menu for that object. You can do this with almost any kind of object in FXRuby, but it sure seems to come up a lot when developers decide to add an FXTreeList to their application. For that reason, I'm going to treat you to a little recipe for how to add one of these right-click pop-up menus to a tree list, bearing in mind that a very similar technique could be applied to other widgets. I'm going to skim over the details about the different parts of the menu itself, but we'll cover that in depth later, in Chapter 13, *Advanced Menu Management*, on page 187.

The first step is to catch the SEL_RIGHTBUTTONRELEASE message that the FXTreeList forwards to its target. If the mouse moved in between the time the button went down (the SEL_RIGHTBUTTONPRESS event) and came back up, the call to moved?() will return true, and in that case we'll disregard the event. Otherwise, we can use the window coordinates reported in the event data to determine which tree item (if any) was hit:

treelistexample.rb

```
treelist.connect(SEL_RIGHTBUTTONRELEASE) do |sender, sel, event|
  unless event.moved?
    item = sender.getItemAt(event.win_x, event.win_y)
    unless item.nil?
      # ...
    end
  end
end
```

The getItemAt() method will return nil if there is no tree item at the specified coordinates. Otherwise, it will return a reference to that FXTreeItem.

The next step is to construct an FXMenuPane and add one or more menu commands to it:

treelistexample.rb

```
treelist.connect(SEL_RIGHTBUTTONRELEASE) do |sender, sel, event|
  unless event.moved?
    item = sender.getItemAt(event.win_x, event.win_y)
    unless item.nil?
      FXMenuPane.new(self) do |menu_pane|
        play = FXMenuCommand.new(menu_pane, "Play Song")
        play.connect(SEL_COMMAND) { play_song_for(item) }
        info = FXMenuCommand.new(menu_pane, "Get Info")
        info.connect(SEL_COMMAND) { display_info_for(item) }
        # ...
      end
    end
  end
end
```

Finally, create the menu pane, call popup() on it to display it onscreen, and then start a nested run loop focused on that menu pane:

treelistexample.rb

```
treelist.connect(SEL_RIGHTBUTTONRELEASE) do |sender, sel, event|
  unless event.moved?
    item = sender.getItemAt(event.win_x, event.win_y)
    unless item.nil?
      FXMenuPane.new(self) do |menu_pane|
        play = FXMenuCommand.new(menu_pane, "Play Song")
        play.connect(SEL_COMMAND) { play_song_for(item) }
        info = FXMenuCommand.new(menu_pane, "Get Info")
        info.connect(SEL_COMMAND) { display_info_for(item) }
        menu_pane.create
        menu_pane.popup(nil, event.root_x, event.root_y)
        app.runModalWhileShown(menu_pane)
      end
    end
  end
end
```

As soon as the user clicks one of the menu commands or clicks outside the pop-up menu, the menu pane will be hidden and the application will fall back out of the event loop started by the call to runModalWhileShown(). Figure 9.5, on the following page, shows what the pop-up menu looks like when I right-click one of the songs in the list. This is an easy bit of code to add to an application, and when used properly, it can really enhance the program's usability.

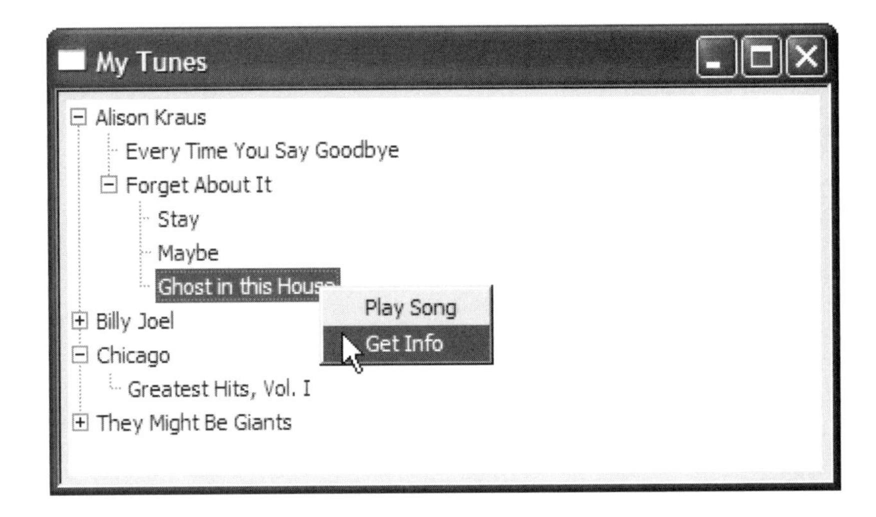

Figure 9.5: ADDING A CONTEXT MENU FOR THE TREE LIST

So, now we have options for dealing with both flat lists of data as well as nested lists of data. Next up, we're going to take a look at one more of the widgets that FXRuby provides for dealing with collections of data, and that's the FXTable widget.

9.4 Displaying Tabular Data with FXTable

The FXTable widget is one of the more complicated widgets in the FOX Toolkit, and it's one that has evolved pretty significantly since it was originally introduced. Newcomers sometimes confuse the FXTable widget with the FXMatrix layout manager, which you can use to lay out a bunch of widgets in rows and columns.[1] The FXTable *does* lay out its contents in rows and columns, but it's not a layout manager per se; in some other toolkits, you may have heard this kind of a widget referred to as a *grid* widget or *spreadsheet* widget.

Storing Data in a Table

Our study of FXTable begins with a look at how to create a table and add some data to it. In this section we're going to learn a little bit about how

1. We used the FXMatrix layout manager while building the Picture Book application, and we'll discuss it in more detail in Section 12.2, *Arranging Widgets in Rows and Columns with a Matrix Layout*, on page 170.

the table actually manages its data internally. We'll see that the table's sparse storage scheme makes it very efficient, and we'll also learn how to define items that can span multiple table cells.

Like the list widgets we looked at in the previous chapter, tables are empty by default. The most efficient way to fill up a table is to use the setTableSize() method:

tableexample1.rb

```
table = FXTable.new(self, :opts => LAYOUT_FILL)
table.setTableSize(10, 10)
```

An important thing to recognize about setTableSize(), and all of the methods that alter the size of the table, is that FXTable makes a distinction between empty cells and those that have some content (or data) associated with them. Both kinds of cells take up space onscreen when the table is drawn, but internally, FXTable allocates storage (in the form of FXTableItem objects) only for those cells that actually have content. This makes the table very efficient in terms of memory use, and it means you can store pretty large tables with very little penalty.

You should also understand that the setTableSize() method is a destructive method. Whether you're initializing the table size or simply resizing it to make it bigger or smaller, setTableSize() begins by destroying all the existing table items. So if your table already contains some data and you just want to grow it by a few rows or columns, calling setTableSize() is not the way to do it. Instead, use some combination of the appendRows(), appendColumns(), insertRows(), and insertColumns() methods.[2]

A *spanning item* is one that takes up more that one position in the table. You can create a spanning item by simply passing in the same item to setItem() for several adjacent rows and columns:

tableexample1.rb

```
table.setItemText(2, 1, "This is a spanning item")
table.setItemJustify(2, 1, FXTableItem::CENTER_X)
spanning_item = table.getItem(2, 1)
table.setItem(2, 2, spanning_item)
table.setItem(2, 3, spanning_item)
table.setItem(3, 1, spanning_item)
table.setItem(3, 2, spanning_item)
table.setItem(3, 3, spanning_item)
```

2. There aren't any methods to prepend rows or columns to a table, but you can use insertRows() or insertColumns(), passing in a value of zero for the starting row or column.

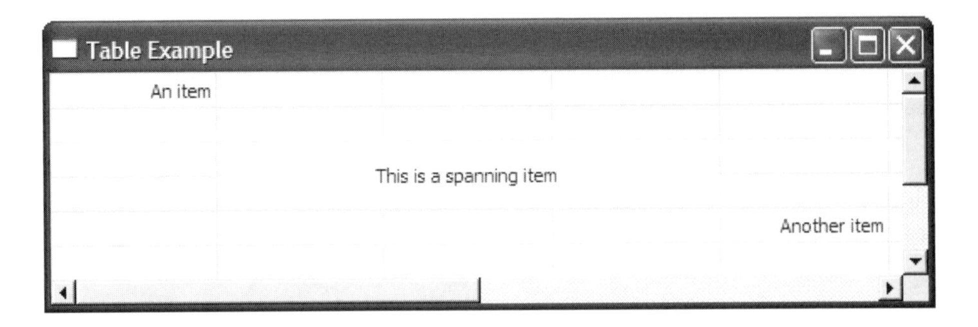

Figure 9.6: TABLE WITH A SPANNING ITEM

In this example, the item at position (2, 1) spans a 3-by-2 block of cells in the table. When this part of the table is drawn, none of the interior grid lines will be drawn. Figure 9.6 shows what the table looks like for this spanning item.

Modifying the Table Display Options

So far we've talked about how you can add to or modify the table data. An equally important topic is the display of that data and more specifically the amount of control the user has over the table's appearance.

By default, both horizontal and vertical grid lines are displayed so that the borders of individual table cells are clearly delineated.[3] If you'd like to turn off the display of grid lines, set either or both of the horizontalGridShown and verticalGridShown attributes to false:

```
table.horizontalGridShown = false
```

All the cells in a row have the same height, and all the cells in a column have the same width. However, different rows can have different row heights, and different columns can have different column widths. By default, the user can't change any of those sizes. You can always change the row heights and column widths programmatically, using methods such as setRowHeight() and setColumnWidth(), but to allow the user to interactively resize them, you must enable either the TABLE_ROW_SIZABLE flag, the TABLE_COL_SIZABLE flag, or both:

```
table.tableStyle |= TABLE_COL_SIZABLE
```

3. As we've already mentioned, the interior grid lines for spanning table items are never drawn.

When one or both of these options is enabled, the user can click the separator between two items in the row (or column) header and drag it from side to side to resize the neighboring rows (or columns).

Speaking of those row and column headers, you can also manipulate their contents to provide (for example) titles for the table columns:

tableexample2.rb

```
table.setColumnText(0, "Ruby 1.8.6")
table.setColumnText(1, "Ruby 1.9")
table.setColumnText(2, "JRuby")
table.setColumnText(3, "Rubinius")
```

If you want to turn off the display of the row header (a pretty common request), first change its mode to LAYOUT_FIX_WIDTH, and then set its width to zero pixels. You can do the same for the column header by setting the columnHeaderMode to LAYOUT_FIX_HEIGHT and the columnHeaderHeight to zero:

tableexample1.rb

```
table.rowHeaderMode = LAYOUT_FIX_WIDTH
table.rowHeaderWidth = 0
table.columnHeaderMode = LAYOUT_FIX_HEIGHT
table.columnHeaderHeight = 0
```

The table shown in Figure 9.6, on the preceding page, has both its row and column headers hidden.

You also have some degree of control over the display of individual table items. Each table item has an associated text string and icon. You can change these values using the setItemText() and setItemIcon() methods.

tableexample2.rb

```
table.setItemText(5, 3, "Timeout")
table.setItemIcon(5, 3, stopwatch_icon)
table.setItemJustify(5, 3, FXTableItem::CENTER_X)
table.setItemIconPosition(5, 3, FXTableItem::BEFORE)
```

The table shown in Figure 9.7, on the following page, includes a number of items with the text right-justified (the default) as well as others with centered text and icons.

Finally, the user can edit the contents of a table cell by double-clicking that cell, typing some new text, and pressing the Enter key. You can disable this feature by setting the editable attribute to false:

```
table.editable = false
```

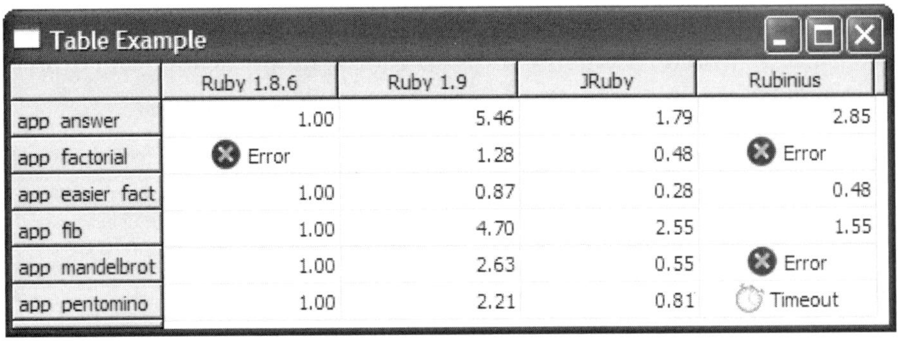

Table Example

	Ruby 1.8.6	Ruby 1.9	JRuby	Rubinius
app answer	1.00	5.46	1.79	2.85
app factorial	Error	1.28	0.48	Error
app easier fact	1.00	0.87	0.28	0.48
app fib	1.00	4.70	2.55	1.55
app mandelbrot	1.00	2.63	0.55	Error
app pentomino	1.00	2.21	0.81	Timeout

Figure 9.7: TABLE ITEMS WITH ICONS

So far we've been focusing on the display aspects of the FXTable: how to put data inside it and how to change its appearance. Like the other widgets we've looked at in this chapter, however, the table is also useful as an input mechanism. To wrap up this section, we're going to take a look at how users can make selections in tables.

Managing the Table Selection

The table is somewhat less flexible than the list widgets in terms of its selection model. It supports only one selection mode, and in that mode you can select either a single cell or a contiguous block of cells. You can't, for example, select one cell in the upper-left corner and another cell in the lower-right corner, without also selecting all the cells in between.

When you click in a cell to begin building up a selection, that cell becomes the *anchor cell*. The anchorRow and anchorColumn attributes for the table contain the row and column indices of the anchor item, assuming that there is one. If you then hold down the `Shift` key and click somewhere else in the table, the selection will be extended from the anchor cell to the cell in which you clicked. As was the case with the list widgets, the current item (identified by the currentRow and currentColumn attributes) is just the last cell you clicked.

It's important to recognize that the selection doesn't "grow" to include both the previously selected cells and the newly selected cells, unless they all happen to lie on the same side of the anchor. In other words, the selection in a table always pivots around the anchor cell. This may be a little counterintuitive at first (it was to me, anyway). The selStartRow, selEndRow, selStartColumn, and selEndColumn attributes will always contain the starting and ending row and column indices for the entire selection, when there is one. Note that because of how the table's selection model works, one of those endpoints—either (selStartRow, selStartColumn) or (selEndRow, selEndColumn)—will be the anchor cell.

When the user clicks a row heading, all the cells in that row will become selected. Likewise, when the user clicks a column heading, all the cells in that column become selected. You can disable this behavior by setting either or both of the TABLE_NO_ROWSELECT and TABLE_NO_COLSELECT options:

```
# Disable row and column selections
table.tableStyle |= TABLE_NO_ROWSELECT|TABLE_NO_COLSELECT
```

The table sends a SEL_COMMAND message when you click a table item, and the message data is an FXTablePos instance. An FXTablePos is just simple data object with row and col accessor methods for reading the row and column of the selected table item.

You can, of course, programmatically modify the selection, although you normally rely on the user to perform those actions interactively. Try as you might, FXTable won't let you trick it into making a selection that violates its selection model. For example, the following code will result in only one cell—the one at (5, 5)—being selected:

```
table.selectItem(0, 0)
table.selectItem(5, 5)
```

To select a range of cells, use the selectRange() method:

```
# Select all of the cells between (0, 0) and (5, 5), inclusively
table.selectRange(0, 0, 5, 5)
```

As was the case for the FXTreeList, the easiest way to keep up with which table items are selected is to store them in an Array whose contents are updated in response to SEL_SELECTED and SEL_DESELECTED messages:

tableexample2.rb

```
selected_items = []
table.connect(SEL_SELECTED) do |sender, sel, pos|
  item = sender.getItem(pos.row, pos.col)
  selected_items << item unless selected_items.include? item
end
table.connect(SEL_DESELECTED) do |sender, sel, pos|
  selected_items.delete(sender.getItem(pos.row, pos.col))
end
```

This concludes our look at the widgets that FXRuby provides for dealing with collections of data, but there are a number of other, similar widgets in the library that you may want to take a look at as well. For example, the FXTable widget uses a pair of FXHeader widgets internally to display its row and column headings, but you can pull that widget out and use it by itself. The FXFoldingList is a sort of cross between an FXTreeList and an FXHeader that allows you to associate multiple columns of data with each item in a tree list. An FXIconList is used by the file dialog box to provide several different kinds of views on a list of files, but you can also repurpose it to display other kinds of lists. You will find documentation for each of these widgets in the FXRuby API documentation, and the standard FXRuby source distribution includes examples for each of them.

Next, we're going to shift gears and take a look at another one of FOX's more complicated widgets, the FXText widget, which you can use to edit large text documents.

Chapter 10

Editing Text with the Text Widget

In Chapter 8, *Building Simple Widgets*, on page 95, we learned how to use the FXTextField widget when we need to get text input from the user. An FXTextField is an appropriate choice when you're dealing with short, single-line strings, such as form data or filenames. It's clearly not a one-size-fits-all solution, however. In this chapter, we'll look at how to use the FXText widget, which you can use to display and edit multiline text documents. FXText is one of the more complicated widgets in the FOX library, and although it has a number of similarities with FXTextField, at first glance its API is a little overwhelming. You'll get a basic introduction to the FXText widget in this chapter, but you should be sure to look up its API documentation to learn about some of its more advanced features as well.

First, the good news. If you simply need a fully featured text-editing component to stick somewhere in your application, you don't have to do much more than construct an FXText widget, optionally initialize its value to some default text, and then ask it for its contents at some later time using its text attribute:

text.rb

```
text = FXText.new(text_frame, :opts => TEXT_WORDWRAP|LAYOUT_FILL)
text.text = "By default, the text buffer is empty."
```

Out of the box, FXText offers almost all functionality you'd expect from a text-editing component. Figure 10.1, on the following page, shows a partial listing of the key bindings that FXText recognizes. For all the keystrokes that move the cursor, you can hold down the Shift key to select the text between where the cursor is located and where it's going.

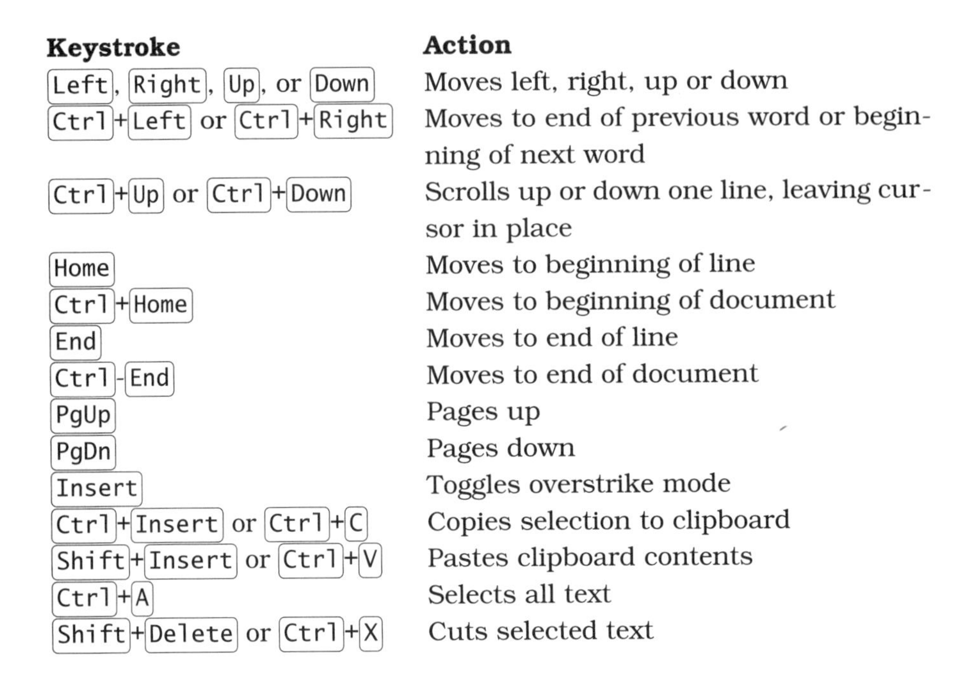

Keystroke	Action
Left, Right, Up, or Down	Moves left, right, up or down
Ctrl+Left or Ctrl+Right	Moves to end of previous word or beginning of next word
Ctrl+Up or Ctrl+Down	Scrolls up or down one line, leaving cursor in place
Home	Moves to beginning of line
Ctrl+Home	Moves to beginning of document
End	Moves to end of line
Ctrl-End	Moves to end of document
PgUp	Pages up
PgDn	Pages down
Insert	Toggles overstrike mode
Ctrl+Insert or Ctrl+C	Copies selection to clipboard
Shift+Insert or Ctrl+V	Pastes clipboard contents
Ctrl+A	Selects all text
Shift+Delete or Ctrl+X	Cuts selected text

Figure 10.1: SOME KEYSTROKES THAT FXTEXT UNDERSTANDS

Because of its inherent capability to format large bodies of text, FXText is also useful for simply displaying text in many circumstances. To make the FXText read-only, just set editable to false:

```
text.editable = false
```

If you want to use FXText in a more sophisticated way, you'll need to dig into its API a bit. Let's do that now, starting with the APIs for adding and removing text from the text buffer.

10.1 Adding and Removing Text

When you're using the FXTextField widget, there's only one way to programmatically change its value, and that's by assigning a new value to its text attribute. This is reasonable since, by definition, you're working with a relatively short string and it takes very little overhead to just replace the whole thing in one shot. It's a different story when you're working with the FXText widget, however. FXText is optimized for working with very large bodies of text, and as a result, it provides a number of methods for modifying that text.

By default, the text buffer for an FXText widget is empty. You can initialize its value by assigning a string to its text attribute, but that's just about the only time you'll want to do that. The problem is that when you assign the text using the text attribute, the FXText widget assumes that it needs to recalculate a number of metrics that it uses internally, such as the positions of all the line starts. This is a computationally expensive operation. When you have a choice, you should instead use one of the other methods that FXText provides. For example, to append some text to the end of the buffer, use the appendText() method:

```
text.appendText(additional_text)
```

The appendText() method accepts an optional second argument, which defaults to false:

text.rb

```
text.appendText(additional_text, true)  # notify target of change
```

If you pass a value of true as the optional second argument to appendText(), FXRuby will send SEL_INSERTED and SEL_CHANGED messages to the text widget's target after the text has been modified:[1]

text.rb

```
text.connect(SEL_INSERTED) do |sender, sel, change|
  puts "The string #{change.ins} was inserted at position #{change.pos}"
end
```

The message data for SEL_INSERTED message is an FXTextChange instance, which includes information about text that is inserted (or replaced or removed) from an FXText widget's text buffer. Use insertText() to insert a string at a specific position in the text buffer:

text.rb

```
text.insertText(pos, inserted_text)
```

You can replace one chunk of text with another using replaceText():

text.rb

```
text.replaceText(pos, amount, replacement_text)
```

---

1. All the methods we'll discuss in this section accept this optional true parameter as a final argument. See the API documentation for FXText for more details about which messages get sent to the text widget's target as a result.

Note that the chunk of text that you're replacing may be shorter or longer than the replacement string; that's why you have to specify how many characters you want to replace.

Finally, you can remove a chunk of text using removeText():

text.rb

```
text.removeText(pos, amount)
```

So far we've glossed over the fact that for user-editable text like that supported by FXText, we may not be able to assume very much about the positions of strings required for the insertText(), replaceText(), and removeText methods' arguments. In the next section, we'll look at some of the methods that FXText provides for determining where we are in the text buffer and how we get to where we want to go.

10.2 Navigating Through Text

The methods we discussed in the previous section assume that you already know the position at which you want to add, replace, or remove some text. You can always read the value of the cursorPos attribute to determine the current cursor position, but sometimes you need to find some position relative to that (or some place completely different, for that matter).

Let's start at the lowest level. If you want to find the position of the previous character (relative to a known position in the text buffer), you can use the dec() method. Likewise, to find the position of the following character, use the inc() method:

```
previous_character_pos = text.dec(text.cursorPos)
```

Why, you may ask, can't we just subtract or add 1 to the current position to find the character at an adjacent position? If you try this, there is in fact a very good chance that it will work just fine. The reason that you want to be careful about this is that FXText (and every other FOX widget that displays or otherwise deals with string values) assumes that it's working with UTF-8 encoded Unicode strings. Now, a lot of smart people have written a lot of words about the Unicode standard and the UTF-8 encoding for Unicode, so we're not going to get into that here. Suffice it to say that a given character—or *code point*, in Unicode parlance—may be represented by more than one byte in the text buffer. So, to accurately find your way from one position to the next, you should always use the inc() and dec() methods.

You can use the wordStart() and wordEnd() methods to determine the position for the beginning or ending of a word that occupies a particular position in the text. For example, to determine the starting position of the current word, use something like this:

```
current_word_start_pos = text.wordStart(text.cursorPos)
```

You can use the leftWord() and rightWord() methods to find the position for the end of the previous word or the beginning of the next word:

```
next_word_start_pos = text.rightWord(text.cursorPos)
```

Along the same lines, you can find the position for the beginning or end of a line using the lineStart() and lineEnd() methods:

```
current_line_start_pos = text.lineStart(text.cursorPos)
```

There are even methods to determine the starting positions of previous, or following, lines in the text. Note that there's a subtle distinction between "lines" of text and "rows" of text. A *line* of text (sometimes referred to as a *logical* line) doesn't end until you reach a newline character in the text buffer, even if the text gets wrapped over several *rows* onscreen when it's displayed. If you've turned off the word wrapping option for FXText, it will always be the case that the line start and row start relative to a given position will be equal, as will the line end and row end relative to that position.

It's important to be familiar with the methods we've discussed in this section, but they address only one aspect of navigating through the text. It may be the case that you're not so much concerned about the current position and how to navigate from that starting point but rather that you're concerned with finding other locations in the text. We'll take a look at that aspect of navigation next.

10.3 Searching in Text

So far we've talked about how to find your way around in the text, relative to a known position in the text buffer. You can use the findText() method to search for a specific string in the text buffer. By default, findText() will return a pair of arrays that tells you where it found the first occurrence of the search string:

findtext.rb

```
text.text =
  "Now is the time for all good men " +
  "to come to the aid of their country."
first, last = text.findText("the")  # returns [7], [10]
```

The first array contains the starting position(s) of all the matches that findText() found. The second array contains the ending position(s), plus 1. That's why the value of last in the previous example is [10] and not [9]. If findText() doesn't find any matches, both return values will be nil:

findtext.rb

```
first, last = text.findText("women")  # returns nil, nil
```

By default, findText() starts its search from the beginning of the text buffer and looks for an exact match of your search string. You can modify the starting position for the search by specifying a value for the :start parameter:

findtext.rb

```
first, last = text.findText("the", :start => 20)  # returns [44], [47]
```

You can also modify the search options, for example, to perform a case-insensitive search or to search backward from a starting position:

findtext.rb

```
first, last = text.findText("ThE", :start => 20,
  :flags => SEARCH_BACKWARD|SEARCH_IGNORECASE)  # returns [7], [10]
```

For more complicated searches, you can use FOX's built-in regular expression engine, FXRex.[2] For example, to find the first four-letter word in the text, we could use a search like this:

findtext.rb

```
first, last = text.findText("\\w{4}",
  :flags => SEARCH_REGEX)  # returns [11], [15]
```

If the regular expression contains capturing groups (delimited by parentheses), the arrays returned by findText() will contain the starting and ending positions for each of those groups:

findtext.rb

```
first, last = text.findText("the (\\w+ (\\w+)) (\\w+)",
  :flags => SEARCH_REGEX)  # returns [7, 11, 16, 20], [23, 19, 19, 23]
```

This last example is trickier than the others we've looked at, so let's break it down. For starters, the first group is just the entire matching expression, and that's what the first elements of the first and last arrays refer to here. The matched expression, "the time for all," starts at position 7 and ends at 23. Now, moving from left to right, the next group

2. For a detailed discussion of FXRex, see the documentation at http://www.fox-toolkit.org/rex.html.

matched the subexpression "time for," which starts at 11 and ends at 19. The next group matches "for," which starts at 16 and ends at 19. Finally, the last group matches "all," which starts at 20 and ends at 23.

FOX's regular expression engine is very powerful, but in some cases the syntax may not be identical to that for Ruby's standard regular expressions. You may find it easier to just extract the text from an FXText widget and then search it using a more familiar Ruby-style regular expression:

findtext.rb

```
if text.text =~ /the (\w+ (\w+)) (\w+)/
  group0, group1, group2, group3 = $~[0], $~[1], $~[2], $~[3]
end
```

The only penalty you pay in this case is that, under the hood, FXRuby creates a new String object that contains the contents of the text buffer whenever you read the value of the text attribute. Depending on the size of the text buffer and how often you need to perform a match, this cost may not be all that prohibitive.

10.4 Applying Styles to Text

A serious shortcoming of FOX and FXRuby is the lack of a widget that can display HTML or rich text. The FXText widget is definitely not that kind of widget, although it provides some minimal support for "styled" text.

The first step is to enable support for styled text by setting the styled attribute to true:

styledtext.rb

```
text.styled = true
```

The next step is define one or more styles to be applied to the text. We do this by first constructing an FXHiliteStyle instance and then setting its attributes. The default new() method for the FXHiliteStyle class isn't all that useful, since it can't initialize the various style colors to reasonable values for an arbitrary FXText widget. It's better to use the from_text() method, which initializes the FXHiliteStyle instance with the current color scheme for the FXText widget that you pass in:

styledtext.rb

```
style1 = FXHiliteStyle.from_text(text)
```

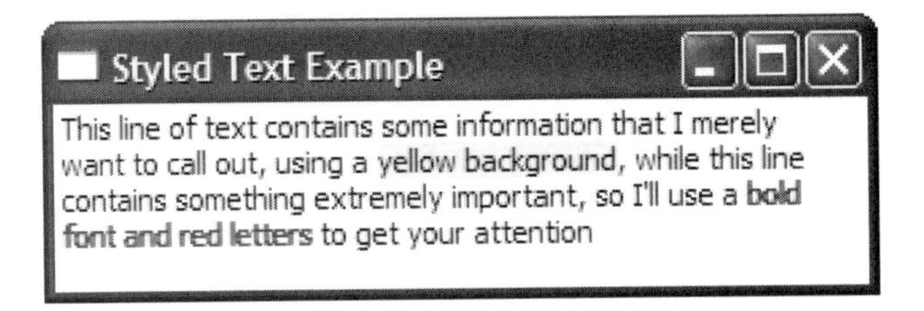

Figure 10.2: DISPLAYING STYLED TEXT IN A TEXT WIDGET

Now modify one or more attributes for this style setting. Suppose you want to display some text highlighted with a yellow background, with some other text bold and in red:

styledtext.rb

```
style1 = FXHiliteStyle.from_text(text)
style1.normalBackColor = "yellow"

style2 = FXHiliteStyle.from_text(text)
style2.normalForeColor = "red"
style2.style = FXText::STYLE_BOLD
```

Next, we need to tell our FXText widget to use this style array:

styledtext.rb

```
text.hiliteStyles = [style1, style2]
```

Finally, use the changeStyle() method to set the style for a specified block of text to a particular style in the style array. Since the first two arguments to changeStyle() are the starting position and length of the text to be styled, we'll use findText() to locate the string of interest:

styledtext.rb

```
first, last = text.findText("yellow background")
start_pos = first[0]
length = last[0] - first[0]
text.changeStyle(start_pos, length, 1)
```

The last argument to changeStyle() is the style index. Note that the "zeroth" style index is reserved for the text widget's default style. That is, when you pass in zero as the last argument to changeStyle(), the text will be displayed using the normal, nonstyled color scheme. Since we're passing in 1 as the style index in this example, FXText will use the yellow-background style to display the phrase "yellow background." Figure 10.2 shows what this example looks like running under Windows.

We've spent the previous few chapters talking about some of the widgets that you can use to take care of the user interface basics. Although displaying information and collecting input from users certainly addresses the functional requirements of most applications, that's not enough to produce the sort of visually rich and aesthetically pleasing application that folks have gotten used to creating. In the next chapter, we'll shift gears a bit and look at some of the tools that FXRuby provides for dressing up GUIs and making them all shiny.

Chapter 11

Creating Visually Rich User Interfaces

So far we've focused on the basics of assembling widgets into a cohesive user interface and how to handle the interaction between the application and its users. If that were all that was required to create an application that people would enjoy working with, there wouldn't be much more for us to talk about. The fact of the matter is that users have gotten used to working with applications that go beyond the basic functional requirements and incorporate various elements that create visual interest.

Fortunately for us, FXRuby provides a number of features for creating visually rich user interfaces. In the process of building the Picture Book application, we've already learned that FXRuby provides extensive support for displaying images. In Chapter 8, *Building Simple Widgets*, on page 95, we got a brief introduction to a different sort of graphical object when we learned how to construct icons and use them to decorate labels, buttons, and other kinds of widgets. Although most of the code we've written so far uses the default application font, FXRuby provides access to all your installed system fonts so that you can use different typefaces throughout your application, when that's an appropriate thing to do. You can also change the shape of the mouse cursor in certain circumstances to provide the user with a visual cue about the state of the application or the kind of operation that they're performing. In this chapter, we'll investigate all these features and see how you can use them effectively in your own applications.

The user interface objects that we're talking about in this chapter are special because, unlike widgets, fonts, cursors, images, and icons are *shared resources*. When you construct a widget like an FXButton, that widget occupies exactly one location in the widget hierarchy. Another way to look at it is that the button has exactly one parent window. In contrast to this, a shared resource can be associated with many other user interface objects. For example, when you construct the application object, it constructs a default FXFont object that is used by all the widgets in your application.

The important thing to take away from this is that it's not necessary to construct multiple instances of these kinds of objects if they all have the same characteristics. For example, suppose that instead of the default application font that you see throughout your application, you want to construct a custom font using the Geneva typeface, for use with a particular FXLabel widget. You would first construct the new FXFont object, and if necessary, call create() on it:

```
geneva_font = FXFont.new(app, "Geneva", 10)
geneva_font.create
my_special_label.font = geneva_font
```

Then you'd assign it to the label.

```
my_special_label.font = geneva_font
```

Now suppose you want to use that same Geneva font, in the same point size, in an FXText widget elsewhere in your application. You *could* construct a new FXFont object with exactly the same properties as the label's font, but this would be a waste of resources. The better choice is to simply assign geneva_font as the FXText widget's font.

```
my_special_text.font = geneva_font
```

With that introduction out of the way, let's take a look at our first shared resource, FXFont.

11.1 Using Custom Fonts

Depending on which dictionary you consult, you may think that *font* refers to either an entire family of sizes and styles for a particular typeface or that it refers to a specific size and style from that family.[1] For

1. You may also read that a font is a "receptacle in a church for the water used in baptism." We're not referring to that particular kind of font.

FXRuby's purposes, an FXFont object corresponds to the second definition. If you need to display the same typeface in two different point sizes, for example, you're going to need to construct two different FXFont objects.

There are three methods for constructing FXFont objects. All of them give you some way to specify your desired font characteristics, such as the typeface name, point size, and weight. FOX will then use those parameters to identify the available system font that best matches what you want. The font constructor you'll probably use most often involves passing in a number of parameters to specify the desired font characteristics. For example, you could use the following code to request a 14-point font using the italicized flavor of the Arial typeface:

fonts.rb

```
label1 =
  FXLabel.new(self, "This label uses a 14 point Arial italic font.")
label1.font = FXFont.new(app, "Arial", 14, :slant => FXFont::Italic)
```

Another method for constructing a font involves passing in a string containing the font description. You'll want to consult the API documentation for the FXFont class for the exact format of this string, but here's an example of how to request a 12-point Times bold font:

fonts.rb

```
label2 =
  FXLabel.new(self, "This label uses a 12 point Times bold font.")
label2.font = FXFont.new(app, "Times,120,bold")
```

The third method for constructing a font involves passing in an FXFontDesc object. An FXFontDesc is just a data object with attributes that correspond to the arguments that you'd pass into the first form of the FXFont.new() method that we looked at (for example, the font name, point size, and so on). In practice, you usually won't construct an FXFontDesc object directly. In many cases, you'll obtain one from an FXFontDialog (which we'll cover in Chapter 14, *Providing Support with Dialog Boxes*, on page 197). A more direct way to get your hands on an FXFontDesc object is to use the listFonts() method.

The listFonts() method returns a list of all the available fonts that match the criteria you specify. This is a powerful and platform-independent method for choosing a font, since it doesn't require you to explicitly identify all the font characteristics.

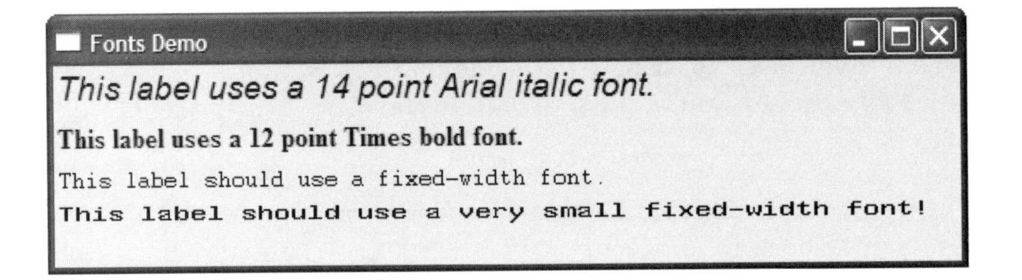

Figure 11.1: EXAMPLES OF CUSTOM FONTS

In this example, we're asking for a list of all the straight (nonitalics) fixed-width fonts and then just choosing the first one:

fonts.rb

```
label3 = FXLabel.new(self, "This label should use a fixed-width font.")
fonts = FXFont.listFonts("", :slant => FXFont::Straight,
  :hints => FXFont::Fixed)
label3.font = FXFont.new(app, fonts.first)
```

If we want to be a little pickier, we can look for the smallest fixed-width font that's size 2 points (20 decipoints) or larger:

fonts.rb

```
label4 = FXLabel.new(self,
  "This label should use a very small fixed-width font!")
fonts = FXFont.listFonts("", :slant => FXFont::Straight,
  :hints => FXFont::Fixed)
sorted_by_size = fonts.sort { |a, b| a.size <=> b.size }
label4.font = FXFont.new(app, sorted_by_size.find { |f| f.size > 20 })
```

Figure 11.1 shows some of the fonts generated by this example under Windows. Note that in this case, the fixed-width font with the smallest point size (shown on the last line) is actually wider than the previous fixed-width font that we selected (and which is shown on the next-to-last line). This is not an error; a font's point size is a relative measure that is usually based on the distance from the top of the tallest ascender to the bottom of the lowest descender.[2]

As is also the case with web design, you should be conservative about the number and kinds of fonts you use in your applications to ensure that they'll work well on a variety of platforms and on monitors running

2. See http://nwalsh.com/comp.fonts/FAQ/cf_8.htm for a good, brief discussion of how to interpret the point size of a font.

at different display resolutions. Consider using listFonts() to increase your odds of finding the appropriate font that meets your application's needs.

Another opportunity you have for sprucing up your application's look is the use of custom mouse cursors to provide visual cues about a change in the application's state or the operation that the user is performing. Let's take a look at how FXRuby uses cursors next.

11.2 Pointing the Way with Cursors

The shape of the cursor is just one of those things you usually don't think about. For a lot of the GUI applications that you'll write, you'll stick with the default cursor provided by FOX. For some applications, however, it's useful to change the shape of the cursor during certain operations to provide a visual cue to the user about what's happening. For example, when I drag a file from one folder to another in the Windows Explorer for the purpose of *moving* it, the cursor shows a little "plus" sign off to the side of the regular arrow cursor, but when I hold down the Alt key while dragging a file, the cursor changes its shape to indicate that I'll be creating a *link* to the original file.

You can change the shape of the cursor for a particular window by assigning an FXCursor instance to its defaultCursor attribute. Whenever the mouse pointer enters that window, the cursor's shape will change to whatever shape you've specified. The FXApp class provides a number of built-in "default" cursors that you can (and should) use when you need to change the cursor's appearance. In the following example, the cursor's shape will change to the built-in DEF_HAND_CURSOR shape whenever the user mouses over the label:

cursors.rb

```
box = FXLabel.new(frame, "Gimme Five!",
  :width => 40, :height => 40,
  :opts => LAYOUT_CENTER_X, :padding => 40)
box.defaultCursor = app.getDefaultCursor(DEF_HAND_CURSOR)
```

Figure 11.2, on the next page, shows what the DEF_HAND_CURSOR shape looks like. If none of the built-in cursors meets your needs, you can always construct your own custom cursors. The easiest way to do this is to use the FXGIFCursor subclass, which can construct a cursor from a GIF image.[3]

3. There's also an FXCURCursor class for constructing cursors from CUR files.

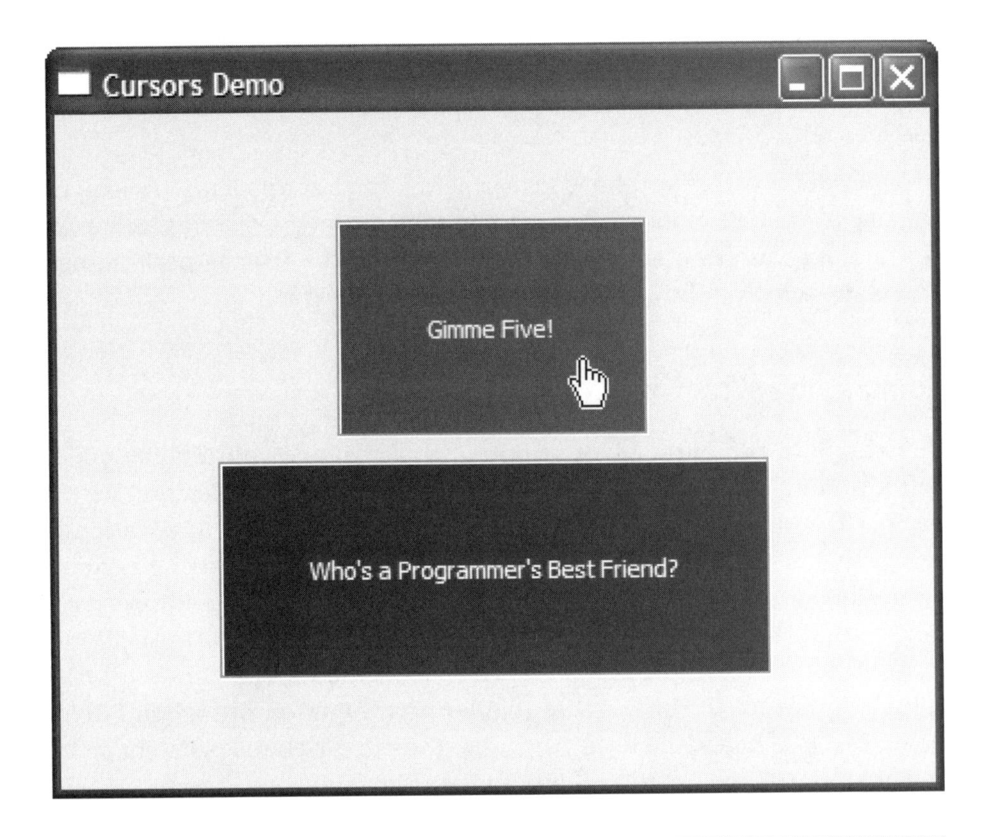

Figure 11.2: TALK TO THE HAND (CURSOR)

cursors.rb

```
box = FXLabel.new(frame,
  "Who's a Programmer's Best Friend?",
  :width => 40, :height => 40,
  :opts => LAYOUT_CENTER_X, :padding => 40)
custom_cursor = FXGIFCursor.new(app,
  File.open("rubycursor.gif", "rb").read)
custom_cursor.create
box.defaultCursor = custom_cursor
```

Figure 11.3, on the facing page, shows what this custom cursor shape looks like, when the cursor is inside the lower box. Note that the size of the GIF image should be 32-by-32 pixels or less; this is because of a limitation on the size of cursors in Windows. Also note that FOX distinguishes between the *default cursor* for a window and the *drag cursor* for a window. The cursor changes to the drag cursor whenever the window is grabbed (which usually happens as a result of the user

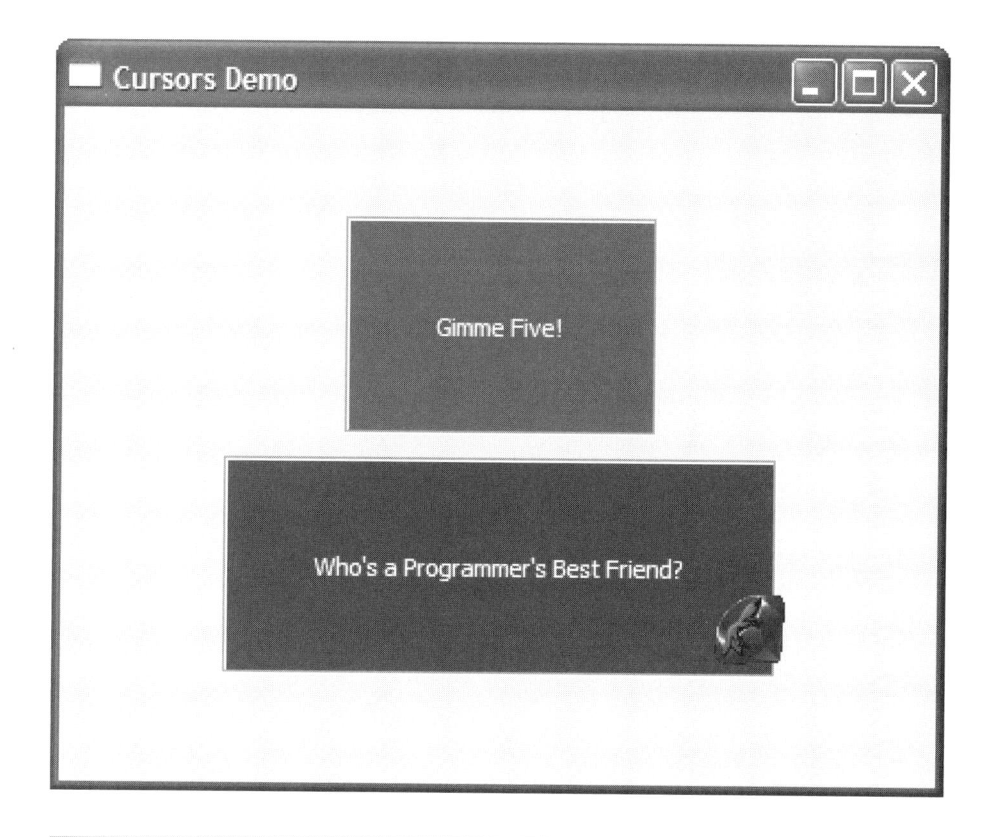

Figure 11.3: USING A GIF IMAGE FOR A CUSTOM CURSOR SHAPE

holding down the mouse button and dragging the mouse). If you change the default cursor for a window, you'll likely want to change the drag cursor for that window as well, using the dragCursor attribute.

There's a special case that comes up often enough for FXRuby to provide a pair of helper methods for it. When your application is doing something time-consuming, such as loading a large file or performing a complicated calculation, you usually want to change the cursor shape to the "busy" cursor (which looks like a wristwatch). You can use the beginWaitCursor() and endWaitCursor() methods to temporarily switch the cursor from its current shape to the busy cursor and back again:[4]

```
app.beginWaitCursor # save current shape and switch to busy cursor
    ... perform time-consuming operation ...
app.endWaitCursor   # revert to previous cursor shape
```

4. FOX calls it the "wait" cursor, I like to call it the "busy" cursor. Deal with it.

You can also use the transactional form of beginWaitCursor(), which will automatically call endWaitCursor() when the block exits:

busy.rb

```
open_button = FXButton.new(self, "Open File")
open_button.connect(SEL_COMMAND) do
  app.beginWaitCursor do
    open_file # this may take awhile...
  end
end
```

It's important to note that, in this example, the user won't be able to do anything else with the program while it's busy opening the file. You need to be really careful with this. If the task that you're performing is going to take a long time but can be done in the background, you should consider performing that task in a separate thread so that your program remains responsive during that time.

Considering the work you did in building the Picture Book application, you already have a lot of experience working with images. In the next couple of sections, we'll review that information and learn a few new tricks in the process.

11.3 Creating and Displaying Images

The easiest way to get started working with FXImage objects is to use one of the format-specific subclasses such as FXJPGImage to construct an image directly from some image data. For example, you can construct an image from a JPEG format file in one line of code:

image.rb

```
birdsnest_image =
  FXJPGImage.new(app, File.open("birdsnest.jpg", "rb").read)
```

FOX doesn't much care where you get the image data from. If the data is online somewhere, you can just as easily use Ruby's standard open-uri library to grab it:

image.rb

```
require 'open-uri'

oscar_image =
  FXJPGImage.new(app, open("http://tinyurl.com/35o8yy").read)
```

Image File Format	Class Name
Windows Bitmap (BMP)	FXBMPImage
Graphics Interchange Format (GIF)	FXGIFImage
Joint Photographic Experts Group (JPEG)	FXJPGImage
Portable Network Graphics (PNG)	FXPNGImage
Tagged Image File Format (TIFF)	FXTIFImage

Figure 11.4: FXIMAGE SUBCLASSES

There are subclasses of FXImage for many popular image file formats. See Figure 11.4 for a listing of the most commonly used file types and the corresponding class names.[5]

Once you have a reference to an FXImage object, there are a number of ways you can use it. The FXImageFrame class is a subclass of FXFrame whose sole purpose is to display an image:

image.rb

```
FXImageFrame.new(tab_book, birdsnest_image,
  :opts => FRAME_RAISED|FRAME_THICK|LAYOUT_FILL)
```

The FXImageFrame widget isn't all that sophisticated. If you run the sample application and resize the window to make it smaller, you'll see that the image doesn't shrink to fit the window's new size; it just gets clipped around its edges. When you're displaying an image of unknown size, you might be better off using an FXImageView widget, which displays the image inside a scrolling window:

image.rb

```
FXImageView.new(tabbook_page, oscar_image, :opts => LAYOUT_FILL)
```

A third use for images is to draw them into device contexts for more general-purpose drawing applications. I'm not going to cover that topic here, but you can check out the dctest.rb example program in the standard FXRuby distribution to see how this works.

In addition to the basic capability for loading and displaying images, FOX provides a number of APIs for manipulating and transforming images. Let's take a look at those features next.

5. FOX also provides support for a number of other, more obscure image file formats.

11.4 Manipulating Image Data

In some circumstances, you may need to make minor modifications to image data. We tackled this in Chapter 5, *Take 2: Display an Entire Album*, on page 35, when we used the scale() method to shrink the original images so that we could see more of them at the same time. The FXImage class provides several additional APIs that support the manipulation and transformation of image data, but they take a little extra effort in terms of setup.

For starters, by default the FXImage throws away its copy of the original image data once it has created the server-side representation. If you need to manipulate the source image data only before you call create() on the image, this default behavior doesn't present a problem. If, on the other hand, you want to be able to manipulate the image data after that initial call to create(), you need to tell FXImage to hold on to its copy of the original image data (what people in the know refer to as the *client-side pixel buffer*) by passing in the IMAGE_KEEP option when you construct the image:

cropimage1.rb

```
@image = FXJPGImage.new(app,
  File.open("birdsnest.jpg", "rb").read,
  :opts => IMAGE_KEEP)
```

Now you can call one or more of the image manipulation APIs to alter the image's client-side copy of the pixel buffer. For example, you can use the crop() method to eliminate portions of the original image. Figure 11.5, on the next page shows a sample image with all of its original content. Let's see what it looks like after cropping away everything but the upper quadrant of the image.

cropimage1.rb

```
@image.crop(0, 0, 0.5*@image.width, 0.5*@image.height)
```

The first two arguments to crop() are the coordinates for the upper-left corner of the region that you want to keep, and the third and fourth arguments are the width and height of that region. Figure 11.6, on page 150, shows what's left of the image after it has been cropped. As expected, the image is one fourth of its original size and contains only the upper-left quadrant's worth of the original image.

The way that crop() actually works is that it resizes the image to the new width and height, copies over the part of the original image that you want to keep, and then fills in any gaps with a fill color (which

Figure 11.5: ORIGINAL IMAGE BEFORE CROPPING

by default is black). In most cases, you'll use crop() as we did in the previous example to retain some region that is a subset of the original image, but crop() is flexible enough to let you do some unusual things. For example, consider this call to crop() for the same original image:

cropimage2.rb

```
@image.crop(0.5*@image.width, 0.5*@image.height,
            @image.width, @image.height)
```

In this example, we're using the center of the image as the upper-left corner of the crop region, which seems reasonable, but we're also saying that the size of the new image should have the same width and height as the original image. Figure 11.7, on page 151, shows the result of this call to crop(). Note that the new parts, which weren't present in the original image, are filled in with black.

Figure 11.6: RESULTING IMAGE AFTER CROPPING

Let's consider a different image manipulation technique. You can create a mirror image of the current image using the mirror() method:

mirrorimage.rb

```
@image.mirror(false, true)
```

The first argument to mirror() indicates whether the image should be mirrored in the horizontal direction (that is, flipped from left to right). The second argument indicates whether the image should be vertically mirrored. In this example, we're mirroring the image only in the vertical direction. Figure 11.8, on page 152, shows what the photo of the bird's nest looks like when it has been mirrored vertically.[6]

We previously noted that if you want to be able to manipulate the client-side pixel buffer after the image is created, you need to be sure to pass in the IMAGE_KEEP option when you construct the image. It's also

6. No birds were harmed in the development of this example program.

Figure 11.7: CROPPING GONE BAD

important to note that when you subsequently manipulate the image data, you need to tell FOX to update the server-side representation of the image by calling the image's render() method. Many of the image manipulation APIs, including scale(), crop(), and mirror(), automatically call render() for you after they've finished rearranging the pixels. Other APIs, such as blend() and gradient(), don't, and it's up to you to call render() on the image after using those APIs.[7]

In addition to scaling, cropping, and mirroring images, FOX provides APIs for rotating, shearing, fading, and blending images; see the FXImage API documentation for more details. This is a pretty useful set of tools, but for anything more sophisticated you're probably better off using an auxiliary library such as Tim Hunter's popular RMagick.[8]

7. The API documentation for the image manipulation methods indicates which ones automatically rerender the image and which ones do not.
8. http://rmagick.rubyforge.org/

Figure 11.8: A MIRROR IMAGE

So far we've really been considering only one aspect of how to use bitmapped image data to enhance the appearance of our applications. In the next section, we'll look at how to use images as icons to provide smaller decorative touches to labels, buttons, and other widgets.

11.5 Creating and Displaying Icons

The main difference between images and icons is that some parts of icons are treated as transparent. You define a transparency color for an icon, and then when FOX draws that icon, the stuff underneath the pixels of that color shows through. Icons are also usually smaller in size than your average image, but in all but a few situations there's no real constraint on an icon's size. Another important difference is that icons can be used in a lot more places than a plain old image. You've already seen how you can use icons as decorations for labels, buttons, and various kinds of list items. In Chapter 13, *Advanced Menu*

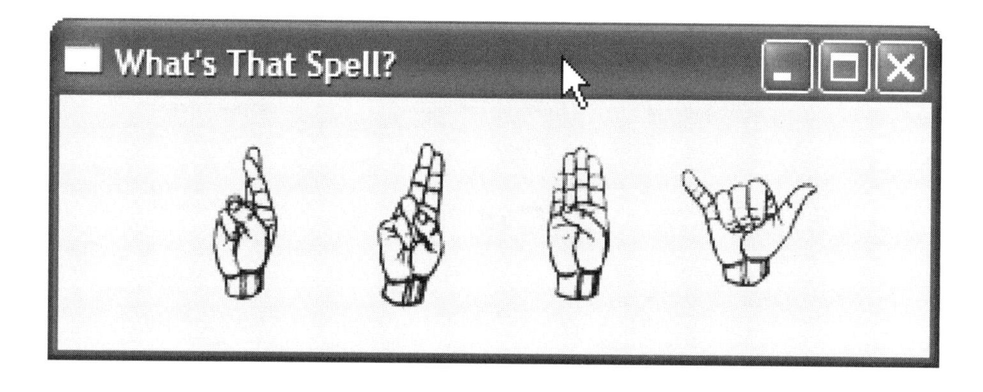

Figure 11.9: GUESSING THE TRANSPARENCY COLOR FOR BMP ICONS

Management, on page 187, you'll see that you can also associate them with menu items.

As was the case with images, the easiest way to get started using icons is to construct one from some image data by using one of the subclasses of FXIcon. For example, you can construct an icon from a GIF file in a single line:

icons.rb

```
gif_icon = FXGIFIcon.new(app, File.open("fxruby.gif", "rb").read)
```

The only tricky part of constructing an icon is that most image file formats (other than GIF) don't inherently support the notion of a single transparency color. For example, the BMP file format doesn't address transparency at all. When you want to construct an icon from a BMP image, you must at least give FOX a hint about which color is the right one. The easiest way to do this is using the IMAGE_ALPHAGUESS option:

icons2.rb

```
r_icon = FXBMPIcon.new(app,
  File.open("Ras1.bmp", "rb").read,
  :opts => IMAGE_ALPHAGUESS)
```

Figure 11.9 shows an example of the IMAGE_ALPHAGUESS option in action. When you specify the IMAGE_ALPHAGUESS option, FOX will guess the transparency color based on the colors of the four corners of the image. And this is usually a pretty good guess; for this example, all four corners of the original BMP images were white, so it correctly guessed that the white regions should be made transparent.

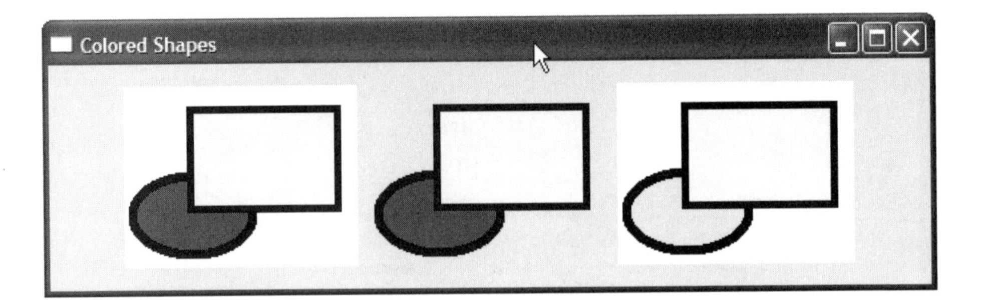

Figure 11.10: FIXING THE TRANSPARENCY COLOR FOR BMP ICONS

If the IMAGE_ALPHAGUESS algorithm doesn't in fact make the right guess, you can explicitly specify which color value should be transparent by passing in that value and the IMAGE_ALPHACOLOR option:

icons3.rb

```
red_transp = FXBMPIcon.new(app,
  File.open("shapes.bmp", "rb").read,
  :opts => IMAGE_ALPHACOLOR)
red_transp.transparentColor = FXRGB(255, 0, 0)
```

Figure 11.10 shows three different results for the transparency color of the same BMP icon. The first result, on the left, shows what we get if we don't say anything about the transparency color: the image is simply drawn opaque, with no transparent regions. The middle result shows what we get if we use the IMAGE_ALPHAGUESS option: since all four corners of the image are white, that's assumed to be the transparency color. The third result, on the right, shows what we get when we specify the IMAGE_ALPHACOLOR option and a transparency color of red (as in the previous code excerpt).

At the other end of the spectrum is the PNG file format, which includes an *alpha* channel for specifying the degree of transparency for each individual pixel. Pixels can be completely opaque, completely transparent, or somewhere in between. FOX renders these kinds of icons by assuming that any pixel that's not completely transparent (and thus has a nonzero alpha value) should be visible. The downside of this is that you can't display partially transparent regions in icons, but the upside is that you're not restricted to a single transparency color as you are with most of the other file formats.

11.6 One More Thing

We discussed this point way back in Section 7.7, *Client-Side vs. Server-Side Objects*, on page 89, but it bears repeating. If you construct an image or icon dynamically, after the program is up and running, be sure to call create() on it to link it with a server-side resource. Otherwise, your program will crash spectacularly. This problem comes up in a number of different situations, but one where it's especially prevalent is in conjunction with adding new items to a list at runtime.

Suppose that you have an FXListBox widget to which items are added at runtime. The list box contains a list of usernames, and each entry in the list has an associated icon that indicates the user's status:

```
def add_user(user_name, status)
  status_icon = make_status_icon(status)
  status_icon.create
  users_listbox.appendItem(user_name, status_icon)
end
```

In this excerpt from our hypothetical program, the application can invoke the add_user() method to add a new user with a given status on the fly. Before adding the list item, we call the make_status_icon() method to construct a new FXIcon instance that graphically indicates the user's status. The key here is to then call create() on the icon object *before* we associate it with a list item. Note that our implementation of make_status_icon() could cache the icon objects if that makes sense. There's no harm in calling create() on an already-created resource, but you definitely want to ensure that the resource has been created before it's ever used.

Constructing a GUI application isn't just about putting all the widgets in the right places and wiring them together. The gratuitous use of colorful icons and fancy fonts is certainly no remedy for poorly designed user interaction, but with the appropriate (and I hope tasteful) use of custom fonts, cursors, images, and icons, you can enhance your user interfaces to make them more visually pleasing to the end users. As more and more users come to expect visually rich user interfaces, the "curb appeal" of the application is a factor that you shouldn't disregard.

Speaking of putting all the widgets in the right places, it's now time for us to take a closer look at how you can use layout managers to place and size the widgets in a user interface. Let's do that in the next chapter.

Chapter 12

Managing Layouts

Layout managers are objects that are responsible for arranging the positions and sizes of other widgets. On its surface, this may sound like a pretty simple assignment, and it's certainly true that in well-designed user interfaces, an application's users won't really be aware of the role that layout managers play. From an application developer's point of view, however, layout managers provide you with a lot of flexibility in terms of how your user interface is organized.

Fundamentally, layout managers give you ways to express not only how individual widgets' sizes and positions are determined but also how groups of widgets are sized and positioned relative to each other. They give you the tools to make everything fit, just the way you want them to work. For those cases where things won't (or shouldn't) all fit on the same screen at the same time, layout managers provide you with options for conditionally displaying different parts of the user interface at different times. For example, some special-purpose layout managers allow you to swap different parts of the application in and out, while others allow you to scroll different portions of a window in and out of view.

Layout managers also help you address some less obvious problems. For example, one of the trickier aspects of creating cross-platform applications is that some resources, such as fonts, can be changed on the fly. These sorts of changes can have a potentially significant impact on the arrangement of the parts of the user interface that display text using those fonts. Layout managers can help you minimize the impact of those changes.

In this chapter, we will start by looking at the packing model, the fundamental layout algorithm that powers many of FOX's most heavily used layout managers. The FXPacker is a pretty complicated layout manager, and although we'll use it in our initial discussion of the packing model, in practice you won't use FXPacker directly all that often. Instead, you'll use one of its subclasses, such as FXHorizontalFrame or FXVerticalFrame.

We'll take a look at those as well and then continue our discussion of layout basics by examining how to create more complicated layouts by nesting layout managers inside each another, how to create fixed layouts (and why you shouldn't), and how to modify the padding and spacing inside layout managers to get just the right look.

Once we have a handle on the fundamentals, we'll turn our attention to some of the more special-purpose layout managers. We already encountered some of these layout managers, such as FXMatrix, FXScrollWindow, and FXSplitter, when we were building the Picture Book application. We'll take a closer look at those layout managers and touch on some of the finer points involved in using them.

We'll also examine the FXTabBook layout manager, which you can use to create tabbed notebook-style views. We'll wrap up the chapter with a more general look at how to solve some more common layout problems using FOX's layout managers.

12.1 Understanding the Packing Model

Are you familiar with the videogame Tetris? The object of Tetris is to maneuver a series of falling geometric shapes so that they will fit into a container. While one of these shapes is falling, you can rotate it or shift it from side to side until you find the best fit for it. Well, the FXPacker layout manager works something like that (although I hope it's less stressful).

When you first construct an FXPacker window, it's like an empty box. The first child widget that you add to the packer will be packed against one of its four sides.

You specify which side you want to pack against by passing in one of LAYOUT_SIDE_TOP, LAYOUT_SIDE_RIGHT, LAYOUT_SIDE_BOTTOM, or LAYOUT_SIDE_LEFT as a layout hint:[1]

packer1.rb

```
packer = FXPacker.new(self, :opts => LAYOUT_FILL)
child1 = FXButton.new(packer, "First",
  :opts => BUTTON_NORMAL|LAYOUT_SIDE_BOTTOM)
```

Here, we've specified that the first child widget, a button, should be packed along the bottom side of the packer. By default, the packer is going to align that button with its left side. We can override that behavior so that the button is instead centered between the packer's left and right sides:

packer2.rb

```
child1 = FXButton.new(packer, "First",
  :opts => BUTTON_NORMAL|LAYOUT_SIDE_BOTTOM|LAYOUT_CENTER_X)
```

If we want the button to be aligned with the packer's right side, we can replace LAYOUT_CENTER_X with LAYOUT_RIGHT:

packer3.rb

```
child1 = FXButton.new(packer, "First",
  :opts => BUTTON_NORMAL|LAYOUT_SIDE_BOTTOM|LAYOUT_RIGHT)
```

So far, the packer is just sizing the button to its default width and height. We can request that the button be stretched horizontally to make it as wide as possible:

packer4.rb

```
child1 = FXButton.new(packer, "First",
  :opts => BUTTON_NORMAL|LAYOUT_SIDE_BOTTOM|LAYOUT_FILL_X)
```

Note that I've left out the hint about how to align the button, since the LAYOUT_FILL_X hint makes that irrelevant.

1. If you don't explicitly specify the side, it defaults to LAYOUT_SIDE_TOP.

Figure 12.1: NOT QUITE WHAT WE EXPECTED?

Now, what if we want to pack *two* buttons against the bottom side of the packer? It seems like we ought to be able to write code like this:

packer5.rb

```
packer = FXPacker.new(self, :opts => LAYOUT_FILL)
child1 = FXButton.new(packer, "Bottom-Right",
  :opts => BUTTON_NORMAL|LAYOUT_SIDE_BOTTOM|LAYOUT_RIGHT)
child2 = FXButton.new(packer, "Bottom-Left",
  :opts => BUTTON_NORMAL|LAYOUT_SIDE_BOTTOM|LAYOUT_LEFT)
```

The LAYOUT_SIDE_BOTTOM hint tells the packer that we want both buttons packed against the bottom side. We specify LAYOUT_RIGHT on the first button and LAYOUT_LEFT on the second. We know that the button's default size is small enough for both of them to fit, right? So, what happens when you run this example?

With that kind of a setup, you just knew that it wasn't going to work, right? Figure 12.1 shows what it looks like running under Windows, but the layout is not quite what we expected. The first button is correctly packed against the packer's bottom edge and aligned with the packer's right side. The second button is correctly aligned with the packer's left side, but it's sitting on top of this invisible shelf, just above the first button. The deal with the packer is that once you pack a widget against a side of the remaining space (aka the "cavity"), it takes up that entire side of the cavity. This is true even if you aren't using LAYOUT_FILL_X or LAYOUT_FILL_Y.

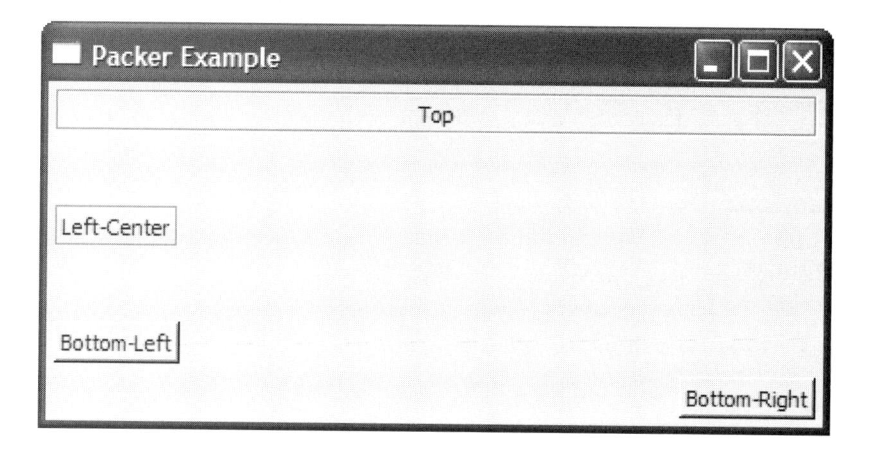

Figure 12.2: AFTER ADDING MORE WIDGETS

Let's add a few more widgets, packed against other sides of the cavity, to see how they are placed as the packer begins to fill up:

packer6.rb

```
packer = FXPacker.new(self, :opts => LAYOUT_FILL)
child1 = FXButton.new(packer, "Bottom-Right",
  :opts => BUTTON_NORMAL|LAYOUT_SIDE_BOTTOM|LAYOUT_RIGHT)
child2 = FXButton.new(packer, "Bottom-Left",
  :opts => BUTTON_NORMAL|LAYOUT_SIDE_BOTTOM|LAYOUT_LEFT)
child3 = FXLabel.new(packer, "Top",
  :opts => FRAME_GROOVE|LAYOUT_SIDE_TOP|LAYOUT_FILL_X)
child4 = FXLabel.new(packer, "Left-Center",
  :opts => FRAME_GROOVE|LAYOUT_SIDE_LEFT|LAYOUT_CENTER_Y)
```

Figure 12.2 shows what this looks like running under Windows. It may help to understand what has happened by looking at Figure 12.3, on the next page. The dashed lines indicate the spaces occupied by each of the child widgets that have been placed in the packer. Note that by the time we added the fourth child widget (the "Left-Center" label) a good bit of the vertical space in the cavity had been eaten up by the previously added widgets.

But let's not forget our earlier goal of placing buttons in the lower-left and lower-right corners of the packer. How do we achieve that kind of layout? For any kind of nontrivial layout, you're going to end up nesting layout managers inside each another. And that leads us into

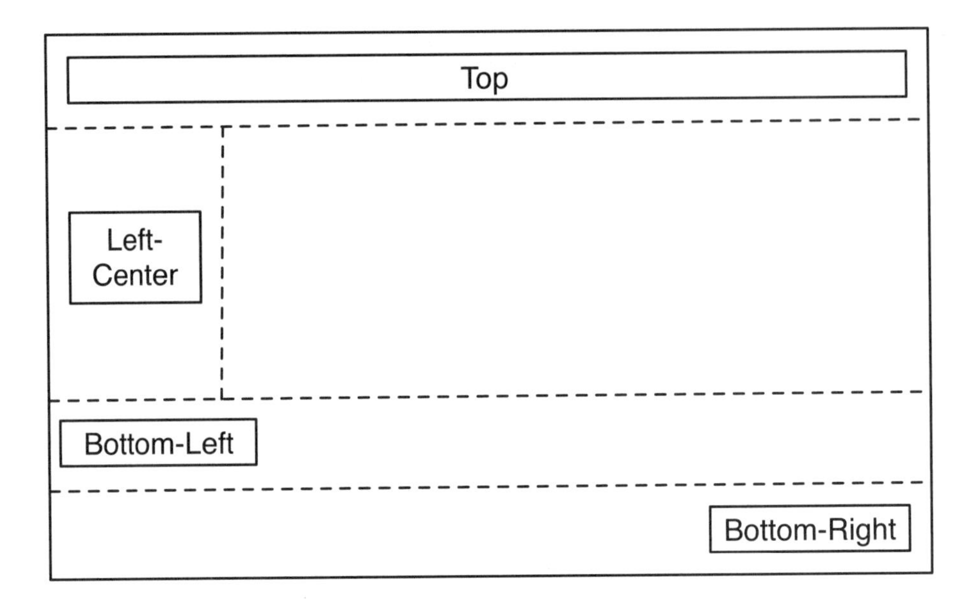

Figure 12.3: WHAT'S GOING ON BEHIND THE SCENES

a discussion of the next set of layout managers, the horizontal and vertical frames.

Creating Simple Layouts with Horizontal and Vertical Frames

The FXHorizontalFrame and FXVerticalFrame layout managers are subclasses of FXPacker that place some additional constraints on the packer model that we've been talking about. As you might guess from their names, the horizontal frame arranges its children horizontally, and the vertical frame arranges its children vertically.

By default, the horizontal frame will just lay out its children from left to right, using their default sizes:

hframe1.rb

```
hframe = FXHorizontalFrame.new(self)
child1 = FXButton.new(hframe, "First")
child2 = FXButton.new(hframe, "Second")
child3 = FXButton.new(hframe, "Third")
```

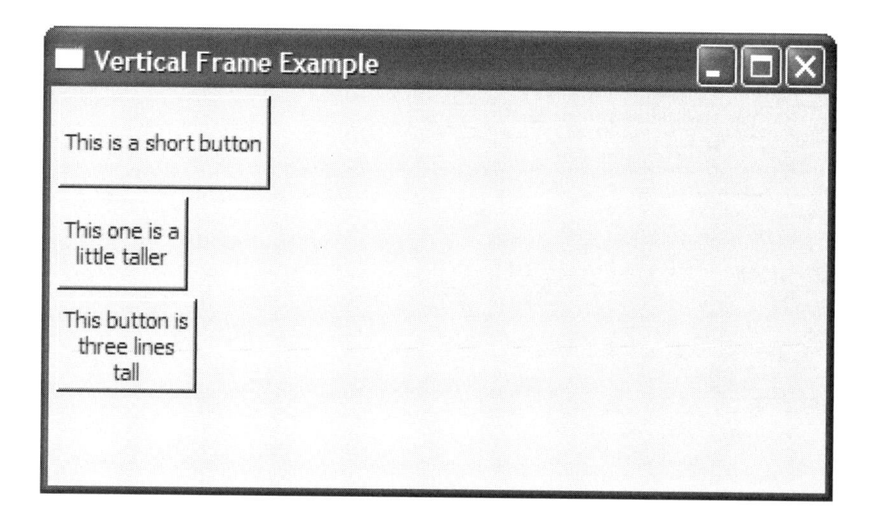

Figure 12.4: VERTICAL FRAME WITH UNIFORM HEIGHTS

As was the case with the FXPacker, you can be more specific about which side the child widget should be aligned with:

hframe2.rb

```
hframe = FXHorizontalFrame.new(self)
child1 =
  FXButton.new(hframe, "Right", :opts => BUTTON_NORMAL|LAYOUT_RIGHT)
child2 =
  FXButton.new(hframe, "Left",  :opts => BUTTON_NORMAL|LAYOUT_LEFT)
```

Note that we're using LAYOUT_LEFT and LAYOUT_RIGHT, not LAYOUT_SIDE_LEFT and LAYOUT_SIDE_RIGHT. The thing to remember is that the packing hints (such as LAYOUT_SIDE_LEFT and LAYOUT_SIDE_RIGHT) are considered by only the FXPacker layout manager.

You can specify the PACK_UNIFORM_HEIGHT packing hint to force all the widgets in a frame to assume the same height:

vframe1.rb

```
vframe = FXVerticalFrame.new(self, :opts => PACK_UNIFORM_HEIGHT)
child1 = FXButton.new(vframe, "This is a short button")
child2 = FXButton.new(vframe, "This one is a\nlittle taller")
child3 = FXButton.new(vframe, "This button is\nthree lines\ntall")
```

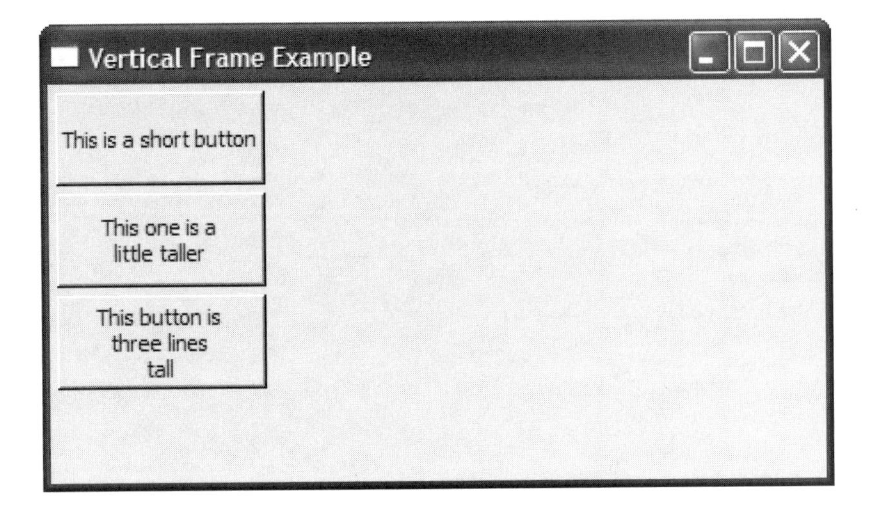

Figure 12.5: VERTICAL FRAME WITH UNIFORM WIDTHS AND HEIGHTS

Note that the PACK_UNIFORM_HEIGHT hint is specified for the frame, not for the individual buttons. When you run this example, you'll see that all three buttons have been sized to the height of the tallest widget (the third button). Figure 12.4, on the preceding page shows what this looks like under Windows. You can also request that the widgets have uniform width.

vframe2.rb

```
vframe = FXVerticalFrame.new(self,
  :opts => PACK_UNIFORM_WIDTH|PACK_UNIFORM_HEIGHT)
child1 = FXButton.new(vframe, "This is a short button")
child2 = FXButton.new(vframe, "This one is a\nlittle taller")
child3 = FXButton.new(vframe, "This button is\nthree lines\ntall")
```

Figure 12.5, shows what this looks like under Windows. Note that each of the buttons is now as wide as the widest widget (the first button).

An understanding of how the packing model works and how to use FXHorizontalFrame and FXVerticalFrame to create simple layouts is essential knowledge for any FXRuby developer, but you'll begin to realize the real power of layout managers when you learn how to nest layout managers inside one another to create more complex layouts. Let's take a look at how to do that next.

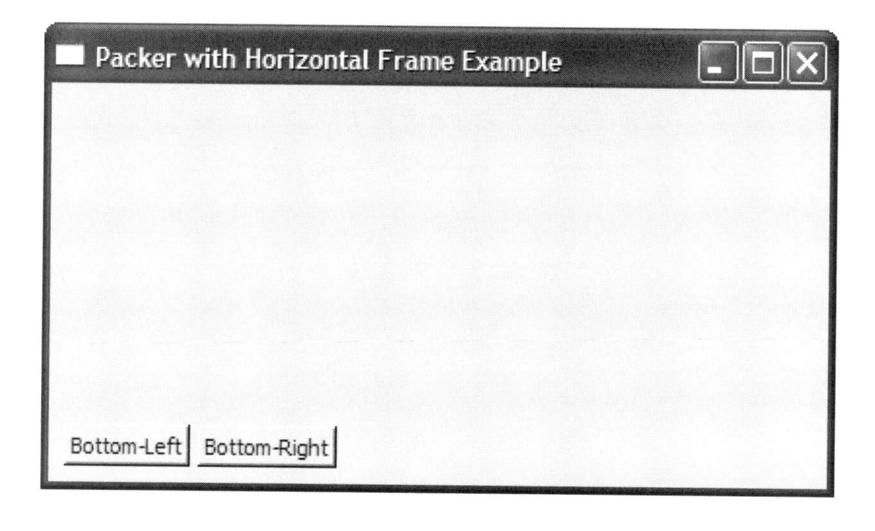

Figure 12.6: PACKER WITH NESTED HORIZONTAL FRAME

Nesting Layout Managers Inside Each Other

Let's revisit the example we looked at in an earlier section, when we tried to figure out how to pack two buttons along the bottom side of a packer. To achieve that layout, we'll put the two buttons inside a horizontal frame and then put that horizontal frame inside the packer:

hframe3.rb

```
packer = FXPacker.new(self, :opts => LAYOUT_FILL)
hframe = FXHorizontalFrame.new(packer, :opts => LAYOUT_SIDE_BOTTOM)
child1 = FXButton.new(hframe, "Bottom-Right",
  :opts => BUTTON_NORMAL|LAYOUT_RIGHT)
child2 = FXButton.new(hframe, "Bottom-Left",
  :opts => BUTTON_NORMAL|LAYOUT_LEFT)
```

Before you run this example, take a look at the code and make sure you understand how the horizontal frame is nested inside the packer. Figure 12.6 shows what this example looks like running under Windows.

This is pretty close. The buttons are now on the same level, but instead of being in opposite corners, they're right next to each other (and butted up against the left side).

The problem has to do with the layout hints that we specified for the horizontal frame. Since we didn't ask for the horizontal frame to stretch, the frame has been sized just large enough to hold the two buttons that

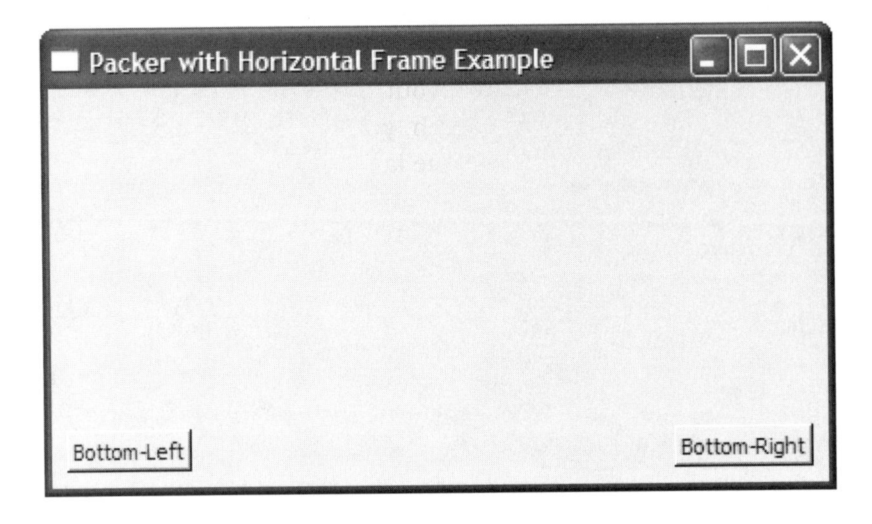

Figure 12.7: PACKER WITH NESTED HORIZONTAL FRAME

it contains; and since we didn't specify which side to align it with, it chose the default alignment of LAYOUT_LEFT. Let's fix that by specifying the LAYOUT_FILL_X hint for the horizontal frame:

hframe4.rb

```
packer = FXPacker.new(self, :opts => LAYOUT_FILL)
hframe = FXHorizontalFrame.new(packer,
  :opts => LAYOUT_SIDE_BOTTOM|LAYOUT_FILL_X)
child1 = FXButton.new(hframe, "Bottom-Right",
  :opts => BUTTON_NORMAL|LAYOUT_RIGHT)
child2 = FXButton.new(hframe, "Bottom-Left",
  :opts => BUTTON_NORMAL|LAYOUT_LEFT)
```

Figure 12.7, shows the final result. Obviously, this is a pretty basic example of nesting layout managers inside each other, but it gives you a taste of how we'll solve some more complicated layout problems. We'll revisit this in more detail in Section 12.6, *Strategies for Using Different Layout Managers Together*, on page 180.

So far, we've been discussing how to achieve various layouts without making any explicit references to the sizes or positions of the widgets being laid out. FOX also supports fixed layouts, where you explicitly specify the positions and/or sizes of the widgets, and we'll take a look at how that works next.

Creating Fixed Layouts

You can, of course, bypass the layout managers altogether and just use fixed layouts. With this approach, you can specify the position of a widget explicitly instead of letting the layout manager figure it out.

fixedlayout.rb

```
@fixed_pos_button = FXButton.new(self, "Fixed Position",
  :opts => BUTTON_NORMAL|LAYOUT_FIX_X|LAYOUT_FIX_Y,
  :x => 20, :y => 20)
```

When you run this example, try resizing the main window. Thanks to the LAYOUT_FIX_X and LAYOUT_FIX_Y layout hints, you'll see that the button stays in the same position, relative to the upper-left corner of the main window, regardless of what you do. If you resize the window so that it's too short (or narrow) to display the button, the button will just be clipped.

You can also fix the size of a widget, using the LAYOUT_FIX_WIDTH and LAYOUT_FIX_HEIGHT layout hints:

fixedlayout.rb

```
@fixed_size_label = FXLabel.new(self, "Fixed Size Label",
  :opts => (LAYOUT_CENTER_X|LAYOUT_CENTER_Y|
            LAYOUT_FIX_WIDTH|LAYOUT_FIX_HEIGHT),
  :width => 120, :height => 40)
```

It's not an all-or-nothing proposition, by the way. If you just want to fix the *x* position of the widget but leave the other parameters up to the layout manager, just pass in the LAYOUT_FIX_X flag and a value for the x attribute. If you are going to specify all four parameters (x, y, width, and height), you can pass in the more compact LAYOUT_EXPLICIT hint instead:

```
FXLabel.new(self, "Fixed Position and Size",
  :opts => LAYOUT_EXPLICIT,
  :x => 20, :y => 20,
  :width => 120, :height => 40)
```

This has the same effect as passing in the LAYOUT_FIX_X, LAYOUT_FIX_Y, LAYOUT_FIX_WIDTH, and LAYOUT_FIX_HEIGHT layout hints.

Now, forget everything I just told you, because fixed layouts are almost *never* the best solution.

The problem with fixed layouts is that they decrease the portability of your user interface to runtime environments with different display characteristics. That label that looks fine with a fixed width of 120 pixels on your system might look gigantic on a system where the user substitutes a smaller font than the one you used. Worse, if the user's font is larger than the one you tested with, some of the widget's label string might be truncated and unreadable. To see this in action, run the example program, and try increasing or decreasing the font size using the spinner widget at the bottom of the screen.

A similar problem has to do with the display size. If you're developing and running the application in full-screen mode on a 1024-by-768 monitor and you're using a fixed layout, deploying to a system running at a different screen resolution will almost certainly be disastrous. Unless you're using some kind of element that always needs to be the same size—say, a fixed-size image or icon—you should avoid using fixed layouts in your applications.

Adding Finishing Touches with Padding and Spacing

By now you may have noticed that when we pack widgets against a given side of the packer (or whatever layout manager we're using), they aren't exactly flush with that surface. So far, there has always been a little bit of breathing room between the widget and the container that it's in. There's also spacing between adjacent child widgets in a container. Obviously, FOX is applying some reasonable defaults to ensure that the layout looks good, and in many cases that's not something you'll want to mess with. In some cases, though, you need to tighten up those gaps between widgets, and for that reason we're going to take a quick look at the padding and spacing parameters.

Figure 12.8, on the next page, illustrates how the padding and spacing values are used during layout. The *padding* for a widget is the amount of space it reserves for itself around its edges. The default padding for most widgets is 2 pixels on each side, but you can change that value for any or all sides. For example, if you want a widget to be flush against the upper-left corner of its parent, you'd want to specify zero padding on the left and top sides, but you might leave the bottom and right padding values at their default settings. You can specify the padding values for a widget at construction time, using some combination of the :padLeft, :padRight, :padTop, and :padBottom keys:

```
spinner = FXSpinner.new(self, 4,
  :opts => SPIN_NORMAL|LAYOUT_SIDE_TOP|LAYOUT_LEFT,
  :padLeft => 0, :padTop => 0)
```

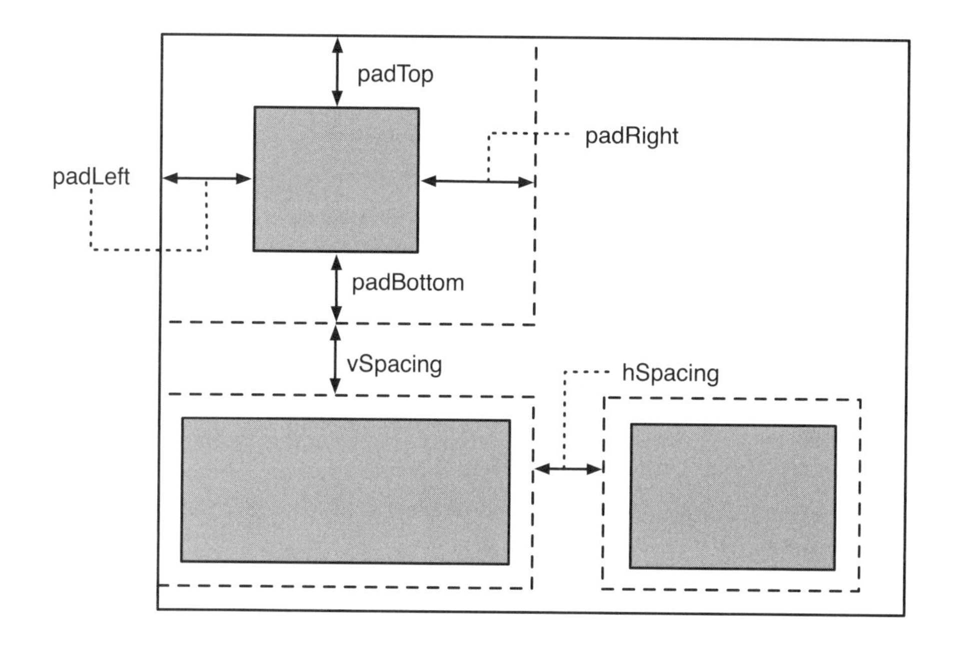

Figure 12.8: PADDING AND SPACING

It's pretty common to want to set the padding on all four sides to zero so that there's no internal padding. For those situations, you can just specify the :padding:

```
spinner = FXSpinner.new(self, 4,
  :opts => SPIN_NORMAL|LAYOUT_SIDE_TOP|LAYOUT_LEFT,
  :padding => 0)
```

You can also change the padding for a widget after it has been constructed, using the padLeft, padRight, padTop, and padBottom attributes:

```
spinner = FXSpinner.new(self, 4,
  :opts => SPIN_NORMAL|LAYOUT_SIDE_TOP|LAYOUT_LEFT)
spinner.padLeft = 0
spinner.padTop = 0
```

The *horizontal and vertical spacing* parameters for a layout manager dictate how much room it will leave between adjacent child widgets as it positions them.

You can specify these values using the :hSpacing and :vSpacing keys at construction time:

```
groupbox = FXGroupBox.new(self, "No horizontal or vertical spacing",
  :hSpacing => 0, :vSpacing => 0)
```

Note that since spacing is considered only in between adjacent widgets, the spacing values aren't used for widgets along the sides of the layout manager. For example, the left edge of the leftmost widget in a horizontal frame will be offset only by its internal padding (more specifically, its padLeft value).

As was the case with padding, you can also change the spacing values for a container after it has been constructed:

```
groupbox = FXGroupBox.new(self, "No horizontal or vertical spacing")
groupbox.hSpacing = 0
groupbox.vSpacing = 0
```

It can be a little tricky to get the hang of padding and spacing values and how they interact with each other. The main thing to remember is that you specify spacing on the layout manager (the container) and padding on the child widgets. Since all layout managers can themselves be children of other layout managers, that means you can also specify the padding for layout managers.

Now that we've covered all the basics of working with layout managers, we'll turn our attention to some of the more special-purpose layout managers that FOX provides. We'll start with the FXMatrix layout manager, which we previously encountered when we were building the Picture Book application.

12.2 Arranging Widgets in Rows and Columns with a Matrix Layout

The FXMatrix layout manager lays out its child widgets in rows and columns. Some other toolkits refer to this kind of layout as a "grid" layout. It's especially useful for laying out forms, with a column of labels on one side and a column of text fields (or other kinds of widgets) on the other. Note that if you want to display tabular data along the lines of a spreadsheet, you're probably better off using the FXTable widget, which we'll look at in Section 9.4, *Displaying Tabular Data with FXTable*, on page 122.

A matrix can be configured with either a fixed number of rows (MATRIX_BY_ROWS) or a fixed number of columns (MATRIX_BY_COLUMNS), and the second argument for FXMatrix.new is that desired number of rows (or columns).

matrix.rb

```
matrix = FXMatrix.new(self, 3, :opts => MATRIX_BY_ROWS|LAYOUT_FILL)
```

You add child widgets to a matrix just as you would any other layout manager, by passing in a reference to the matrix as the parent for each child widget. Where the matrix actually places those widgets when it lays them out may surprise you, however.

Figure 12.9, on the next page, illustrates the layout for an FXMatrix widget configured as MATRIX_BY_ROWS with three rows. The first child widget you add becomes the first widget in the first row of the matrix (no surprise there). The second widget you add becomes the first widget in the *second* row of the matrix. This pattern continues until you've filled up the first column of the matrix (by adding the first element of each row), and then you start over again with the second column. If the matrix is configured as MATRIX_BY_COLUMNS, you'll instead be filling up a row at a time.

Making the FXMatrix behave properly in response to resizing can be a little tricky sometimes. We need to understand how the layout hints for the matrix's child widgets affect the overall layout of the matrix.

Within a particular cell of a matrix, the usual layout hints work as expected. If you've specified LAYOUT_FILL_X for a child widget, that widget will stretch horizontally to fill up the entire width of the matrix cell that it's in. Likewise, if you specify LAYOUT_CENTER_Y, that child will be centered vertically. The part that's up in the air is how much of its total space the FXMatrix will allocate to that particular cell.

First, the good news. All things being equal, FXMatrix will allocate enough space to each cell to ensure that the child widget at that location "fits." But what if the matrix has room to spare? Your first guess might be that if you simply specify LAYOUT_FILL_X and/or LAYOUT_FILL_Y for the matrix itself, all of its contents will stretch accordingly. Well, that would be a good guess, but you'd be wrong.

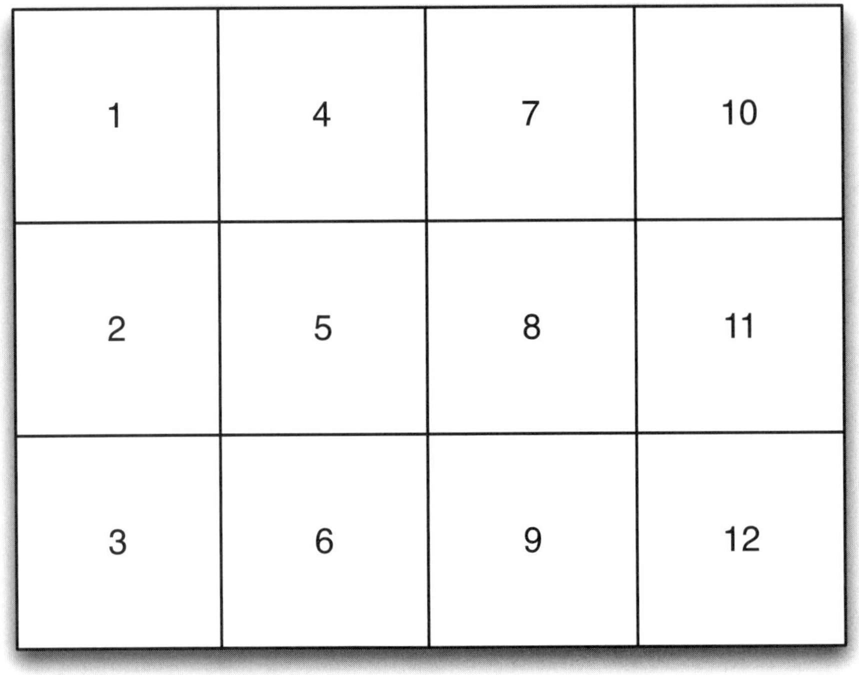

1	4	7	10
2	5	8	11
3	6	9	12

Figure 12.9: LAYOUT ORDER FOR A MATRIX WITH THREE ROWS

Consider this simple matrix, with nine child widgets arranged in three columns:

matrix2.rb

```
matrix = FXMatrix.new(self, 3, :opts => MATRIX_BY_COLUMNS|LAYOUT_FILL)
FXLabel.new(matrix, "Lyle Johnson",
  :opts => JUSTIFY_LEFT|FRAME_LINE|LAYOUT_FILL_X)
FXLabel.new(matrix, "Madison", :opts => JUSTIFY_LEFT|FRAME_LINE)
FXLabel.new(matrix, "AL", :opts => FRAME_LINE)
FXLabel.new(matrix, "Homer Simpson",
  :opts => JUSTIFY_LEFT|FRAME_LINE|LAYOUT_FILL_X)
FXLabel.new(matrix, "Springfield", :opts => JUSTIFY_LEFT|FRAME_LINE)
FXLabel.new(matrix, "CT", :opts => FRAME_LINE)
FXLabel.new(matrix, "Bob Smith",
  :opts => JUSTIFY_LEFT|FRAME_LINE|LAYOUT_FILL_X)
FXLabel.new(matrix, "Walla Walla", :opts => JUSTIFY_LEFT|FRAME_LINE)
FXLabel.new(matrix, "WA", :opts => FRAME_LINE)
```

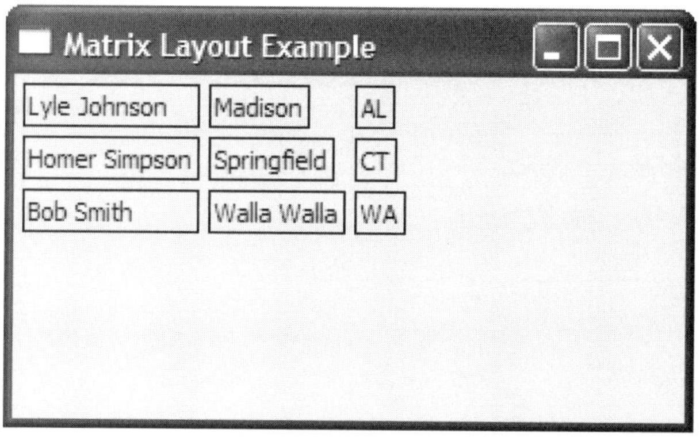

Figure 12.10: MATRIX WITHOUT LAYOUT_FILL_COLUMN

I've added the FRAME_LINE frame style for each of the labels so that you can more clearly see the boundaries of each of those widgets. Figure 12.10 shows what the example looks like running under Windows. When you run this example, your first reaction might be to suspect that FXRuby isn't honoring the LAYOUT_FILL layout hint that you specified for the FXMatrix. After all, it's clear that the matrix hasn't stretched to fill up the main window, right?

Well, as it turns out, the matrix *is* in fact filling up the entire main window. You can make a quick change to the code to prove this to yourself.

matrix3.rb

```
matte = FXPacker.new(self, :opts => LAYOUT_FILL)
matte.backColor = "red"
matrix = FXMatrix.new(matte, 3,
  :opts => MATRIX_BY_COLUMNS|LAYOUT_FILL, :padding => 20)
```

By introducing an intermediate FXPacker with a red background and placing the matrix inside it, we can see that the matrix really is filling up all of the available space (see Figure 12.11, on the next page). So, what gives?

The key to getting individual rows and columns of FXMatrix to stretch and take up the slack space is to use the LAYOUT_FILL_ROW and LAYOUT_FILL_COLUMN layout hints.

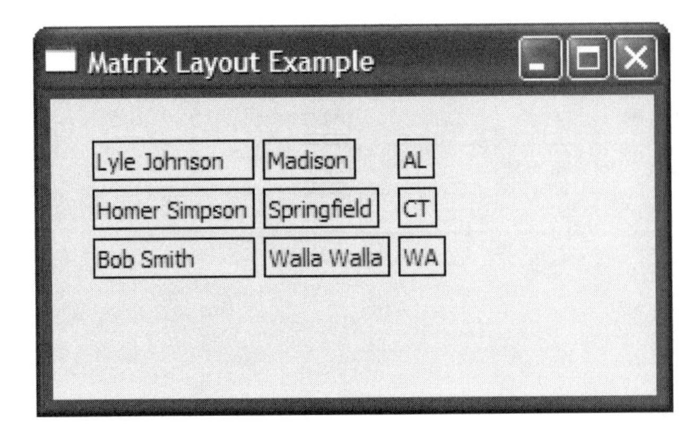

Figure 12.11: MATRIX WITHOUT LAYOUT_FILL_COLUMN (WITH RED MATTE)

If all of the widgets in a column specify the LAYOUT_FILL_COLUMN hint, then that column will stretch horizontally.

matrix4.rb

```
matrix = FXMatrix.new(self, 3, :opts => MATRIX_BY_COLUMNS|LAYOUT_FILL)
FXLabel.new(matrix, "Lyle Johnson",
  :opts => JUSTIFY_LEFT|FRAME_LINE|LAYOUT_FILL_X|LAYOUT_FILL_COLUMN)
FXLabel.new(matrix, "Madison",
  :opts => JUSTIFY_LEFT|FRAME_LINE|LAYOUT_FILL_COLUMN)
FXLabel.new(matrix, "AL", :opts => FRAME_LINE)
FXLabel.new(matrix, "Homer Simpson",
  :opts => JUSTIFY_LEFT|FRAME_LINE|LAYOUT_FILL_X|LAYOUT_FILL_COLUMN)
FXLabel.new(matrix, "Springfield",
  :opts => JUSTIFY_LEFT|FRAME_LINE|LAYOUT_FILL_COLUMN)
FXLabel.new(matrix, "CT", :opts => FRAME_LINE)
FXLabel.new(matrix, "Bob Smith",
  :opts => JUSTIFY_LEFT|FRAME_LINE|LAYOUT_FILL_X|LAYOUT_FILL_COLUMN)
FXLabel.new(matrix, "Walla Walla",
  :opts => JUSTIFY_LEFT|FRAME_LINE|LAYOUT_FILL_COLUMN)
FXLabel.new(matrix, "WA", :opts => FRAME_LINE)
```

Figure 12.12, on the facing page, shows how our example looks, when the layout hint LAYOUT_FILL_COLUMN is specified for each of the labels in the first column. Note that if we were to forget that hint for any one of these, the stretching would not occur. Also, if more than one column's widgets all have this layout hint specified, then the slack space will be divided proportionally.

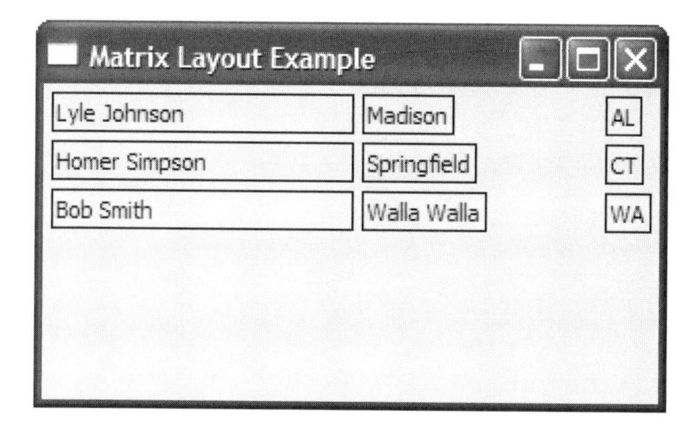

Figure 12.12: MATRIX WITH LAYOUT_FILL_COLUMN ON FIRST COLUMN

The FXMatrix layout manager is one that you won't necessarily use in a lot of applications, but it solves a particular problem very well, so it's a good one to be familiar with. In the next section, we'll take a look at another layout manager that we encountered while building the Picture Book application, the FXSplitter.

12.3 Dynamically Resizing Layouts with a Splitter Layout

The layout managers we've talked about so far enforce layout constraints automatically. Assuming that you've specified the appropriate layout hints, they will determine suitable sizes and locations for all of their child widgets, without any intervention on your part. In some cases, however, it's useful to provide the user with tools for interactively resizing parts of the user interface, and FXRuby offers the FXSplitter layout manager for that purpose.

We got an introduction to the FXSplitter class in Chapter 6, *Take 3: Manage Multiple Albums*, on page 55 when we used it to display the album list and album view side by side. In practice, an FXSplitter will usually contain just two child windows, the "left" and "right" subpanels (or the top and bottom subpanels, if it's a vertical splitter). There's actually no restriction on the number of child windows in a splitter, however, and the splitter will draw handles between each of the subpanels and allow you to resize them accordingly.

By default, the split is from left to right; that is, the first child of the FXSplitter appears on the left side of the split, and the second child appears on the right (and so on, if there are more than two children). You can configure the split to go from top to bottom by passing in the SPLITTER_VERTICAL flag:

```
splitter.splitterStyle |= SPLITTER_VERTICAL
```

You can change the space allocated to either side of a split by grabbing the splitter handle and dragging it from side to side. While you're dragging the splitter handle, a semitransparent line will be drawn across the window to show you where the split will be placed when you stop dragging. When you release the splitter handle, the adjacent subpanels are resized according to the handle's new location.

If the splitter is configured in tracking mode, the panels on either side of the splitter are resized dynamically, while you're dragging the splitter:

```
splitter.splitterStyle |= SPLITTER_TRACKING
```

This is a bit more expensive, computationally speaking, since the subpanels' contents are continuously laid out and redrawn.

Usually, you'll want to set the initial sizes of the splitter's subpanels to some default widths (or heights) and then let the user resize them as needed. It's considerate to save the sizes of the subpanels to the registry[2] when the application exits and then restore them the next time the application starts up. The best practice for doing so is to write the size of the splitter's first panel to the registry just before exiting the application:

splitter.rb

```
app.reg.writeIntEntry("Settings", "splitSize", @splitter.getSplit(0))
app.exit(0)
```

Read the split size back in your main window's create() method and use it to configure the splitter, just before showing the main window:

splitter.rb

```
def create
  super
  @splitter.setSplit(0, app.reg.readIntEntry("Settings", "splitSize"))
  show(PLACEMENT_SCREEN)
end
```

2. We don't cover the FOX registry in this book, but you can read more about it at http://www.fox-toolkit.org/registry.html.

This example assumes that your splitter contains only two subpanels. Obviously, if your splitter contains more than two subpanels, you'll want to save (and restore) the sizes of all but the last one.

Next, let's take a look at the FXScrollWindow layout manager.

12.4 Managing Large Content with Scrolling Windows

We got an introduction to the FXScrollWindow class back in Chapter 5, *Take 2: Display an Entire Album*, on page 35 when we used it as the basis for the album view. As we learned there, FXRuby provides the FXScrollWindow class as a sort of decorator class for other layout managers. When you construct a widget as a child of a scroll window, the scroll window takes care of displaying vertical and horizontal scroll bars, and it ensures that the correct part of the content is visible when the user scrolls through it.

You should add only one child window to an FXScrollWindow. Almost always, that child window will be one of the other layout managers that we've seen. Internally, the scroll window will construct some additional child widgets (for the vertical and horizontal scroll bars), so if you were to directly inquire about the list of child windows, you'd see more than one. For that reason, you should take care to always refer to the scroll window's content area using the contentWindow attribute.

In most cases, you'll want to just add your content to the scroll window and then let the user decide which portion of the content they want to view by adjusting the scroll bars. If it's necessary to programmatically adjust the viewport of the scroll window so that it's showing a particular area of interest, you can use the setPosition() method to do that, but it's a little tricky. The coordinates you must pass into setPosition() are the desired x and y coordinates of the upper-left corner of the content window, relative to the upper-left corner of the viewport window. What that means in practice is that you'll always be passing in negative values to setPosition().

So, for example, if you want to adjust the content so that the part that's visible inside the scroll window's viewport is the part whose upper-left corner is at position (100, 100), you need to pass in (-100, -100) to setPosition():

```
scroll_window.setPosition(-100, -100)
```

If you want to move the content so that it is centered within the viewport, you need to account for the difference in sizes between the content and the viewport. The following bit of code should work in most circumstances:

scrollwindow.rb

```
x = 0.5*(@scroll_window.contentWindow.width -
  @scroll_window.viewportWidth)
y = 0.5*(@scroll_window.contentWindow.height -
  @scroll_window.viewportHeight)
@scroll_window.setPosition(-x, -y)
```

Now let's take a look at the tabbed notebook layout manager.

12.5 Organizing Windows with Tabbed Notebooks

The FXTabBook layout manager is so named because it resembles a notebook with tabbed pages. When you click one of the tabs, the page associated with that tab is raised to the top of the stack of pages, and although the entire row of tabs is always visible, only one page (the top page) in the notebook is visible at a time. The FXTabBook is frequently used in dialog boxes that allow the user to modify an application's settings; each tabbed page in the dialog box presents a different category of settings. It also shows up in text-editing or word-processing applications, where each tabbed page displays a different document.

It's not very difficult to add a tabbed notebook to your application. Start by constructing an FXTabBook widget:

tabbook.rb

```
tabbook = FXTabBook.new(self, :opts => LAYOUT_FILL)
```

Next, add the tab items and tabbed notebook pages in pairs. A tab item is an instance of the FXTabItem class. A tab page is usually some kind of layout manager, but it can in fact be any kind of widget.

tabbook.rb

```
basics_tab = FXTabItem.new(tabbook, " Basics ")
basics_page = FXVerticalFrame.new(tabbook,
  :opts => FRAME_RAISED|LAYOUT_FILL)
contact_tab = FXTabItem.new(tabbook, " Contact ")
contact_page = FXVerticalFrame.new(tabbook,
  :opts => FRAME_RAISED|LAYOUT_FILL)
extras_tab = FXTabItem.new(tabbook, " Extras ")
extras_page = FXVerticalFrame.new(tabbook,
  :opts => FRAME_RAISED|LAYOUT_FILL)
```

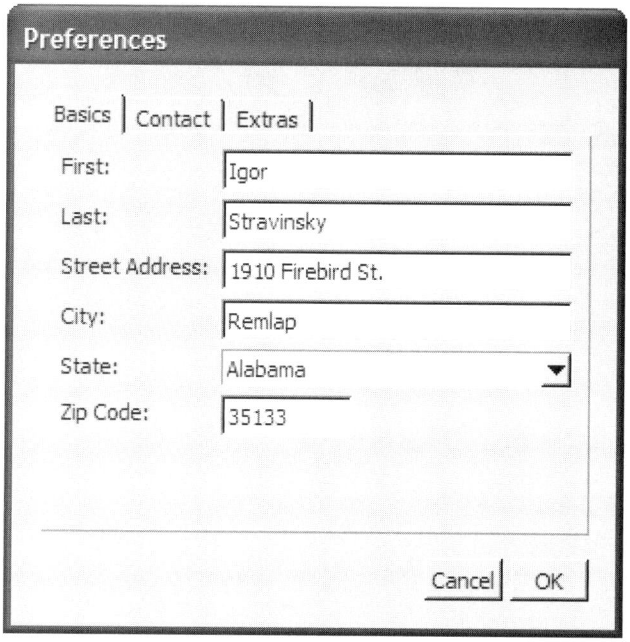

Figure 12.13: A PREFERENCES DIALOG BOX THAT USES A TABBED NOTEBOOK

Figure 12.13 shows what this FXTabBook looks like when it's displaying the first tab (the Basics tab).[3]

If you're merely interested in displaying tabbed pages, that's really all there is to it. If you want to be notified whenever the user selects a new tab, however, you can catch the SEL_COMMAND message that the FXTabBook sends to its target after the new page is displayed:

tabbook.rb

```
tabbook.connect(SEL_COMMAND) do |sender, sel, data|
  puts "User selected tab number #{data}"
end
```

You might want to use this technique if it's resource-intensive to display the content associated with a particular page in a tabbed notebook. For

3. The code excerpt that I've listed here doesn't show all the code required to actually build up the form that you seen in the screenshot, since that code is not directly related to how FXTabBook works. The full source code is available online.

example, if a page is displaying some dynamically updated content, such as a counter or an animated image, you might want to suspend the update of that content when the user selects a different tab and then reactivate the updates when the user navigates back to that page.

This concludes our overview of some of the more special-purpose layout managers available in FXRuby. Before we wrap up this chapter, however, we are going to tackle the more general question of how to use all these layout managers together to solve some common layout problems.

12.6 Strategies for Using Different Layout Managers Together

For the most part, this chapter has focused on how to use the different layout managers in isolation. Want to lay out a group of widgets in rows and columns? Use an FXMatrix. Is the widget too big to fit onscreen? Consider putting it inside an FXScrollWindow. And while it's true that you need to get familiar with how all these layout managers work on a stand-alone basis before you can use them at all, the real fun begins when you start using them together to solve more complicated layout problems.

We touched on this idea in Section 12.1, *Nesting Layout Managers Inside Each Other*, on page 165, when we looked at how we could nest an FXHorizontalFrame inside an FXPacker to achieve a layout that would have been difficult or impossible to achieve using either of the two layout managers by themselves.

Indeed, this is one of the most important skills you'll learn as you begin developing your own FXRuby applications: how to break down a complex layout into a number of smaller, more manageable pieces and then glue those pieces together using other layout managers.

For example, if your impression is that you're looking at things stacked on top of other things, you probably want to use an FXVerticalFrame. Let's consider a relatively straightforward example for starters. Figure 12.14, on the next page is a mock-up of a program that provides a GUI front end to a translation service.

When you look at this application's main window, you should see five elements stacked on top of each other. From the top, we have a label ("Source Text"), a text area, a second label ("Translated Text"), a second text area, and finally a row of controls.

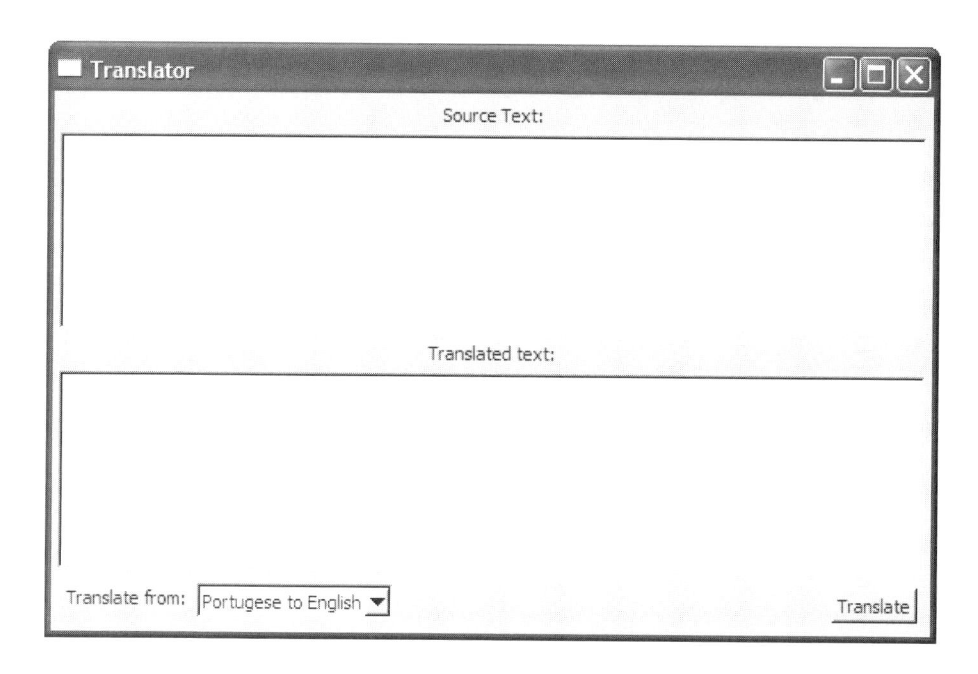

Figure 12.14: MOCK-UP OF A GUI FRONT END TO A TRANSLATION SERVICE

When you're looking at things stacked on top of other things, your mind should go to the FXVerticalFrame. A reasonable first attempt at this layout might look something like the following:

layoutexample1.rb

```
frame = FXVerticalFrame.new(self)
FXLabel.new(frame, "Source Text:")
source_text = FXText.new(frame)
FXLabel.new(frame, "Translated text:")
translated_text = FXText.new(frame, :opts => TEXT_READONLY)
controls = FXHorizontalFrame.new(frame)
```

The controls horizontal frame at the end holds the combo box of translation modes as well as the Translate button in the lower-right corner:

layoutexample1.rb

```
FXLabel.new(controls, "Translate from:")
translations = FXComboBox.new(controls, 15,
  :opts => COMBOBOX_STATIC|FRAME_SUNKEN|FRAME_THICK)
translate_button = FXButton.new(controls, "Translate",
  :opts => BUTTON_NORMAL)
```

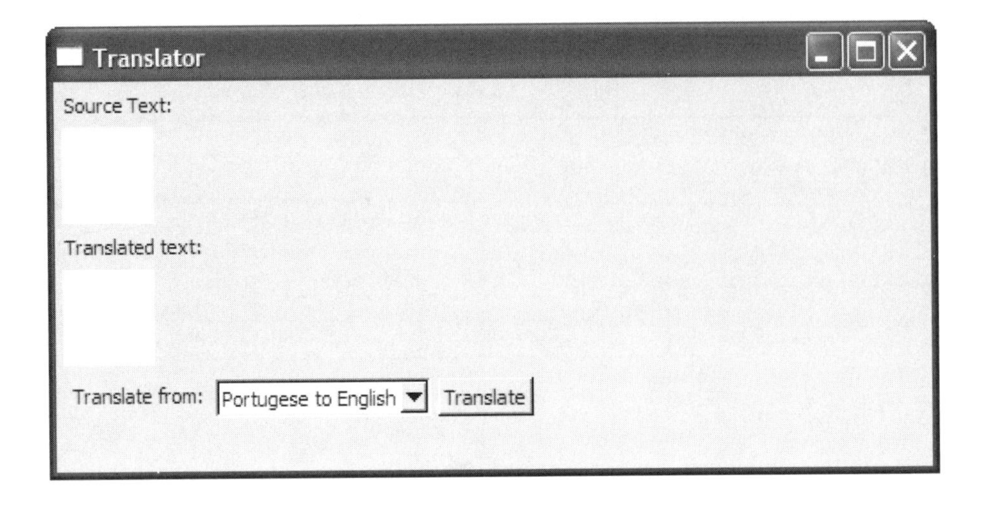

Figure 12.15: A FIRST ATTEMPT AT THE LAYOUT

Let's run this first cut of the layout and see how it looks. Figure 12.15 shows what this version looks like under Windows.

The most charitable thing you could say about it is that, as promised, the widgets are stacked on top of each other as expected. Before we improve on the look of this application, let's talk about the next important skill that you'll need to master: knowing how and when to use the different layout hints to influence how the layout managers do their jobs.

In most layouts, you'll apply at least one of the "fill" hints (LAYOUT_FILL_X or LAYOUT_FILL_Y) to layout managers themselves. In particular, you will often find you want to use the LAYOUT_FILL_X layout hint for each of the children of an FXVerticalFrame.[4] Let's do that for the child widgets of the vertical frame in this example. While we're at it, let's also set the LAYOUT_RIGHT hint on the Translate button so that it will be packed against the right side of the controls horizontal frame.

4. Likewise, you'll often want to use LAYOUT_FILL_Y for each of the children of an FXHorizontalFrame.

layoutexample2.rb

```
frame = FXVerticalFrame.new(self, :opts => LAYOUT_FILL)
FXLabel.new(frame, "Source Text:", :opts => LAYOUT_FILL_X)
source_text = FXText.new(frame, :opts => LAYOUT_FILL_X)
FXLabel.new(frame, "Translated text:", :opts => LAYOUT_FILL_X)
translated_text = FXText.new(frame, :opts => TEXT_READONLY|LAYOUT_FILL_X)
controls = FXHorizontalFrame.new(frame, :opts => LAYOUT_FILL_X)
FXLabel.new(controls, "Translate from:")
translations = FXComboBox.new(controls, 15,
  :opts => COMBOBOX_STATIC|FRAME_SUNKEN|FRAME_THICK)
translate_button = FXButton.new(controls, "Translate",
  :opts => BUTTON_NORMAL|LAYOUT_RIGHT)
```

Figure 12.16, on the next page, shows what this version looks like under Windows.

Already, it's starting to look more like the final product, but there are still a few problems. We'd like for the two text areas to grow to take up as much space as possible, while the other widgets (the two labels, and the row of controls along the bottom) continue to take as much as space as they're taking now. This behavior should hold even if we resize the main window.

If you play around with this latest version of the example, you'll quickly find that that's not the case.

Let's attempt a fix by changing the LAYOUT_FILL_X hints on the two FXText widgets to LAYOUT_FILL (which, as you recall, includes both LAYOUT_FILL_X and LAYOUT_FILL_Y):

layoutexample3.rb

```
frame = FXVerticalFrame.new(self, :opts => LAYOUT_FILL)
FXLabel.new(frame, "Source Text:", :opts => LAYOUT_FILL_X)
source_text = FXText.new(frame, :opts => LAYOUT_FILL)
FXLabel.new(frame, "Translated text:", :opts => LAYOUT_FILL_X)
translated_text = FXText.new(frame, :opts => TEXT_READONLY|LAYOUT_FILL)
controls = FXHorizontalFrame.new(frame, :opts => LAYOUT_FILL_X)
FXLabel.new(controls, "Translate from:")
translations = FXComboBox.new(controls, 15,
  :opts => COMBOBOX_STATIC|FRAME_SUNKEN|FRAME_THICK)
translate_button = FXButton.new(controls, "Translate",
  :opts => BUTTON_NORMAL|LAYOUT_RIGHT)
```

For one final touch, let's nest each of the FXText widgets inside a frame so that we can create a thick, sunken border around each of them. In this case, it doesn't matter whether we use a horizontal frame or vertical frame, since each frame has only one child widget to keep up with.

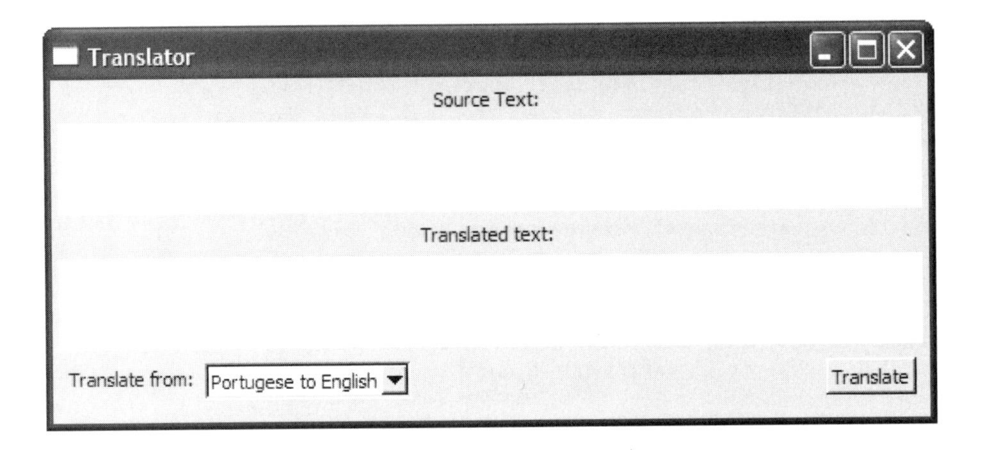

Figure 12.16: AFTER ADDING LAYOUT HINTS

layoutexample4.rb

```
source_text_frame = FXHorizontalFrame.new(frame,
  :opts => FRAME_SUNKEN|FRAME_THICK|LAYOUT_FILL,
  :padding => 0)
source_text = FXText.new(source_text_frame,
  :opts => LAYOUT_FILL)
FXLabel.new(frame, "Translated text:", :opts => LAYOUT_FILL_X)
translated_text_frame = FXHorizontalFrame.new(frame,
  :opts => FRAME_SUNKEN|FRAME_THICK|LAYOUT_FILL,
  :padding => 0)
translated_text = FXText.new(translated_text_frame,
  :opts => TEXT_READONLY|LAYOUT_FILL)
```

If you run the example at this point, the layout should finally resemble our original concept as shown in Figure 12.14, on page 181.

That last step that we took, nesting the text areas inside additional frames for the sole purpose of providing some decoration around them, may strike you as wasteful. Well, don't let it.

As you consider various options for nesting layouts inside each another, one consideration that you should never spend too much time worrying about is the number of widgets that you're creating along the way. If the solution that makes the most sense and is easiest for you to maintain involves using a large number of horizontal and vertical frames nested inside each other, go for it. One of the advantages of using FOX is that it's very resource-friendly, and it's very "cheap" to create and destroy widgets on the fly when you need to do that.

The final thing you'll learn about working with layout managers is that, for almost every layout challenge you encounter, there's more than one way to tackle it! Creating complicated layouts in user interfaces is as much an art as it is a science.

At the beginning of this chapter, I noted that most users aren't really going to be aware of the role that layout managers play in an application's appearance. That also goes for pull-down menus and toolbars, which are so commonplace in GUI applications that the role they play is often underappreciated. In the next chapter, we're going to take a closer look at how you can best integrate menus and toolbars into your FXRuby applications.

Chapter 13

Advanced Menu Management

It's easy to underestimate the usefulness of well-designed menus, but they are an important feature of any GUI application. The first stop for new users of your application will almost always be the menu bar. For those users, menus provide a sort of learning and discovery tool that gives them an overview of the application's features. Other users may have been working with the application for some time, but they use it so infrequently that they can't immediately recall how to access some of the application's more obscure functionality. For those users, menus provide a familiar "refresher course" in how to get things done.

Back in Chapter 5, *Take 2: Display an Entire Album*, on page 35, when we extended the Picture Book application to allow for creating new photo albums and importing photos into those albums, we got an introduction to the process of adding menu bars with pull-down menus to an FXRuby application. In this chapter, we'll look at some of the more advanced options for exposing an application's functionality. We'll begin by looking at some alternatives to the standard menu pane that allow us to provide cascading and scrolling menus. After that we'll take a look at some of the other kinds of menu items you can add to a pull-down menu. We'll wrap up the chapter by looking at a closely related subject, how to add a toolbar (or toolbars) to an application.

13.1 Creating Cascading and Scrolling Menus

After working through the Picture Book example, you know the basic steps of adding a pull-down menu to an application:

1. Construct an FXMenuBar widget as a child of the main window.

2. Construct one or more FXMenuPane widgets, owned by the main window, for each pull-down menu you want to display. So, for example, you might have one menu pane for the File menu and another menu pane for the Edit menu.
3. Construct an FXMenuTitle widget as a child of the menu bar to establish a link between the menu bar and the menu pane.
4. Add one or more FXMenuCommand widgets to the menu pane, each of which represents an action that the user can carry out. Use the connect() method to associate a block of Ruby code with each of those menu commands.

There are a couple of useful variations on the standard FXMenuPane widget that we've used thus far. *Cascading menus* are menu panes that are nested in other menu panes. For example, suppose you already have a File menu, with New, Open..., Save, and Save As... commands:

menuexample.rb

```
file_menu_pane = FXMenuPane.new(self)
file_new_command = FXMenuCommand.new(file_menu_pane, "New")
file_open_command = FXMenuCommand.new(file_menu_pane, "Open...")
file_save_command = FXMenuCommand.new(file_menu_pane, "Save")
file_save_as_command = FXMenuCommand.new(file_menu_pane, "Save As...")
file_menu_title = FXMenuTitle.new(menu_bar, "File",
  :popupMenu => file_menu_pane)
```

Now you'd like to add an Export submenu, with commands like Export as GIF, Export as PNG, and so on. Start by constructing the new menu pane, just as you did for the File menu:

menuexample.rb

```
export_menu_pane = FXMenuPane.new(self)
export_gif_command =
  FXMenuCommand.new(export_menu_pane, "Export as GIF")
export_jpeg_command =
  FXMenuCommand.new(export_menu_pane, "Export as JPEG")
export_png_command =
  FXMenuCommand.new(export_menu_pane, "Export as PNG")
export_tiff_command =
  FXMenuCommand.new(export_menu_pane, "Export as TIFF")
```

Now, add an FXMenuCascade widget to the File menu pane, alongside the existing FXMenuCommand widgets:

menuexample.rb

```
export_cascade = FXMenuCascade.new(file_menu_pane, "Export",
  :popupMenu => export_menu_pane)
```

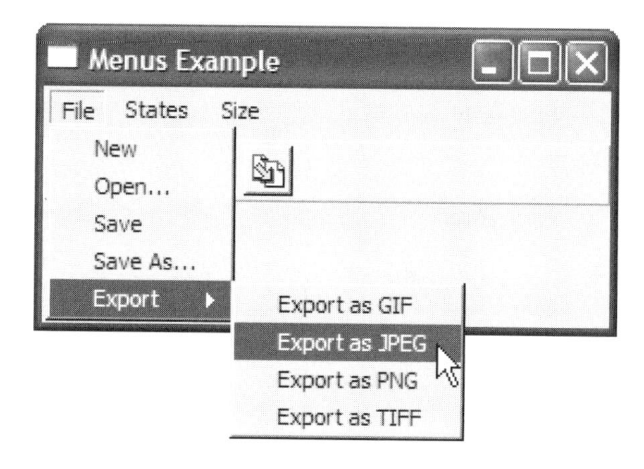

Figure 13.1: A CASCADING MENU PANE

Figure 13.1 shows what this cascading menu pane looks like when it's expanded. As you can see, the FXMenuCascade is awfully similar to the FXMenuTitle widget that we use to attach menus directly to the menu bar. You can even nest another cascading menu in export_menu_pane if you'd like, but don't get carried away with it. Deeply nested menus are really difficult to use, and you should use them sparingly.

Another trick that you may find useful, when you have a lot of information to try to pack into a menu, is a scrolling menu pane. It's especially useful when the menu items are generated programmatically and you don't know in advance how many items the menu pane will contain.

Since FXScrollPane is subclassed from FXMenuPane, it can be used anywhere that a nonscrolling menu pane could be used. The first argument to FXScrollPane.new is the owner window for the menu pane, and the second argument is the number of visible items that should be displayed:

menuexample.rb

```
states_menu_pane = FXScrollPane.new(self, 8)
$state_names.each do |state_name|
  FXMenuCommand.new(states_menu_pane, state_name)
end
states_menu_title = FXMenuTitle.new(menu_bar, "States",
  :popupMenu => states_menu_pane)
```

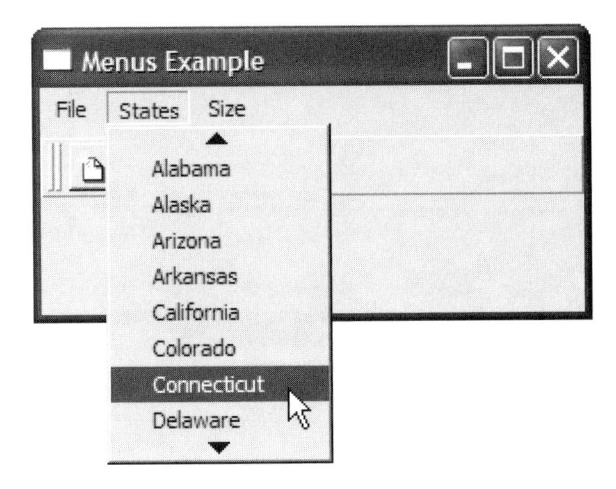

Figure 13.2: A SCROLLING MENU PANE

Figure 13.2 shows what this scrolling menu pane looks like. Note the arrows at either end of the menu pane. If you hover the mouse cursor over either of these arrows, the menu pane will scroll its contents up or down. Like cascading menus, scrolling menu panes should be used sparingly because they're a little difficult for users to deal with.

Cascading and scrolling menus are just a couple examples of the possible variations on the standard menus that we used in the Picture Book application. In the next section, we will take a look at some alternatives to the standard FXMenuCommand button that we have come to know and love.

13.2 Adding Separators, Radio Buttons, and Check Buttons to Menus

You already know how to use an FXMenuCommand widget to provide a user interface to an imperative command, such as Open or Save. You can add an FXMenuSeparator widget to a menu pane to create a visual break between groups of related commands:

```
FXMenuSeparator.new(menu_pane)
```

The FXMenuRadio and FXMenuCheck widgets give you a way to incorporate the same kinds of functionality that the FXRadioButton and FXCheckButton widgets provide. As you learned in Section 8.1, *Making Choices*

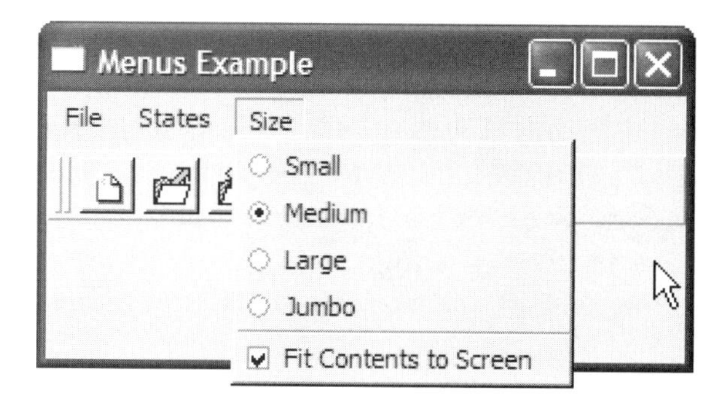

Figure 13.3: A MENU WITH CHECK AND RADIO BUTTON ITEMS

with Radio Buttons, on page 101, the preferred way to ensure that the choices for radio items remain mutually exclusive is to associate each of them with the same FXDataTarget:

menuexample.rb

```
@size = FXDataTarget.new(1)
size_pane = FXMenuPane.new(self)
FXMenuRadio.new(size_pane, "Small",
  :target => @size, :selector => FXDataTarget::ID_OPTION)
FXMenuRadio.new(size_pane, "Medium",
  :target => @size, :selector => FXDataTarget::ID_OPTION+1)
FXMenuRadio.new(size_pane, "Large",
  :target => @size, :selector => FXDataTarget::ID_OPTION+2)
FXMenuRadio.new(size_pane, "Jumbo",
  :target => @size, :selector => FXDataTarget::ID_OPTION+3)
size_menu_title = FXMenuTitle.new(menu_bar, "Size",
  :popupMenu => size_pane)
@size.connect(SEL_COMMAND) do
  # @size.value holds the index of the selected size
end
```

Here's a similar example for an FXMenuCheck item:

menuexample.rb

```
@fit_to_screen = FXDataTarget.new(false)
FXMenuCheck.new(size_pane, "Fit Contents to Screen",
  :target => @fit_to_screen, :selector => FXDataTarget::ID_VALUE)
```

Figure 13.3 shows a menu containing a group of FXMenuRadio buttons, separated from a single FXMenuCheck button by an FXMenuSeparator item.

Pull-down menus like the kinds that we've been building so far are essential for all but the simplest of GUI applications. They're especially useful for beginners or infrequent users of an application because they provide a sort of teaching tool for people who are learning how to use the application. As users become more and more familiar with an application, however, they're going to want more direct access to commonly used functions, and one way to provide that immediate access is through the use of toolbars. In the next couple of sections, we'll learn how to add toolbars to an FXRuby application.

13.3 Adding Toolbars to an Application

This is a short section, because there's not a *lot* to say about the FXToolBar widget. For the most part, you can think of it as another kind of layout manager (and it is in fact derived from the FXPacker class).

A common use for the FXToolBar is to fill it with a number of icon-adorned buttons (what Alan Cooper refers to as *butcons*) that provide easy access to commonly used functions. These are just regular FXButton widgets, but with the proper combination of layout hints and icon sizes, we can ensure that they're all the same size. One piece of the puzzle is to make sure PACK_UNIFORM_WIDTH layout hint is set on the toolbar:

menuexample.rb

```
tool_bar = FXToolBar.new(top_dock_site, tool_bar_shell,
  :opts => PACK_UNIFORM_WIDTH|FRAME_RAISED|LAYOUT_FILL_X)
```

You might also want to include the PACK_UNIFORM_HEIGHT option to see what effect that has on the toolbar's appearance. Next, you want to add one or more FXButton widgets for the different toolbar commands:

menuexample.rb

```
new_button = FXButton.new(tool_bar,
  "\tNew\tCreate new document.",
  :icon => new_icon)
open_button = FXButton.new(tool_bar,
  "\tOpen\tOpen document file.",
  :icon => open_icon)
save_button = FXButton.new(tool_bar,
  "\tSave\tSave document.",
  :icon => save_icon)
save_as_button = FXButton.new(tool_bar,
  "\tSave As\tSave document to another file.",
  :icon => save_as_icon)
```

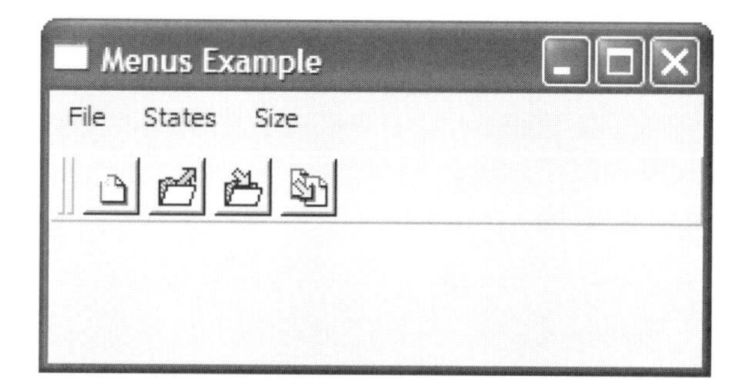

Figure 13.4: USE A TOOLBAR FOR IMMEDIATE ACCESS TO COMMONLY USED COMMANDS.

Figure 13.4 shows what this toolbar looks like, when the program is running under Windows.

Note the format of the label string for each of the buttons. Back in Section 8.3, *Providing Hints with Tooltips and the Status Bar*, on page 108, we talked about how you can embed tab characters inside the label string for a button to separate the button's label from its tooltip message and status line help message. For these buttons in the toolbar, the label string starts out with a tab character, which means they won't have a label displayed on the button. For example, the first button will display the tooltip "New" and the status line help message "Create new document," but the surface of the button will show only its icon.

The really significant difference between the FXToolBar and other layout managers is that it can be configured so that the user can drag it off of the main window so that it "floats" elsewhere onscreen. Let's see how that works next.

13.4 Creating Floating Menu Bars and Toolbars

So far we've dealt only with a stationary menu bar or toolbar. It might get narrower or wider as you resize the main window, but it stays in the same place. FXRuby also provides for floating menu bars and toolbars that can be dragged away from their "docks," positioned somewhere else on the screen, and even reattached to the main window in some other location. Depending on the type of application that you're developing, this can be an extremely useful feature to implement.

The FXMenuBar and FXToolBar classes are both descended from the FX-DockBar base class. A *dock bar* can be docked inside a *dock site*, it can be located somewhere on the surface of the main window, or it can float away from the main window inside some other parent container (usually, an FXToolBarShell window).

Let's walk through a brief example to see how this works. First, we need to construct an FXToolBarShell widget that will act as the toolbar's home away from home when it's floating around:

menuexample.rb

```
tool_bar_shell = FXToolBarShell.new(self)
```

Next, construct one or more dock sites that provide places for the toolbar to land when it's ready to come back home. It is perfectly acceptable to designate only one dock site, but for the purposes of this example, we'll set up two dock sites: one along the top side of the main window, another along the bottom:

menuexample.rb

```
top_dock_site = FXDockSite.new(self,
  :opts => LAYOUT_FILL_X|LAYOUT_SIDE_TOP)
bottom_dock_site = FXDockSite.new(self,
  :opts => LAYOUT_FILL_X|LAYOUT_SIDE_BOTTOM)
```

The user can drag the floating toolbar to either of these positions on the main window, and it will reattach itself (dock) there. It's important to note that when the toolbar is floating, the dock sites will hide themselves and allow other nearby widgets to take up that space if they choose. Now we can construct the FXToolBar itself:

menuexample.rb

```
tool_bar = FXToolBar.new(top_dock_site, tool_bar_shell,
  :opts => PACK_UNIFORM_WIDTH|FRAME_RAISED|LAYOUT_FILL_X)
```

The first argument to FXToolBar.new is the initial dock site, and the second argument is the shell. Now we need to add a "grip," a handle that the user can grab to tear the toolbar away from the dock site:

menuexample.rb

```
FXToolBarGrip.new(tool_bar,
  :target => tool_bar, :selector => FXToolBar::ID_TOOLBARGRIP,
  :opts => TOOLBARGRIP_DOUBLE)
```

I prefer the look of the double-lined grip, but if you'd like just a single line, pass in TOOLBARGRIP_SINGLE as the option instead. At this point, you can add all the application-specific widgets to the toolbar. It's not

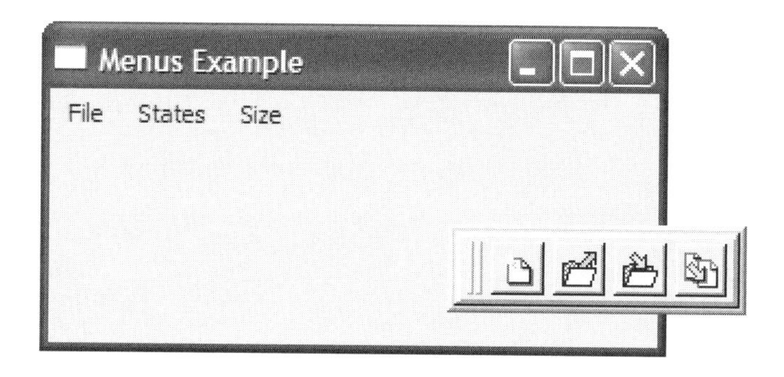

Figure 13.5: FLOATING TOOLBAR

strictly necessary to make the FXToolBarGrip widget the first child widget in the FXToolBar, but it's probably best to make it either the first or last widget to avoid cluttering up the appearance of the tool buttons.

You've already seen what the toolbar looks like in the docked position, in Figure 13.4, on page 193. Figure 13.5 shows what the toolbar looks like after it's been "undocked" and dragged off to the side.

Up until this point, we've focused on how to handle interaction with the application's main window, but it's also sometimes useful to isolate certain interactions in a separate top-level window known as a *dialog box*. FXRuby provides a number of built-in standard dialog boxes, such as the FXFileDialog that we used when we were building the Picture Book application. You can also create custom dialog boxes for handling application settings or other functionality. We'll take a look at all these topics in the next chapter.

Chapter 14

Providing Support with Dialog Boxes

So far we've been talking about how to use FXRuby to build up the main window of your application's user interface. Everything has focused on the user's primary interaction with the application. FXRuby also provides a different sort of top-level window known as a *dialog box*, and that's the focus of this final chapter.

A dialog box is similar to the main window in that it "floats" on the desktop and serves as a top-level container for a bunch of other widgets. Like the main window, a dialog box can incorporate a title bar, a menu bar, a status bar, and other sorts of decorations for resizing or closing the window. Despite these similarities, you shouldn't confuse dialog boxes with the main program. In most cases, they are transient and remain onscreen only for a short time while the user interacts with them, and they always play secondary, supporting roles in an application.

You've already encountered one kind of dialog box in Section 5.3, *Import Photos from Files*, on page 42, when we used the FXFileDialog to request from the user the names of the photo files to import. FXRuby includes a number of other standard dialog boxes for use in your applications. In this chapter, we're to take a brief tour of some of the most commonly used standard dialog boxes provided by FXRuby. We'll also talk about what's involved in creating custom dialog boxes, for those situations where none of the standard dialog boxes fit the bill. Let's begin by revisiting our old friend, the FXFileDialog dialog box.

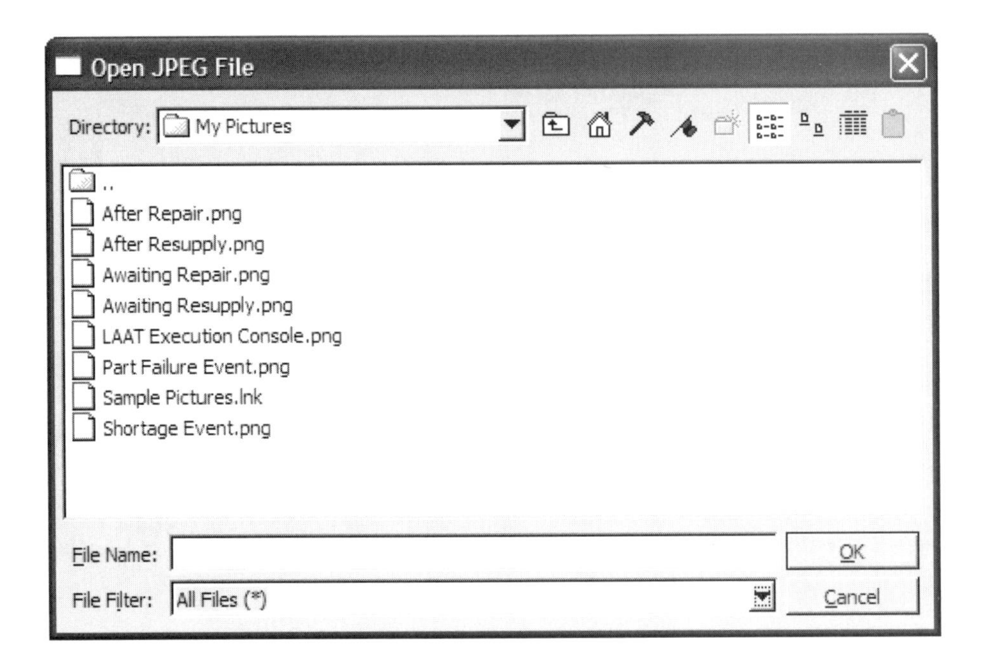

Figure 14.1: USE FXFILEDIALOG TO SELECT FILES.

14.1 Selecting Files with the File Dialog Box

The FXFileDialog, shown in Figure 14.1, is probably the most frequently used of the standard dialog boxes. You can use the FXFileDialog when you want the user to select an existing file or files (for example, during an Open operation) or when you want ask the user for the name of a file that you're about to write to (for example, during a Save operation). For example, suppose you want the user to select an existing JPEG file on disk:

filedialog.rb

```
dialog = FXFileDialog.new(self, "Open JPEG File")
dialog.patternList = [
  "All Files (*)",
  "JPEG Files (*.jpg, *.jpeg)"
]
dialog.selectMode = SELECTFILE_EXISTING
if dialog.execute != 0
  open_jpeg_file(dialog.filename)
end
```

When you call execute() on the FXFileDialog, it will display itself, allow the user to select a file, and then wait for the user to click either the OK or Cancel button. If execute() returns zero, the user clicked Cancel; otherwise, the user clicked OK. At this point, you can check the value of the dialog box's filename attribute to read the full path to the selected file.

The file dialog box sports most of the features you'd expect from this kind of widget and a few you may not have seen before (such as setting bookmarks for frequently visited directories). As shown in the previous example, you can initialize the patternList to an array of strings that indicate the available file filters. The file selection mode has to do with whether you're able to select only a single file or multiple files. A selectMode of SELECTFILE_EXISTING means the user can select only an existing file; this would be an appropriate setting for loading a document. We could instead allow for the selection of multiple files.

If you don't explicitly set the patternList, it will default to All Files (*).

filedialog.rb

```
dialog = FXFileDialog.new(self, "Open JPEG File(s)")
dialog.patternList = [
  "All Files (*)",
  "JPEG Files (*.jpg, *.jpeg)"
]
dialog.selectMode = SELECTFILE_MULTIPLE
if dialog.execute != 0
  dialog.filenames.each do |filename|
    open_jpeg_file(filename)
  end
end
```

The FXFileDialog provides a number of options that allow you to configure its appearance and behavior; see the API documentation for the FXFileDialog and FXFileSelector classes for more details.

It's worth noting here that the FXFileDialog is specifically geared toward dealing with individual files (or groups of them, as the case may be). Although you can use the SELECTFILE_DIRECTORY selection mode to limit the selection in a file dialog to directories only, that can result in an awkward user experience in my opinion. For those situations where you want the user to select a directory, and only a directory, the FXDirDialog may be a better choice. We'll take a look at that dialog box next.

14.2 Selecting a Directory with the Directory Dialog Box

You can use the FXDirDialog when you need the user to select a *single* directory, and only a directory. For anything more complicated, you should probably stick with an FXFileDialog.

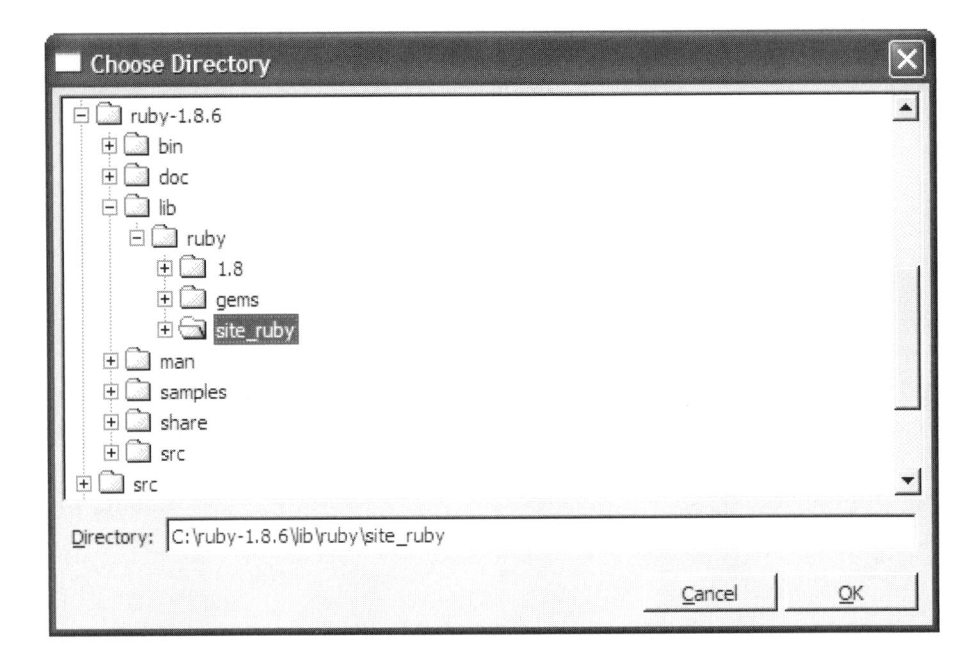

Figure 14.2: USE A DIRECTORY DIALOG BOX TO SELECT A SINGLE DIRECTORY.

Because the FXDirDialog has this very simple function, it's also straightforward to configure and use. In most cases, you'll simply initialize the directory attribute to some path in the file system, display the dialog box, and then retrieve the selected directory from the directory attribute:

dirdialog.rb

```
dialog = FXDirDialog.new(self, "Choose Directory")
dialog.directory = "/Users/lyle"
if dialog.execute != 0
  open_directory(dialog.directory)
end
```

Note that if you don't initialize the directory attribute before displaying the dialog box, it defaults to the current working directory.

Figure 14.2 shows how the directory dialog box displays the file system as a tree structure. To choose an existing directory, simply navigate to it in the directory tree list, and click the OK button. To create a new directory, right-click the parent directory for the new directory, and choose the New command from the pop-up menu.

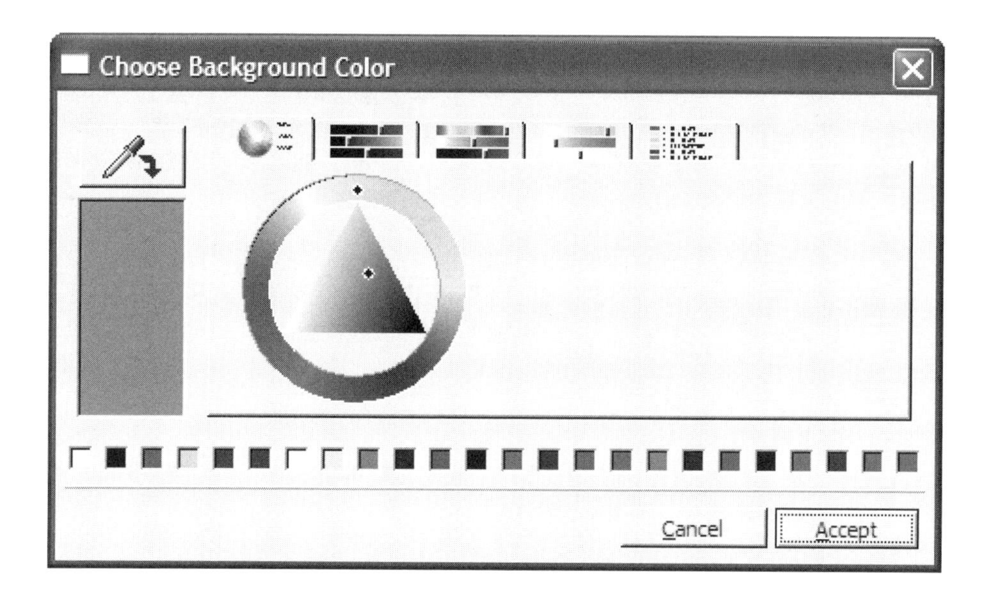

Figure 14.3: COLOR DIALOG BOX IN HSV DIAL MODE

Dialog boxes are not merely useful for collecting information about files and directories. In the next few sections, we'll look at the standard dialog boxes for dealing with colors and fonts.

14.3 Choosing Colors with the Color Dialog Box

You can use the FXColorDialog when you need the user to select (or modify) a color value. Because there are so few settings, it's easy to integrate the color dialog box into an application:

colordialog.rb

```
dialog = FXColorDialog.new(self, "Choose Background Color")
dialog.rgba = FXRGB(255, 0, 0) # initialize color to red
if dialog.execute != 0
  self.backColor = dialog.rgba
end
```

If you don't want to use the default initial color (black), you can of course initialize the color value before displaying the dialog box by setting the value of the rgba attribute.[1]

1. The attribute name rgba refers to the fact that the color consists of Red, Green, Blue,

Although the color dialog box is easy to use from an application developer's perspective, its wide variety of options can make it a little bewildering for end users. The color dialog box contains five tabs, each of which displays the currently selected color using a different color model.

- The first tab displays a dial for adjusting the Hue, Saturation, and Value (HSV) components of the color.[2] You can see what this page of the FXColorDialog looks like in Figure 14.3, on the previous page.
- The second tab displays a set of slider bars for setting the Red, Green, Blue, and Alpha components of the color.
- The third tab displays a set of slider bars, again for setting the HSV components of the color.
- The fourth tab displays a set of slider bars for setting the Cyan, Magenta, Yellow, and Key (CMYK) components of the color.[3]
- The last tab displays a list of color names.

In addition, the color dialog box incorporates on its left side a "color picker" button that enables you to select a color from anywhere onscreen as the new color, and along the bottom, a collection of predefined color wells.

14.4 Selecting Fonts with the Font Dialog Box

We made reference to the FXFontDialog in Section 11.1, *Using Custom Fonts*, on page 140, when we discussed that the font dialog box returns information about the selected font using an FXFontDesc object. As with the other dialog boxes that we've been looking at in this chapter, the usage pattern for an FXFontDialog is to initialize its settings, display the dialog box to let the user interact with it, and then retrieve the selection information once the user's done. Figure 14.4, on the next page, shows a font dialog, with the bold, 16-point version of the Book Antiqua typeface selected.[4]

---

and Alpha components. If you're thinking that something like color might have been a better name for this attribute, I'd have to agree with you.

2. See http://en.wikipedia.org/wiki/HSV_color_space for a discussion of the HSV color model.
3. See http://en.wikipedia.org/wiki/CMYK_color_model for a discussion of the CMYK color model.
4. Depending on your operating system and the fonts installed, this particular font may or may not be available on your system.

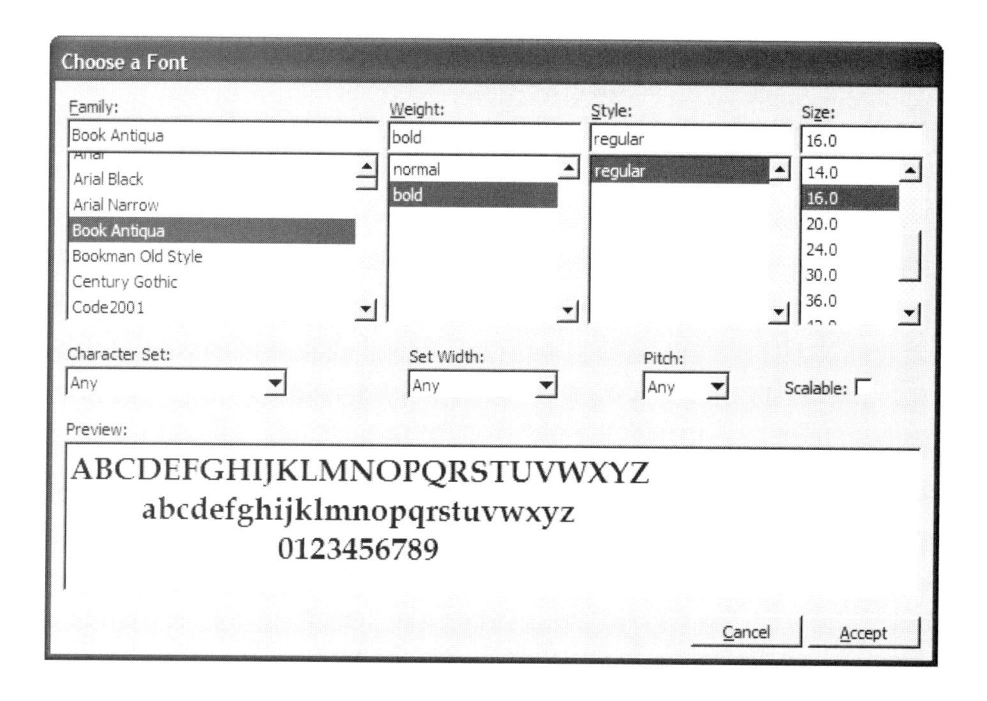

Figure 14.4: SELECTING FONTS IN A FONT DIALOG BOX

Working with the font dialog box is a little trickier than working with the file, directory, or color dialog since we're passing back and forth FXFontDesc objects and not actual FXFont objects. The following code excerpt demonstrates the typical pattern of interaction with an FXFontDialog:

fontdialog.rb

```
dialog = FXFontDialog.new(self, "Choose a Font")
dialog.fontSelection = button.font.fontDesc
if dialog.execute != 0
  new_font = FXFont.new(app, dialog.fontSelection)
  new_font.create
  button.font = new_font
end
```

The first step is to extract the initial font settings (as an FXFontDesc object) from an existing font via its fontDesc attribute. We can use that font description to initialize the FXFontDialog's fontSelection attribute. This step isn't strictly necessary; the font dialog box will come up with some default settings if you don't initialize the fontSelection attribute in advance.

Figure 14.5: DISPLAYING A WARNING USING A MESSAGE BOX

Once the user is finished interacting with the font dialog box and has made their selection, we need to retrieve the font description from the font dialog's fontSelection attribute and use it to construct a new FXFont object. As we discussed in Chapter 11, *Creating Visually Rich User Interfaces*, on page 139, it's crucial that we call create() on the newly constructed FXFont object before we assign it to a widget.

14.5 Alerting the User with Message Boxes

Compared to the other standard dialog boxes, a message box is very simple. It provides for only the most basic interaction with the user. For example, the following FXMessageBox displays the warning message shown in Figure 14.5:

messagebox.rb

```
FXMessageBox.warning(
  self,
  MBOX_OK,
  "Buyer Beware",
  "All Sales are Final!"
)
```

Unlike the other dialog boxes that we've looked at, an FXMessageBox is usually constructed and displayed in one shot using a class method like warning(). Since we configured this message box using the MBOX_OK option, it displays only an OK button, and there's no need for us to check the return value of the warning() method. If the message box includes more than one termination button, you'll want to inspect the return value of the method to determine which button the user clicked.

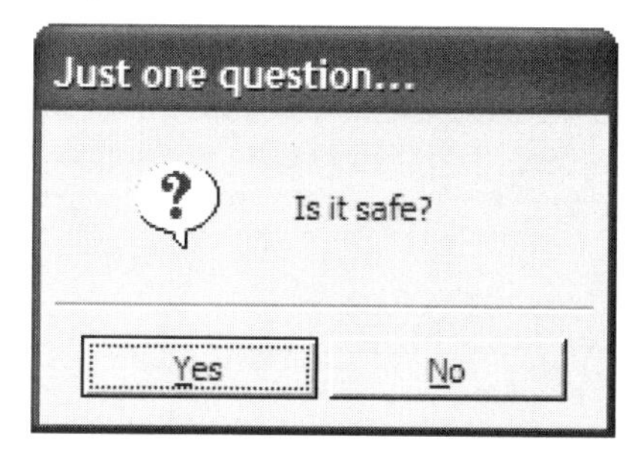

Figure 14.6: ASKING A QUESTION USING A MESSAGE BOX

For example, the message box shown in Figure 14.6 asks a question that can be answered with yes or no:

messagebox.rb

```
answer = FXMessageBox.question(
  self,
  MBOX_YES_NO,
  "Just one question...",
  "Is it safe?"
)
if answer == MBOX_CLICKED_YES
  ask_again()
end
```

The FXMessageBox class also provides information() and error() class methods for displaying those kinds of messages. For a complete listing of the message box options, and possible return values, see the API documentation for the FXMessageBox class.

14.6 Creating Custom Dialog Boxes

If your application has a requirement that can be satisfied by using one of the standard dialog boxes, it's preferable to stick with the standard so that your application's users are treated to a consistent and familiar user interface. For many applications, however, you'll need to develop one or more custom dialog boxes to handle application-specific functionality. In this section, we'll walk through the creation of a typical Preferences dialog box that you might include in an application.

Fortunately, most everything you have learned up to this point with respect to creating user interfaces in FXRuby is relevant to creating custom dialog boxes in FXRuby. As noted in the introduction to this chapter, dialog boxes are like main windows in many ways. The first step in creating a custom dialog box is to subclass FXDialogBox:

tabbook.rb

```
class PreferencesDialog < FXDialogBox
  def initialize(owner)
    super(owner, "Preferences", DECOR_TITLE|DECOR_BORDER|DECOR_RESIZE)
end
```

Now we need to add a row of terminating buttons along the bottom of the dialog box. The name may sound kind of ominous, in an Arnold Schwarzenegger kind of way, but we're just talking about the buttons that you use to dismiss the dialog box once you're done interacting with it. It's fairly common to see OK and Cancel buttons and possibly also an Apply button if that makes sense for the dialog box you're building. We're going to add a horizontal frame along the bottom side of the window, and then add first an OK button, followed by a Cancel button. Here's the code for the add_terminating_buttons() method:

tabbook.rb

```
def add_terminating_buttons
  buttons = FXHorizontalFrame.new(self,
    :opts => LAYOUT_FILL_X|LAYOUT_SIDE_BOTTOM|PACK_UNIFORM_WIDTH)
  FXButton.new(buttons, "OK",
    :target => self, :selector => FXDialogBox::ID_ACCEPT,
    :opts => BUTTON_NORMAL|LAYOUT_RIGHT)
  FXButton.new(buttons, "Cancel",
    :target => self, :selector => FXDialogBox::ID_CANCEL,
    :opts => BUTTON_NORMAL|LAYOUT_RIGHT)
end
```

Because we add the OK button first and pass in the LAYOUT_RIGHT layout hint, that button will be packed against the right side of the horizontal frame. When we subsequently add the Cancel button, it too will get packed against the right side of the remaining space in the horizontal frame, which means that it will appear to the left of the OK button. This is a pretty standard arrangement for those two buttons, but if you'd prefer that the OK button be on the left and the Cancel button be on the right, you can swap the order of those two statements.

We're also taking advantage of the fact that the FXDialogBox class from which PreferencesDialog is subclassed defines two message identifiers, ID_ACCEPT and ID_CANCEL, that we can send directly from the OK and Cancel buttons to the dialog box to dismiss it. If the user clicks our OK button, it will send a message of type SEL_COMMAND, with identifier ID_ACCEPT, back to the dialog box object. When the dialog box receives that message, it will hide itself and ensure that the call to execute() that originally launched the dialog box returns a nonzero value. If the dialog box receives the ID_CANCEL message instead, it will ensure that execute() returns zero.

Now that we have the terminating buttons squared away, we can turn to the main attraction. We're going to display the preferences settings in an FXTabBook, using the same example that we introduced back in Section 12.5, *Organizing Windows with Tabbed Notebooks*, on page 178. Let's begin by writing an add_tab_book() method that constructs the FXTabBook and adds a couple of tab items and empty pages. We'll worry about the content for the pages in a moment.

tabbook.rb

```
tabbook = FXTabBook.new(self, :opts => LAYOUT_FILL)
basics_tab = FXTabItem.new(tabbook, " Basics ")
basics_page = FXVerticalFrame.new(tabbook,
  :opts => FRAME_RAISED|LAYOUT_FILL)
contact_tab = FXTabItem.new(tabbook, " Contact ")
contact_page = FXVerticalFrame.new(tabbook,
  :opts => FRAME_RAISED|LAYOUT_FILL)
extras_tab = FXTabItem.new(tabbook, " Extras ")
extras_page = FXVerticalFrame.new(tabbook,
  :opts => FRAME_RAISED|LAYOUT_FILL)
```

Earlier in this chapter, when we were talking about how to use the standard dialog boxes, we established a pattern of initializing the dialog box with some default data, displaying it to the user to collect their inputs, and then retrieving those inputs when the dialog box is dismissed. We want to take the same tack with our custom dialog boxes, although we'll have to do a little more of the heavy lifting since we're dealing with our own custom data types and settings instead of some built-in type (like the FXFontDesc that we used with an FXFontDialog).

It's important to remember that the presence of a Cancel button on a dialog box implies a sort of contract with the user. If the user decides they don't want to keep the changes they've made to the settings, they can always back out of the deal by cancelling the dialog box and rest assured that the real application settings will be undisturbed. For that reason, I never let the dialog box code directly change the application settings. When it's time to display a Preferences dialog box or some other kind of custom dialog, I make a *copy* of the current application settings and pass that copy into the dialog box. If the user subsequently clicks the OK button to dismiss the dialog box, I retrieve that copy and then extract the needed information from it. If on the other hand the user clicks the Cancel button to dismiss the dialog box, I can just forget about the copy that the dialog box was using, and I don't have to worry about undoing any changes.

To keep things simple, let's focus on how we could handle the settings for the Basics tab, which deals with name and address information. We're going to take advantage of the FXDataTarget class to handle getting data into and out of the individual widgets in the form.[5] Internally, the PreferencesDialog will just use a hash of FXDataTarget instances:

tabbook.rb

```
@prefs = {
  :first_name => FXDataTarget.new,
  :last_name => FXDataTarget.new,
  :street => FXDataTarget.new,
  :city => FXDataTarget.new,
  :state => FXDataTarget.new,
  :zip_code => FXDataTarget.new
}
```

Now let's build up the contents for the first page, the one associated with the Basics tab. To keep this code out of the dialog box's initialize() method, we'll put it in a separate instance method called construct_basics_page():

tabbook.rb

```
def construct_basics_page(page)
  form = FXMatrix.new(page, 2,
    :opts => MATRIX_BY_COLUMNS|LAYOUT_FILL_X)
  FXLabel.new(form, "First:")
  FXTextField.new(form, 20,
    :target => @prefs[:first_name], :selector => FXDataTarget::ID_VALUE,
    :opts => TEXTFIELD_NORMAL|LAYOUT_FILL_X|LAYOUT_FILL_COLUMN)
  FXLabel.new(form, "Last:")
  FXTextField.new(form, 20,
    :target => @prefs[:last_name], :selector => FXDataTarget::ID_VALUE,
    :opts => TEXTFIELD_NORMAL|LAYOUT_FILL_X|LAYOUT_FILL_COLUMN)
  FXLabel.new(form, "Street Address:")
  FXTextField.new(form, 20,
    :target => @prefs[:street], :selector => FXDataTarget::ID_VALUE,
    :opts => TEXTFIELD_NORMAL|LAYOUT_FILL_X|LAYOUT_FILL_COLUMN)
  FXLabel.new(form, "City:")
  FXTextField.new(form, 20,
    :target => @prefs[:city], :selector => FXDataTarget::ID_VALUE,
    :opts => TEXTFIELD_NORMAL|LAYOUT_FILL_X|LAYOUT_FILL_COLUMN)
  FXLabel.new(form, "State:")
```

5. You remember data targets, right? We talked about them in Section 7.5, *Using Data Targets for GUI Update*, on page 86.

```
  states = FXListBox.new(form,
    :target => @prefs[:state], :selector => FXDataTarget::ID_VALUE,
    :opts => (LISTBOX_NORMAL|FRAME_SUNKEN|
              LAYOUT_FILL_X|LAYOUT_FILL_COLUMN))
  FXLabel.new(form, "Zip Code:")
  FXTextField.new(form, 10,
    :target => @prefs[:zip_code], :selector => FXDataTarget::ID_VALUE,
    :opts => TEXTFIELD_NORMAL|LAYOUT_FILL_COLUMN)
end
```

Note that for each of the FXTextField widgets, as well as the FXListBox that holds the state name, we're using one of the data targets from the @prefs hash. The widgets will take their initial settings from the data in those data targets, and whenever the user changes some setting in a widget, the data target's value will be updated automatically.

To integrate this dialog box with the application, we'd need to add a Preferences... menu command in one of the application's menus. When that menu command is invoked, it will first construct a new PreferencesDialog instance:

tabbook.rb

```
dialog = PreferencesDialog.new(self)
```

Next, it should initialize the dialog box's copy of the preferences data from the current application settings:

tabbook.rb

```
dialog.prefs[:first_name].value = user_name.first_name
dialog.prefs[:last_name].value  = user_name.last_name
dialog.prefs[:street].value     = user_address.street
dialog.prefs[:city].value       = user_address.city
dialog.prefs[:state].value      = user_address.state
dialog.prefs[:zip_code].value   = user_address.zip_code
```

The last step is call execute() on the dialog box to display it. If execute() returns nonzero, we'll extract the modified application settings from the dialog box's copy and push those back to the model:

tabbook.rb

```
if dialog.execute != 0
  user_name.first_name    = dialog.prefs[:first_name].value
  user_name.last_name     = dialog.prefs[:last_name].value
  user_address.street     = dialog.prefs[:street].value
  user_address.city       = dialog.prefs[:city].value
  user_address.state      = dialog.prefs[:state].value
  user_address.zip_code = dialog.prefs[:zip_code].value
end
```

To keep things straightforward for this example, we've relied on a Ruby hash, a really basic data structure. As a result, the code required to get data into and out of the dialog box is pretty verbose. Depending on the amount of data you're dealing with in a custom dialog box, you may find it helpful to create custom data types that allow the rest of your application code to interact with the dialog box in a more compact way.

14.7 Looking Ahead

As I noted at the beginning of the book, this isn't a comprehensive book on FXRuby development. My hope is that now that you've finished reading this book, you have enough of a foundation to head out into the world and learn about some of the more advanced aspects of FOX and FXRuby.

For example, one of the many cool things about FOX that we didn't address at all is its support for OpenGL-based 2D and 3D graphics applications. You can use FXRuby's FXGLViewer widget to construct a complex 3D scene graph that supports selection, rotation, zooming, and a number of other sophisticated features right out of the box, or you can drop down to the more basic FXGLCanvas widget when you need to exercise more control over how the scene is presented to the user.

FOX also provides a number of special-purpose widgets, such as dials, spinners, and sliders, that you can use alongside the other widgets that we looked at in Chapter 8, *Building Simple Widgets*, on page 95. You know how to look up the documentation for those classes to learn more about their specific capabilities, and you can apply the techniques that you've learned from this book for responding to messages from those widgets and associating them with data targets.

As one of this book's reviewers noted, the development of a GUI application is not merely a technical exercise. In this book we've discussed numerous issues related to the implementation of GUIs with FXRuby, but designing an intuitive and easy-to-use GUI application is a challenge in and of itself. Knowing why to make certain choices is perhaps even more important than knowing how to implement those choices. I'm a big fan of the previously mentioned *About Face* [Coo95], but there are a number of other fine books on user interface design that you can (and should) consult on this discipline.

In closing, let me encourage you to join us on the FOX and FXRuby mailing lists, whether it's to ask questions or to share your own experiences with other software developers.Section 1.4, *Where to Get Help*, on page 3, provides details about how to subscribe to those lists (as well as other sources of information). There are always going to be people who are new to Ruby and FXRuby, and now that you've got this head start on FXRuby application development, we could really use your help!

Bibliography

[Coo95] Alan Cooper. *About Face: The Essentials of User Interface Design*. John Wiley & Sons, New York, 1995.

[GHJV95] Erich Gamma, Richard Helm, Ralph Johnson, and John Vlissides. *Design Patterns: Elements of Reusable Object-Oriented Software*. Addison-Wesley, Reading, MA, 1995.

Index

G

H

I

K

L

M

N

O

P

R

S

T

U

V

W

Y

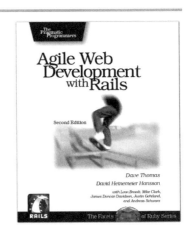

Ruby Everywhere

From day-to-day chores to help you be more productive, to integrating enterprise technologies, Ruby can help.

Everyday Scripting with Ruby

Don't waste that computer on your desk. Offload your daily drudgery to where it belongs, and free yourself to do what you should be doing: thinking. All you need is a scripting language (free!), this book (cheap!), and the dedication to work through the examples and exercises. Learn the basics of the Ruby scripting language and see how to create scripts in a steady, controlled way using test-driven design.

Everyday Scripting with Ruby: For Teams, Testers, and You
Brian Marick
(320 pages) ISBN: 0-9776166-1-4. $29.95
http://pragprog.com/titles/bmsft

Enterprise Integration with Ruby

See how to use the power of Ruby to integrate all the applications in your environment. Learn how to • use relational databases directly and via mapping layers such as ActiveRecord • harness the power of directory services • create, validate, and read XML documents for easy information interchange • use both high- and low-level protocols to knit applications together

Enterprise Integration with Ruby
Maik Schmidt
(360 pages) ISBN: 0-9766940-6-9. $32.95
http://pragprog.com/titles/fr_eir

Where to Go Next

Take your Ruby on Rails application to the next level, or hone your Ruby skills.

Advanced Rails Recipes

A collection of practical recipes for spicing up your web application without a lot of prep and cleanup. You'll learn how the pros have solved the tough problems using the most up-to-date Rails techniques (including Rails 2.0 features)

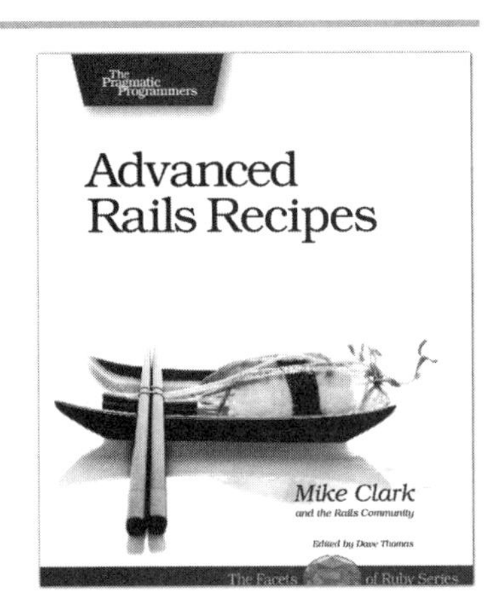

Advanced Rails Recipes
Mike Clark
(300 pages) ISBN: 978-0-9787392-2-5. $32.95
http://pragprog.com/titles/fr_arr

Best of Ruby Quiz

Sharpen your Ruby programming skills with twenty-five challenging problems from Ruby Quiz. Read the problems, work out a solution, and compare your solution with answers from others.

• Learn using the most effective method available: *practice* • Learn great Ruby idioms • Understand sticky problems and the insights that lead you past them • Gain familiarity with Ruby's standard library • Translate traditional algorithms to Ruby

Best of Ruby Quiz
James Edward Gray II
(304 pages) ISBN: 0-9766940-7-7. $29.95
http://pragprog.com/titles/fr_quiz

Real World Tools

Learn real-world design and architecture for your project, and a very pragmatic editor for Mac OS X.

Release It!

Whether it's in Java, .NET, or Ruby on Rails, getting your application ready to ship is only half the battle. Did you design your system to survive a sudden rush of visitors from Digg or Slashdot? Or an influx of real-world customers from 100 different countries? Are you ready for a world filled with flaky networks, tangled databases, and impatient users?

If you're a developer and don't want to be on call at 3 a.m. for the rest of your life, this book will help.

Design and Deploy Production-Ready Software
Michael T. Nygard
(368 pages) ISBN: 0-9787392-1-3. $34.95
http://pragprog.com/titles/mnee

TextMate

If you're coding Ruby or Rails on a Mac, then you owe it to yourself to get the TextMate editor. And, once you're using TextMate, you owe it to yourself to pick up this book. It's packed with information that will help you automate all your editing tasks, saving you time to concentrate on the important stuff. Use snippets to insert boilerplate code and refactorings to move stuff around. Learn how to write your own extensions to customize it to the way you work.

TextMate: Power Editing for the Mac
James Edward Gray II
(200 pages) ISBN: 0-9787392-3-X. $29.95
http://pragprog.com/titles/textmate

Leading Your Team

See how to be a pragmatic project manager and use agile, iterative project retrospectives on your project.

Manage It!

Manage It! is a risk-based guide to making good decisions about how to plan and guide your projects. Author Johanna Rothman shows you how to beg, borrow, and steal from the best methodologies to fit your particular project. You'll find what works best for *you*.

• Learn all about different project lifecycles • See how to organize a project • Compare sample project dashboards • See how to staff a project • Know when you're done—and what that means.

Your Guide to Modern, Pragmatic Project Management
Johanna Rothman
(360 pages) ISBN: 0-9787392-4-8. $34.95
http://pragprog.com/titles/jrpm

Agile Retrospectives

Mine the experience of your software development team continually throughout the life of the project. Rather than waiting until the end of the project—as with a traditional retrospective, when it's too late to help—agile retrospectives help you adjust to change *today*.

The tools and recipes in this book will help you uncover and solve hidden (and not-so-hidden) problems with your technology, your methodology, and those difficult "people issues" on your team.

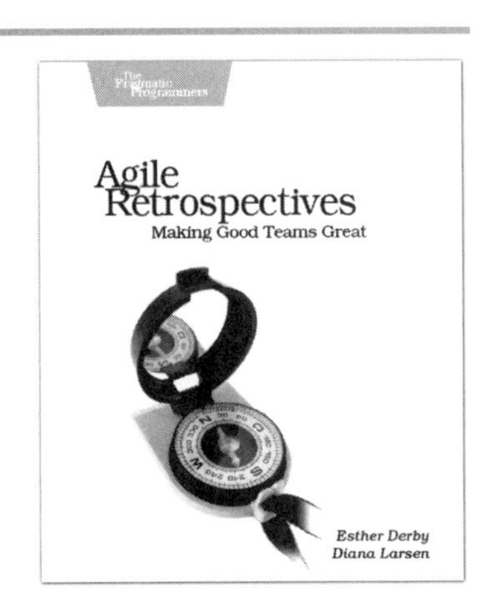

Agile Retrospectives: Making Good Teams Great
Esther Derby and Diana Larsen
(170 pages) ISBN: 0-9776166-4-9. $29.95
http://pragprog.com/titles/dlret

Getting It Done

Start with the habits of an agile developer and use the team practices of successful agile teams, and your project will fly over the finish line.

Practices of an Agile Developer

Agility is all about using feedback to respond to change. Learn how to apply the principles of agility throughout the software development process • establish and maintain an agile working environment • deliver what users really want • use personal agile techniques for better coding and debugging • use effective collaborative techniques for better teamwork • move to an agile approach

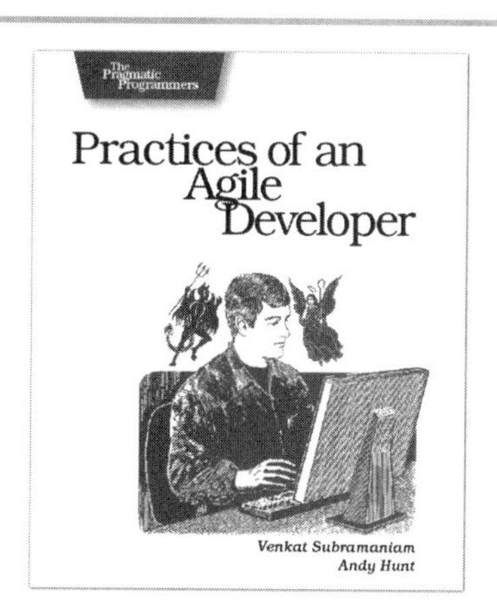

Practices of an Agile Developer: Working in the Real World
Venkat Subramaniam and Andy Hunt
(189 pages) ISBN: 0-9745140-8-X. $29.95
http://pragprog.com/titles/pad

Ship It!

Page after page of solid advice, all tried and tested in the real world. This book offers a collection of tips that show you what tools a successful team has to use, and how to use them well. You'll get quick, easy-to-follow advice on modern techniques and when they should be applied. **You need this book if:** • You're frustrated at lack of progress on your project. • You want to make yourself and your team more valuable. • You've looked at methodologies such as Extreme Programming (XP) and felt they were too, well, extreme. • You've looked at the Rational Unified Process (RUP) or CMM/I methods and cringed at the learning curve and costs. • **You need to get software out the door without excuses**

Ship It! A Practical Guide to Successful Software Projects
Jared Richardson and Will Gwaltney
(200 pages) ISBN: 0-9745140-4-7. $29.95
http://pragprog.com/titles/prj

The Pragmatic Bookshelf

The Pragmatic Bookshelf features books written by developers for developers. The titles continue the well-known Pragmatic Programmer style and continue to garner awards and rave reviews. As development gets more and more difficult, the Pragmatic Programmers will be there with more titles and products to help you stay on top of your game.

Visit Us Online

FXRuby's Home Page
http://pragprog.com/titles/fxruby
Source code from this book, errata, and other resources. Come give us feedback, too!

Register for Updates
http://pragprog.com/updates
Be notified when updates and new books become available.

Join the Community
http://pragprog.com/community
Read our weblogs, join our online discussions, participate in our mailing list, interact with our wiki, and benefit from the experience of other Pragmatic Programmers.

New and Noteworthy
http://pragprog.com/news
Check out the latest pragmatic developments in the news.

Save on the PDF

Save on the PDF version of this book. Owning the paper version of this book entitles you to purchase the PDF version at a terrific discount. The PDF is great for carrying around on your laptop. It's hyperlinked, has color, and is fully searchable.

Buy it now at pragprog.com/coupon.

Contact Us

Phone Orders:	1-800-699-PROG (+1 919 847 3884)
Online Orders:	www.pragprog.com/catalog
Customer Service:	orders@pragprog.com
Non-English Versions:	translations@pragprog.com
Pragmatic Teaching:	academic@pragprog.com
Author Proposals:	proposals@pragprog.com